Caribbean Cookbook

Rita G. Springer was born in Barbados and educated there at Queen's College. Cooking had always been her principal hobby and, after her marriage, she studied the subject professionally. From 1954–7 she served as a visiting lecturer on Food and Nutrition to students at the Housecraft Centre, Bridgetown, and also as a supervisor at evening classes in Home Economics. She came to England in 1964 and, during her stay, gained the certificate in Nutrition awarded by the Royal Society of Health, which entitled her to Associate Membership of the Society.

Other cookery books available in Pan

Rita G. Springer

Caribbean Cookbook

Pan Books London and Sydney

First published 1968 by Evans Brothers Ltd
This edition published 1979 by Pan Books Ltd,
Cavaye Place, London SW10 9PG
9 8 7 6
© Rita G. Springer 1968 and 1975
ISBN 0 330 25873 7
Set, printed and bound in Great Britain by
Cox & Wyman Ltd, Reading

for my daughter Helen,
and my grand-daughter, Karen

Contents

Introduction

I have been encouraged by many friends and interested people to write this book on Caribbean Cookery. The quantities of ingredients of some popular dishes have never been written down, but handed on verbally from generation to generation. An original dish can thus vary greatly in flavour when prepared in different areas.

In addition, many experienced and successful cooks are guided only by the reaction of their senses, as to the correct ingredients necessary for a specific recipe. This is often baffling to a young housewife, or anyone studying cookery in our Caribbean territories with a view to achieving an approved standard.

A further aim in this book is to present, in simple form, some facts of the history of our cosmopolitan foods, with emphasis on their food values, showing how to balance them in menus for good nutrition, and suggesting ways of economizing in buying and using them. Popular 'one-pot' meals are also to be included as these save time, energy and fuel. In these days of high food costs, shortage of domestic help and the necessity for housewives to work outside their homes, meal-planning and its preparation have to be wisely supervised.

With the increasing demand for Caribbean foods by visitors to our shores, hoteliers are continually seeking ways and means of presenting local produce in attractive forms. At present the popular trend in catering is to revive many of our grandmothers' favourite recipes. Many menus are improved in this way.

Although the recipes given in this book relate to ways in which foods are prepared in the Caribbean area, they may be used very widely in other countries of the world, to a greater or lesser extent, depending on the availability and cost of the basic products. In fact we have adopted culinary methods from several sources: European colonists – English, French, Spanish, Dutch – also Chinese, Indians, Americans, the Guyanese on the South American border, and the Hondurans on the Central American border. These, with a few remaining elements of African cookery, have caused Caribbean peoples to inherit a legacy which affords as unique, exotic and delectable a cuisine, as would satisfy the taste of the most exacting gourmet. The national dishes and favourite recipes of these various groups are interchanged and enjoyed by all. Indeed, we in the Caribbean are very proud of our cookery and spend a great deal of time and care in preparing meals. There is much competition among housewives, of all income groups, especially at festival or party occasions.

It is not very difficult these days to obtain most of the foods mentioned in this book. Many foodshops, markets and supermarkets in urban centres throughout Britain, the USA and Canada stock the basic ingredients for Chinese and Indian foods, as well as those from Europe. An increasing number stock at least some African and Caribbean fresh fruits, vegetables and spices, especially those favoured by the local West Indian community.

In Britain several firms specialize in importing these foods and act as wholesalers to local shops and markets. One of the largest importers is Dien Brothers (Food Importers) Ltd, Coal Wharf Road, London w12. Dien Brothers have a list of the relevant retail outlets in Britain. Mr D. Dien of this firm can supply, on application, the names and addresses of those retail shops and markets in your area which specialize in selling Caribbean foods.

For other countries, including the USA and Canada, it is suggested that in case of difficulty the advice of the local Caribbean Tourist Board is sought.

I should like to thank Miss Gwen Denny, Inspector of School Nutrition, and Senator Odessa Gittens, both of Barbados, West Indies, for their advice and encouragement during the preparation of the book. Others I would like to thank include the Management of the Hilton Hotel, Port of Spain, Trinidad, the Management of the Shaw Park Hotel, Ocho Rios, Jamaica, and Miss Denise Hope of the Office of the Barbados Tourist Board in London.

1 Measures and temperatures

Standard measures

Three standards for weights and measures are generally used –
Metric, Imperial and American or Canadian. All quantities given in
this book are based on the American standard, but for reference the
British standard Imperial is also quoted here.

The British standard measuring cup holds 300 ml ($\frac{1}{2}$ pint). The
American standard cup is 8 fluid ounces, half the American pint
which is sixteen fluid ounces.

Liquid measures

Quantity	Metric	British Standard Imperial	American or Canadian Standard
3 teaspoons	1 table-spoon	1 tablespoon	1 tablespoon
2 tablespoons	30 ml	$\frac{1}{4}$ gill	$\frac{1}{8}$ cup
4 tablespoons	60 ml	$\frac{1}{2}$ gill	$\frac{1}{4}$ cup
8 tablespoons	150 ml	1 gill ($\frac{1}{4}$ pint Imperial)	$\frac{1}{2}$ cup
12 tablespoons	225 ml	$1\frac{1}{2}$ gills	$\frac{3}{4}$ cup
16 tablespoons	300 ml	2 gills ($\frac{1}{2}$ pint Imperial)	1 cup
$\frac{1}{2}$ pint	300 ml	10 fluid ounces ($\frac{1}{2}$ pint)	8 fluid ounces
2 cups	600 ml	20 fluid ounces (1 pint)	16 fluid ounces (1 pint)
4 cups	1.2 litres	1 quart (Imperial)	1 quart

Measuring various foods

*All recipes in this book will make 4–6 servings, except where otherwise
stated.* For successful results, it is essential that all measuring is done
accurately. All measurements given are level. Use standard 8 oz
measuring cups (American) in glass or plastic, preferably one for
liquids and another for dry ingredients. A set of measuring spoons
in plastic or aluminium is also required.

Dry ingredients
Fill the measuring cup or spoon to overflowing and level off with a knife edge. A rounded spoonful is as much over the top of the spoon as there is in the spoon.

Liquids
Stand the measuring cup on a level surface and measure carefully.

Syrup
Syrup or molasses leaves the cup or spoon more readily if the measures are greased or wetted with cold water.

Sugar
Roll out any lumps before measuring brown sugar and sift granulated, caster and icing sugar.

Shortening
This may be butter, margarine, lard or a mixture of these. To measure $\frac{1}{2}$ cup of shortening, fill a measuring cup $\frac{1}{2}$ full of water and put in shortening until it reaches the cup level. Shortening may easily be cut in quantities required, bearing in mind that $100 \text{ g} = \frac{1}{4} \text{ lb} = \frac{1}{2}$ cup.

Oil or melted fat
Dip measuring spoon in fat and be sure to lift it out quite full.

Equivalent measures

450 g (1 lb) bananas	3–4 cups
450 g (1 lb) fine breadcrumbs	4 cups
450 g (1 lb) butter	2 cups
450 g (1 lb) grated cheese	4 cups
1 square plain chocolate	$\frac{1}{4}$ cup grated
450 g (1 lb) cocoa	4 cups
1 coconut grated	4 cups
450 g (1 lb) cornmeal	3 cups
12–14 egg yolks	1 cup
8–10 egg whites	1 cup
25 g (1 oz) powdered gelatine	2 tablespoons
450 g (1 lb) lard	2 cups
450 g (1 lb) margarine/butter	2 cups
450 g (1 lb) minced meat (raw)	2 cups (packed)
450 g (1 lb) molasses (cane syrup)	$1\frac{1}{3}$ cups
1 medium onion, chopped	$\frac{1}{3}$ cup

450 g (1 lb) rice	2 cups
Rind of 1 orange (grated)	1–2 teaspoons
Rind of 1 lime (grated)	$\frac{1}{2}$–1 teaspoon
450 g (1 lb) dried peas or beans	2 cups
450 g (1 lb) raisins/currants	3 cups
450 g (1 lb) peanuts (shelled)	3 cups
450 g (1 lb) brown sugar	3 cups
450 g (1 lb) granulated/caster sugar	2 cups
450 g (1 lb) icing sugar	$3\frac{1}{2}$–4 cups
450 g (1 lb) large tomatoes	4–5 medium

Oven temperatures

Oven settings vary according to different makes and sizes of ovens, therefore the following temperatures may not indicate precisely the conditions in individual ovens. However, they will act as a basic guide.

Gas thermostat	Temperature of oven		Oven heat
$\frac{1}{4}$–2	130–150°C	250–300°F	Very slow
2–4	150–180°C	300–350°F	Slow
4–6	180–200°C	350–400°F	Moderate
6–8	200–230°C	400–450°F	Hot
8–9	230–240°C	450–475°F	Very hot

Baking tips

1 Set the oven to the required temperature about 10 minutes before the dish under preparation is finished, so as to allow time for the temperature to be reached before the start of baking.

2 The setting on a thermostat registers the temperature in the centre of the oven. The top will be hotter, the bottom cooler.

3 Bake small cakes and pastry at the top of the oven, large cakes in the centre and rich fruit cakes on a lower shelf.

4 When baking rich fruit cakes and gingerbread, grease and line the pans with two thicknesses of greaseproof paper, to prevent mixture from burning.

5 Test large cakes by inserting a knife or skewer in the centre. If it comes out clean the cake is finished.

6 Dishes of custards should be put in a pan of boiling water while baking to maintain an even, slow temperature which allows mixture to set gradually. Custard is finished when a knife inserted in the centre comes out clean. Test pumpkin pie in the same way.

7 Avoid opening the oven until after the first $\frac{1}{2}$ hour, especially when baking sponge cakes and light batter mixtures.

8 When roasting chickens or large joints of meat, cover with aluminium foil until the last 15–20 minutes of baking. Then raise the oven temperature, and allow the meat to brown. The use of foil precludes the necessity for basting.

9 When using a meat thermometer, be sure that it is pushed into the thickest part of the meat. The thermometer should not touch the bone.

10 If baking on more than one oven shelf at the same time, avoid crowding of pans. Space must be allowed for circulation of hot air for the best results.

2 Herbs, condiments, dressings and seasonings

The success and popularity of Caribbean cookery are undoubtedly due to the subtle ways in which the foods are seasoned and garnished with herbs, spices and condiments to suit the various types of food. Everyday and simple dishes may thus be made more enjoyable and flavourful. There is a very wide variety from which to choose, and personal tastes and experience prompt the correct choices.

The most popular seasonings used for meats, fish, stews, soups, poultry dressings and savoury dishes are: onion, chives, eschalot, thyme, sweet marjoram, parsley, celery, garlic, bay leaves, etc. These are generally used fresh or green. Dried pepper powders are commonly used, especially when hot fresh peppers are scarce, such as paprika (dried sweet pepper), cayenne and chili powder (from red hot pepper), black and white pepper. Cloves, curry powder, gourmet powder (containing monosodium glutamate), garlic and celery salts are also popular. Soy sauce, cassareep, tomato ketchup, mustard, Worcester sauce add flavour to certain dishes. Cinnamon, nutmeg, mace, ginger, lime or orange rinds are chiefly used in sweet dishes, such as desserts, puddings, bread and cakes.

A *bouquet garni* is used in flavouring stews and soups. It consists of a few sprigs of thyme, sweet marjoram, a bay leaf, eschalot or chives, parsley, or a similar mixture of herbs as desired.

A basic marinade for meats
To season pieces of meat or poultry for stewing, and liver, chops etc., they should be marinated for about an hour, to soak up the blended flavourings. To marinate two to three pounds of meat, mix together the following:

1½ tablespoons salt
2 teaspoons sugar
2 tablespoons malt vinegar
1 medium onion (sliced)
2 tablespoons cooking sherry or rum

1 teaspoon paprika *or*
1 teaspoon chili or black pepper
½ teaspoon celery salt
½ teaspoon garlic salt *or*
1 large clove garlic (chopped)
1 tablespoon soy sauce (for chicken)

15

This mixture is rubbed well into the meat and allowed to stand for the required period. After browning the meat, the residue of the marinade with the sliced onion is added with water for cooking and making gravy. Alternatively, the meat pieces may be shaken out of the marinade, dredged in seasoned flour and fried. The residue of marinade, with a little brown colouring and butter added, may be heated, thickened with a little flour, and used as a separate gravy.

Fish fillets, steaks and small fish may be marinated similarly, using lime or lemon juice in preference to vinegar, omitting the sugar, and using less salt for the same amount of fish.

French dressing

For marinating vegetables, a French dressing is desirable, and each type of vegetable should be treated separately before arranging them in a salad. A simple French dressing is as follows:

1 teaspoon salt
2 teaspoons sugar
¼ teaspoon white pepper

¼ cup vinegar (white) *or* lime juice
1 teaspoon salad oil (optional)
1 teaspoon grated onion

Shake well before using.

Seasoned flour

This is used for dredging all kinds of meat, fish, etc. before frying. Mix together:

1 cup flour
1 teaspoon salt
1 teaspoon white *or* black pepper
½ teaspoon powdered cloves

1 tablespoon sugar
1 teaspoon paprika
2 teaspoons seasoning *or* gourmet powder (optional)

Combine this mixture well, store it in a glass jar until ready for use.

Seasoning mixture

1 medium onion
2–3 blades chives *or* eschalot
piece of red pepper
¼ teaspoon powdered cloves

½ teaspoon salt
sprig of thyme *or* marjoram
1 clove garlic
1 teaspoon lime juice

Mince or chop onion very finely, also green seasonings and garlic. Mix in the other ingredients and chop well together with a knife.

Score the flesh deeply in places and put a little mixture in each incision. Fish fillet pieces, flying fish and pork for roasting may be made very tasty, prepared with this seasoning mixture. This method of seasoning is typically Barbadian style.

Italian dressing

¼ cup salad oil
¼ cup white vinegar
1 teaspoon salt
½ teaspoon white pepper
½ teaspoon celery salt

¼ teaspoon cayenne pepper
¼ teaspoon dry mustard
1 clove garlic (minced)
1 teaspoon tomato ketchup

Mix ingredients together in bottle. Cover and shake well.

Salad cream

¼ cup evaporated milk
1 tablespoon malt vinegar
½ teaspoon salt

¼ teaspoon mixed mustard
½ teaspoon sugar

Beat the milk adding the vinegar slowly, add the seasonings and stir until very thick.

Salad cream (Rich)

½ teaspoon mixed mustard
¼ teaspoon salt
¼ teaspoon sugar

¼ cup thick cream
1 tablespoon malt vinegar

Mix together mustard, salt and sugar; stir in the cream. Add the · vinegar drop by drop, beating it very well until thick.

Mayonnaise dressing

1 tablespoon lime juice
1 tablespoon vinegar
1 egg yolk
½ teaspoon salt
1 teaspoon hot water

1 cup salad oil
⅛ teaspoon cayenne pepper
¼ teaspoon mustard
¼ teaspoon caster sugar

Mix dry ingredients with beaten egg yolk. Add vinegar and mix well. Then add ¾ cup oil very gradually, beating constantly with rotary beater, or electric beater until mixture thickens. Alternate lime juice with rest of oil and beat well. Mayonnaise dressing should not be mixed in salads until just before serving.

Pickled onions

450 g (1 lb) small pickling onions
1 teaspoon brown sugar
few peppercorns
salted water

2 teaspoons mixed spice
about 2 cups malt vinegar
1 teaspoon salt

Peel onions with a stainless steel knife and put them in salted water until all have been peeled. Then drain thoroughly. Pack in bottles ¾ full and cover with vinegar and spices.

Pickled hot peppers

225 g (½ lb) hot peppers (large, cut in pieces; small, used whole)
2 cups white vinegar
1 tablespoon salt
50 g (2 oz) sugar
¼ cup rum
few peppercorns
2 tablespoons chopped onion

Cut peppers in pieces, taking out seeds. Leave bird peppers whole, removing stems. Put vinegar, salt, sugar and onion in a saucepan; add peppers. Bring to the boil and simmer for 5 minutes. Cool, add peppercorns and rum, put into sterilized jars, cover and allow to steep for a few days before using.

Tomato sauce or ketchup

1.35 kg (3 lb) tomatoes
1 cup vinegar
½ cup sugar
1 tablespoon salt
1 teaspoon mixed spices
½ teaspoon cayenne pepper

Cut tomatoes in quarters. Place in heavy saucepan and simmer with salt and vinegar until soft. Strain through coarse muslin or nylon sieve, and return purée to saucepan, adding sugar. Continue to simmer till mixture starts to thicken, then add spice, stir well and flavour to taste. When ketchup is very thick pour into hot bottles and seal immediately.

Mango chutney

4 cups under-ripe mangoes (diced)
1 cup raisins
1 cup dates
100 g (4 oz) green ginger
1 teaspoon mustard seed
4 cups sugar
50 g (2 oz) salt
2 cloves garlic
2 hot peppers
4 cups malt vinegar
225 g (½ lb) onions

Cut up dried fruit and peppers; add to vinegar and allow to steep until the next day. Prepare diced mangoes, add sugar, crushed ginger, garlic, chopped onions and other seasonings. Boil all ingredients together gently until chutney is thick and brown.

Mango chow

6–8 half-ripe mangoes
½ cup currants
½ cup raisins
2 tablespoons finely chopped onion
½ teaspoon mixed powdered spices
2 cups vinegar
1 cup sugar
½ teaspoon white pepper
salt to taste
1 tablespoon green ginger (grated)

Peel and dice the mangoes; cook with half the vinegar until soft. Strain through a coarse sieve. Boil the fruit, onion, spices and seasonings in the rest of the vinegar. Combine mango purée with the sugar; allow to simmer and cook until thick. Cool and bottle.

3 One-dish meals

Nowadays, one-pot meals are used by all housewives as they are time and money-saving, nourishing, quick and easy to prepare and are usually favourite dishes with everyone. At the same time, different foods are mixed together in such a way as to preserve the valuable properties of the nutrients.

Hot Pot

225 g ($\frac{1}{2}$ lb) stewing steak
225 g ($\frac{1}{2}$ lb) Irish potatoes
325 g ($\frac{3}{4}$ lb) yellow yams *or* sweet potatoes
100 g ($\frac{1}{4}$ lb) tomatoes
bouquet garni
seasoned flour

1 large onion
100 g ($\frac{1}{4}$ lb) chochos
2 tablespoons butter *or* margarine
225 g ($\frac{1}{2}$ lb) carrots
piece red pepper

Wash meat and cut into serving pieces. Dip in seasoned flour. Brown in fat, and allow to cook in small quantity of water for 20 minutes. Prepare yam or sweet potato, Irish potato, carrot, onion and chocho, cutting into serving pieces of desired size. Remove pan from heat. Arrange ingredients in pan in the following order: one layer yam and Irish potato, one layer meat and other vegetables. Continue in alternate layers as above until all ingredients are included. Pour on desired amount of hot water and add a few pats of butter or margarine, and other seasonings. Cover and simmer until vegetables are tender and meat cooked. Serve hot.

Pigeon pea stew

225 g ($\frac{1}{2}$ lb) salt beef
2 cups pigeon peas (Gunga)
100 g ($\frac{1}{4}$ lb) Irish potatoes
100 g ($\frac{1}{4}$ lb) carrots
1 onion, chopped
2 large tomatoes

100 g ($\frac{1}{4}$ lb) pumpkin
50 g (2 oz) butter *or* margarine
4 cups water
salt, pepper, thyme
1 blade escallion, chopped
1 clove garlic, pounded

Soak salt beef for at least half an hour in cold water. Cut into small pieces. Peel, wash and dice pumpkin, carrots, potatoes. Wash peas. Lightly fry seasonings in saucepan. Add meat, peas and pumpkin and water to cover. Simmer, covered, for about 1 hour. Remove pumpkin, mash, and return to pot. About 15 minutes before stew is ready, add potatoes and carrots. Cook until these are tender.

Cook-up rice

150 g (6 oz) stewing beef
100 g (¼ lb) salted beef
1 blade chive (escallion)
1 onion, sliced
225 g (½ lb) carrots, diced
2 cups rice

4 cups water
1 red sweet pepper
25 g (1 oz) margarine
4–6 lettuce leaves
1 large tomato

Put salted meat to soak in cold water. Drain. Wash and cut beef and salted meat into small pieces. Cook in 2 cups water, with chive and sliced onion. Add salt, if necessary. When meat is cooked, add carrots and rice, and continue cooking until rice is done. Mix in margarine.

Arrange lettuce on platter. Heap cooked rice mixture in centre, and decorate with sliced tomato and sweet pepper.

Mutton-bean casserole

450 g (1 lb) stewing mutton
1 large tin baked beans
1 small tin condensed tomato soup
1 teaspoon mixed herbs

salt and pepper to taste
25 g (1 oz) fat
1 clove garlic

Cut up meat, and fry until lightly brown. Mix together the contents of the tins, and the garlic finely chopped, herbs and seasoning. Finally add the meat, place in a casserole, cover and cook in a slow oven.

Shrimp and potato casserole

675 g (1½ lb) parboiled potatoes
1 cup shelled shrimps
2 hard boiled eggs
25 g (1 oz) margarine
½ cup sliced onions

1½ cups white sauce
50 g (2 oz) grated cheese
½ cup breadcrumbs
1 cup sliced cooked carrots
salt and pepper to taste

Line buttered baking dish with layer of sliced potatoes, brushed with melted margarine. Put layer of white sauce, sprinkle over the grated cheese, sliced onion, chopped eggs and shrimps, sliced carrots, white sauce and lastly a layer of sliced potatoes. Top with breadcrumbs, rest of grated cheese and margarine. Sprinkle a little salt and white pepper to taste between layers. Bake in a moderate oven for about 45 minutes.

Macaroni with vegetables and mince

225 g (½ lb) macaroni
150 g (6 oz) minced meat (raw)
100 g (¼ lb) carrots
100 g (¼ lb) onions
2 teaspoons soy sauce

2 tomatoes
2 celery stalks *or* 1 chocho
1 oz margarine
chopped parsley
salt and pepper to taste

Break macaroni in pieces and cook in some boiling salted water and drain. Stand it aside. Sauté sliced onions, minced meat and diced carrots in the hot margarine in the saucepan. Add salt and pepper to taste and about ½ cup water and simmer until vegetables are tender. Add more water, if necessary to prevent burning. Lastly stir in soy sauce, chopped celery and cooked macaroni. Cook for 5 minutes more. Serve hot with slices of tomato and chopped parsley.

Tamale casserole

1 cup chopped onion
1 cup chopped green pepper
800 g (1¾ lb) minced beef
1 cup grated tomato
1½ cups whole-kernel corn, drained
1 clove garlic, minced
1 teaspoon sugar

1 teaspoon salt
½ teaspoon chili pepper
1 cup grated cheese
¾ cup yellow corn meal
½ teaspoon salt
1 tablespoon butter *or* margarine
2 cups cold water

Cook onion and green pepper in a little hot fat till just tender. Add meat and brown lightly. Add next 6 ingredients. Simmer for 20 to 25 minutes, until thick. Add cheese and stir till melted. Pour into greased baking dish and set aside.

Stir corn meal and salt into cold water. Cook and stir until very thick. Add butter; mix well. Spoon over hot meat mixture in lengthwise strips. Bake casserole in moderate oven about 40 minutes.

Callaloo and rice

2 cups rice
675 g (1½ lb) callaloo leaves
1½ tablespoons margarine
1 tablespoon lime juice
2 small tomatoes
1 clove garlic

1 cup water
225 g (½ lb) salt meat, cut in pieces
1 whole green pepper
12 okras
1 onion
escallion

Cut meat in pieces and simmer in water for about 10 minutes. Wash and cut up leaves, okras, garlic, tomatoes, onion and escallion. Add these to the meat with salt to taste, butter, whole green pepper. Cover saucepan tightly and simmer for 5 minutes. Then add lime juice, sprinkle in rice and cook until rice grains and leaves are soft. Serve hot.

4 Milk, egg and cheese cookery

Milk is the most important food for infants, children and adults in sickness or health. It is very easily digested. It contains 88% water and has more nutrients than any other food. It is rich in bone and body building material but is deficient in iron and Vitamins C and D. Vitamin D is, however, synthesized in the body from the sunshine, so there is no serious lack of this vitamin in the area.

In the Caribbean there is a general shortage of fresh cows' milk, although dairy farms are on the increase, but some tuberculin tested and pasteurized milk is available.

Condensed milk is widely used but should not be substituted for fresh milk. Because of the large amount of sugar it contains, it has the advantage of keeping for several days without refrigeration. Store in a covered jam jar to protect it from dust and insects.

Evaporated milk is pure sterilized tinned milk which has half the water removed and may be reconstituted by mixing one part evaporated milk to one part water.

Whole milk powder is pure milk dried having only the water removed to allow for long storage in tins. Follow the directions on the tin for reconstituting it.

Dried skimmed milk powder is dried like whole milk powder, but has most of the fat removed in processing. It is rich in calcium and protein. It is inexpensive, good value for money, and should be more widely used, especially in milk cookery, etc.

The value of milk in any form cannot be over-estimated. It may be used as a beverage, plain or flavoured, with porridge or cereal, in custards, soups, ice cream and with stewed fruit.

Milk is easily contaminated and must be handled carefully. Whenever in doubt as to its purity it should be scalded before use, covered and refrigerated, if possible, or kept in a cool place in a bowl of cold water.

Sour milk should not be thrown away. It may be used in cakes and scones with a little bicarbonate of soda as a raising agent.

Goats' milk is very nutritious and sometimes available. It is rich in iron and digestible, similar to human milk, and unlike cows' milk, it is free from tuberculin bacteria.

Cheese
Cheese is a milk product rich in protein and fat. Cheddar cheese is the most economical to buy. Cream cheese is rich in fat but more expensive. All kinds of cheese should be kept cool wrapped in waxed paper in a refrigerator or under a cheese dish in a cool place. Mould on cheese may be pared off and discarded; the cheese is still wholesome. Hard pieces of cheese may be grated and used in cheese cookery. Always cook cheese dishes at low or medium temperatures. Quick cooking at high temperatures makes it tough and stringy. Cheese is useful for combining with main dishes, soups, salads, sandwiches etc and adds extra nourishment.

Butter
Butter is also made from cows' milk and is about ⅘ths fat. It is salted during its manufacture. In the Caribbean area ordinary butter is often referred to as table butter to distinguish it from *cooking butter* which is a highly salted orange-coloured pure butter imported from the UK. It is widely used in meat and fish cookery and sometimes in cake and bread making. Imported *margarine* which is cheaper, is obtained in similar form. This butter and margarine have a cheesy taste which adds much to the appetizing flavour of dishes in which they are used. The salt preserves it for a long period and refrigeration is not so necessary.

There are local margarine factories in the area, and these supply a fair amount of margarine which is fortified with Vitamins A and D, thus making it nutritionally an excellent substitute for butter. Table, as well as coloured cooking margarines are made.

Eggs
Eggs may be considered with dairy produce and cheese as they are so often used together in foods. These are rich in high quality protein; the yolk also contains some Vitamin A, iron and fat. Use them daily, cooked in a variety of ways or mixed in dishes.

Like milk and cheese, they must be kept cool. If refrigerated, cool them to room temperature before beating them for making cakes. Test them in a bowl of water for freshness. A stale egg floats to the top, a fresh one will sink to the bottom. Eggs will retain their freshness for 2–3 weeks without refrigeration if kept in a box of sand and turned daily.

Eggs are graded and sold in a variety of sizes. Discretion must be used in buying them in different places. Farm eggs are guaranteed fresher than those sold in grocery shops. To ensure freshness, break each separately in a saucer before mixing with other ingredients.

Low or medium heat is used when cooking eggs. Popular methods of cooking are boiled (soft or hard), scrambled, fried, poached, omelettes.

Boiled eggs

Put number of eggs required in a saucepan and cover them with cold water over medium heat. Bring to boiling point, then allow them to simmer for 2–4 minutes for soft to medium cooked eggs, and 10 minutes for hard boiled eggs; large eggs need longer cooking time.

Scrambled eggs

Use 1½–2 eggs per person.

6 eggs
⅓ cup milk
¾ teaspoon salt

¼ teaspoon white pepper
2 tablespoons butter *or* margarine

Beat eggs lightly with a fork. Add salt, pepper and milk. Mix well. Heat butter in pan over low heat. Pour in mixture and as it begins to set, use a spatula to turn mixture until it sets throughout, but remove it from the heat while still moist and serve at once. Chopped onion, grated cheese, shredded fried fish or tomato may be added for variation.

Bacon and fried eggs

6 eggs
6 (or more) rashers bacon
salt, pepper

Remove bacon rinds if necessary. Place rashers in a warm pan and fry slowly without using extra fat. Fry until the fat is cooked or seems transparent, lightly brown on both sides, but not crisp. Remove bacon from the pan and put aside to keep warm. Fry eggs in the bacon fat removing any fried bits adhering to the pan. Add extra oil if necessary. Fry eggs one at a time, carefully breaking them in a saucer and slipping them into the pan. Sprinkle with salt and pepper. As soon as white sets, ease round the edges with the spatula and spoon the fat over the egg until a white film forms over the yolk. Remove it from the pan and fry the other eggs. Lay a rasher of bacon on each egg and serve hot.

Poached eggs

Break each egg in a saucer and put them one after the other in fast boiling, slightly salted water. Cook for 2–3 minutes or until they are set and remove them with a fish slice or large spoon. Serve hot on buttered toast, with grated cheese or shredded fried fish.

Creamed eggs

6 eggs, hard-boiled
2 cups white sauce (medium)
dash Worcester sauce
Cheddar or Parmesan cheese

1 tablespoon chopped chives *or* onion
breadcrumbs
butter

Slice eggs into casserole. Stir chives into hot sauce and pour over eggs, add Worcester sauce. Cover top generously with breadcrumbs, then with grated cheese. Dot with butter and cook in moderate oven until top is golden and crisp. This is very good served as a luncheon dish with a green or tomato salad.

Creole omelette

1 onion (minced)
1 tablespoon tomato (minced) *or*
1 teaspoon ketchup
oil for frying
1 clove garlic

green pepper
4 beaten eggs
100 g ($\frac{1}{4}$ lb) ham
$\frac{1}{4}$ cup breadcrumbs (soaked in milk)
1 tablespoon butter

Sauté minced onion, tomato and chopped garlic. Add breadcrumbs, remove from heat and allow to cool. Add beaten eggs. Mix well and add bits of ham and green pepper. Put butter in pan. When hot pour in omelette and fry over low flame. Turn the whole over once. Serve hot.

Omelettes

Keep a separate frying pan for making omelettes, if possible; a pan 25 cm (8 in) in diameter for a 3–4 egg omelette. Avoid overbeating eggs, i.e. until frothy. Use a fork for beating and add a little water (1 teaspoon to 2 eggs) instead of milk, which makes them tough.

Plain omelette

4 eggs
2 teaspoons water
1 tablespoon butter
salt and pepper to taste

Beat eggs and water with fork for about $\frac{1}{2}$ minute. Add salt and pepper. Melt butter in pan. When butter is very hot (do not allow it to brown or omelette will stick), pour in eggs. Stir a little, and when cooked, lift the edges with a spatula and carefully turn over omelette from one side to the centre, then over to the other side, folding it in three. Turn on to plate and serve hot. For savoury omelettes, fish, cheese, onion, minced ham etc. may be used as fillings. Add fillings after pouring eggs in pan, and cook in the same way.

Custards

Soft Custards to be used as sauces, may be flavoured with any kind of essence, nutmeg, chocolate, coffee etc. The consistency should be like that of thin cream. Use low heat and stir constantly while cooking. To prevent a skin forming on top, sprinkle a little water or sugar over the top and cover until it is ready for use: 2 eggs to 600 ml (1 pint) milk makes a good sauce.

Baked Custards: 3–4 eggs to 600 ml (1 pint) of milk makes a solid mixture which will hold its shape when turned out after baking. The dish containing the mixture should be kept in a pan of water during the baking period in the oven at a low enough temperature to prevent it from boiling and causing the eggs to coagulate. When finished, a knife blade put into the custard should be clean when removed.

Soft custard or sweet sauce

2 eggs (beaten lightly)
2 cups milk
2 tablespoons sugar

$\frac{1}{2}$ teaspoon essence
pinch of salt

Heat the milk, sugar and salt, preferably in a double boiler or over low heat; mix some of the hot milk with the eggs and pour all into the double boiler and stir until mixture thickens and coats the back of the spoon. Remove from heat, cool and add essence.

Baked custard

3–4 eggs
2–2½ cups milk
½ teaspoon grated nutmeg *or*
  essence

3 tablespoons sugar
pinch of salt
1 teaspoon butter

Beat eggs lightly with the other ingredients. Put into a greased baking dish. Sprinkle a little nutmeg on the top, if used. Dot butter on the top. Place dish in a pan of hot water in the oven. (Replace hot water if it dries up during baking period.) Cook at low heat, about 140°C, 275°F or Gas 1, for about one hour or until finished and set firmly. This custard may also be steamed in the top of a double boiler until set.

Rice and milk or rice pudding

2 cups cooked rice
2 cups milk
1 egg

2 tablespoons sugar
¼ cup raisins (optional)
¼ teaspoon nutmeg

Whisk egg, add sugar and milk. Mix in other ingredients and bake in a moderate oven until lightly brown.

Macaroni cheese (1)

225 g (½ lb) macaroni
100 g (4 oz) cheese, grated
2 tablespoons butter

salt to taste
1 cup (medium) white sauce (p40)

Boil macaroni in salted boiling water for 20 minutes. Wash with cold water and drain. Put alternate layers of macaroni, cheese and sauce in a greased baking dish with a layer of macaroni last. Dot with butter, sprinkle with breadcrumbs and cheese. Bake in moderately hot oven for about ½ hour.

Macaroni cheese (2)

225 g (½ lb) macaroni (cooked)
100 g (4 oz) cheese, grated
2 tablespoons butter
2 eggs

1 medium tomato (sliced)
1 small sliced onion
1 cup milk
salt to taste

Butter a baking dish and put alternate layers of macaroni, grated cheese, sliced onion and tomato, finishing with layer of macaroni. Pour over the milk, beaten eggs and salt mixture, add a little grated cheese and dot with butter. Bake in a moderate oven for about ½ hour.

Cheese soufflé

1 cup soufflé sauce (p40)   ½ cup biscuit *or* bread crumbs
½ cup grated cheese   3 eggs (separated)
¼ teaspoonful white pepper   1 small minced onion

Mix all ingredients together except the eggs. Beat the yolks and add them to the mixture. Then carefully fold in egg whites, previously beaten until stiff, pour in a baking dish and bake in moderate oven for about 1 hour. Serve immediately.

Egg-cheese casserole

4 eggs   2 tablespoons grated cheese
1 tablespoon butter   salt and pepper to taste
4 tablespoons flour

Beat eggs lightly. Mix in butter, 1½ tablespoons grated cheese, salt, pepper and flour. Beat until thick and creamy, sprinkle with grated cheese and bake in a large casserole or individual moulds for about ½ hour in a medium hot oven.

Birds' nests

Cut slices of bread, about 2.5 cm (1 in) thick, and cut into rings using a large or a small biscuit cutter. Fry the rings in butter until brown. Place them on a buttered baking dish. Break an egg in each ring, sprinkle a few drops of milk, salt and pepper and chopped onion over them, and bake in a moderate oven until eggs are set.

Cheese strata

8 slices bread or toast   4 eggs (slightly beaten)
¼ cup butter or margarine   2½ cups milk
2½ cups dried processed cheese   1 teaspoon salt
¼ teaspoon mustard

Trim crusts from bread, butter each slice and divide in 4. Place alternate layers of bread and cheese in buttered baking dish and finish with layer of cheese. Mix eggs, milk and seasonings and pour over layers. Bake in a slow oven for 45 minutes. Cool a little and cut in squares for serving.

5 Soups

There are many advantages in serving soups:
1 Scraps of vegetables, meat and bones may be used up instead of being thrown away, thus avoiding wastage.
2 All the flavour and food value of the ingredients are retained as the liquid in which they are cooked is the main part of the dish.
3 Time and fuel are saved by cooking in one pot.

Thick hearty soups are very popular as main dishes or even complete meals. These comprise root and green vegetables, green or dried peas, added to any available fresh or salted meat, bones, salt or fresh fish, or even peanuts. Grated cheese, milk or cream may be added to soups after cooking to give extra nourishment.

Thin soups, purées and broths are served as first courses of more formal meals, to young children and during illness and convalescence. Stock for soup (with pieces of meat, bones and vegetables) is usually freshly made, other ingredients being added as desired, thus the keeping of a stockpot is not customary in the Caribbean area.

Garnishes and accompaniments for soups

Thin soups and broths are served with crisp biscuits, toast and dumplings as desired.

Purées or sieved soups are improved when garnished with grated cheese, chopped parsley or croutons.

Thick soups, like stews, rarely need extra accompaniments as they are flavourful and filled with pieces of meat, vegetables and dumplings.

For *creamed soups* cups of white sauce may be blended with the ingredients in the particular recipe and chopped parsley or shredded cheese used for garnishing.

Green corn soup

12 ears juicy young corn
225 g (½ lb) salt meat
few pieces of fat chicken
salt and pepper to taste
2 tablespoons vinegar
small piece fresh green pepper

1 large onion
bunch of mixed herbs
few blades eschalot
10 cups water
chopped parsley

Grate corn off cobs, rub chicken with vinegar and 1 tablespoon salt and stand aside. Put cobs to boil in saucepan with water, and with salt meat cut in pieces, for about ½ hour to extract all the milk. Remove the cobs and put in the grated corn, pieces of chicken and seasonings. Simmer for about 2 hours, stirring often. Serve with chopped parsley.

Breadfruit soup

1 medium sized breadfruit
100 g (¼ lb) salt meat   ⎫ previously
100 g (¼ lb) fresh meat   ⎭ soaked
1 large onion

8 cups of water
bunch of herbs
½ teaspoon pepper
salt to taste

Boil peeled and sliced fruit in water with meat, cut in pieces. When tender, crush smoothly and return to saucepan with remainder of ingredients. Stir occasionally and simmer for 1 hour. Strain through a colander before serving with pieces of meat.

Rabbit or chicken soup

900 g–1.35 kg (2–3 lb) rabbit *or* chicken
6 cups water
thyme and sweet marjoram
1 tablespoon vinegar
2 or 3 cloves

1 dessertspoon Worcestershire sauce
450 g (1 lb) potatoes
2 onions
salt and pepper to taste
1 clove garlic (crushed)
1 teaspoon sugar

Wash and cut up the meat. Put it into a saucepan with water and simmer until tender. Add seasonings and boiled crushed potatoes. Just before serving, stir in 1 dessertspoon Worcestershire sauce.

Eddoe soup (White, Chinese or Tannia)

900 g (2 lb) eddoes
100 g (¼ lb) salt meat
3–4 blades eschalot or chives
salt and pepper to taste

100 g (¼ lb) fresh meat
1 medium onion, bunch thyme
6 cups water
1 dessertspoon chopped parsley

Peel eddoes, cut in pieces and put in water to boil with salt and fresh meat also cut in small pieces. Crush eddoes when cooked, add seasonings and simmer till smooth. Lastly add 1 dessertspoon chopped parsley before serving.

Fish soup (Jack, Flying Fish or any small fish)

450 g (1 lb) flying fish	1 tablespoon tomato ketchup
6 cups water	2 blades eschalot or chives
2 or 3 English potatoes	sprig of marjoram
1 tablespoon butter *or* margarine	salt and pepper to taste
1 medium onion	1 tablespoon vinegar or lime juice

Wash and clean the fish with lime and salt. Put all ingredients in saucepan to simmer for about 2 hours crushing potatoes when cooked and adding butter or margarine when nearly finished. Before serving stir in 1 tablespoon vinegar or lime juice.

Green pea soup (Pigeon or Gunga)

225 g (½ lb) salted meat *or*	Black or white pepper *or*
225 g (½ lb) soup beef or bones	a piece of fresh pepper
2½ cups green peas	bunch of herbs
450 g (1 lb) yam or potatoes	1 tablespoon tomato ketchup
1 dessertspoon salt	1 large onion
or to taste	8 cups water

Put peas, beef cut in pieces or bones, and salt in water. When peas are soft, add sliced potatoes or yam and seasonings. Cover and simmer for ½ hour more. Serve with dumplings. Dried or red peas soaked overnight may be substituted for green peas.

Dumplings for soup or stew

1½ cups flour *or*	2 tablespoons sugar
1 cup flour plus ½ cup cornmeal	1 dessertspoon margarine *or* butter
½ teaspoon salt	1 teaspoon baking powder
½ cup water or milk	pinch of powdered mixed spice
	or nutmeg

Mix dry ingredients together. Rub in fat and add liquid to make a soft dough. Drop by spoonfuls in soup and cook for 10 minutes.

Bean soup (White beans or bonavist, etc.)

2½ cups white beans, dried	225 g (½ lb) peeled pumpkin
8 cups of water	bunch of herbs
100 g (¼ lb) salt meat	salt and pepper to taste
1 onion	

Boil the beans in the water after having soaked them overnight. When beginning to soften add the salt meat, onion and pumpkin and herbs. When the pumpkin is quite soft, take it out, mash it smoothly and return to the soup. Heat thoroughly and serve.

Chip chip soup

4 cups chip chips (small molluscs or shell fish)
3 tablespoons butter
1 onion (chopped)
6 cups water
225 g ($\frac{1}{2}$ lb) potatoes or eddoes
salt and pepper to taste
2 limes
1 tablespoon tomato ketchup
a sprig of thyme

Remove sand from chip chips by washing thoroughly. Wash with lime juice and pour boiling water over to scald them. Drain and place them in 6 cups of water and cook them for 15 minutes. Strain off the liquid using it as stock, adding the seasonings and sliced vegetables. When vegetables are cooked, strain the mixture through a sieve and add cooked chip chips, having removed the shells. Mix in the butter and ketchup last and gently reheat before serving.

Pumpkin soup

450 g (1 lb) pumpkin
2 onions
$\frac{1}{2}$ cup split peas (soaked beforehand)
pepper and salt to taste
225 g ($\frac{1}{2}$ lb) salt meat and bones
2 cabbage leaves (cut finely)
piece of thyme
1 tablespoon butter

Slice and lightly fry onions in butter. Add peeled and cut pumpkin, then the rest of ingredients. Cover with water and simmer for about 1 hour. Strain before serving.

Split pea soup

2$\frac{1}{4}$ cups split peas (green or yellow)
1 ham bone or 225 g ($\frac{1}{2}$ lb) salt meat
2 large sliced onions
1 teaspoon salt or salt to taste
piece of fresh pepper or
$\frac{1}{2}$ teaspoon pepper
225 g ($\frac{1}{2}$ lb) pumpkin or carrots
bunch of mixed herbs

Cover peas with 5 cups of cold water and soak overnight. Add ham bone or salt meat, onion and seasonings. Bring to boil, cover, reduce heat and simmer for 1$\frac{1}{2}$ hours. Stir occasionally. Remove bone; cut up meat. Return meat to soup and add vegetables. Cook slowly, uncovered, for 30 to 40 minutes. Add salt and serve.

Rice soup

225 g (½ lb) beef
50 g (2 oz) rice
1 small onion

5 cups water
1 tablespoonful chopped parsley
salt and black pepper

Put beef, cut in pieces, in water and bring slowly to the boil, then simmer gently for 1½ hours. Add the rice and the onion, which must be finely chopped. Simmer till the rice is properly cooked – for about 30 minutes. Add the chopped parsley and seasoning.

Chilled cucumber soup

3 tablespoons flour
½ teaspoon paprika
1 chicken bouillon cube
1 tablespoon lemon juice *or*
1 teaspoon lime juice
1 teaspoon sherry

1½ teaspoons salt
3 cups milk
1 tablespoon grated onion
¼ teaspoon pepper
3 cups shredded cucumber

Sprinkle flour and seasoning over the milk and mix thoroughly. Place over a saucepan of boiling water, add stock cube, onion and cucumber. Stir constantly until the soup thickens – for about 10 to 15 minutes. Remove from heat and stir in the lemon juice, a teaspoon of sherry and some green colouring (optional). Chill thoroughly, stir well before serving and if liked a little chopped parsley can be sprinkled on the top of each serving.

Tomato soup

450 g (1 lb) fresh *or* tinned tomatoes
2 carrots
2 onions
bacon rinds
25 g (1 oz) sugar
salt and pepper to taste

1 cup milk
2 potatoes
bunch of mixed herbs
25 g (1 oz) margarine
2 tablespoons flour

Fry bacon rinds in a heavy saucepan, add half the margarine and fry the sliced onions lightly. Chop up the tomatoes and dice the potatoes and carrots. Add to the saucepan, place on lid and cook gently over a low heat for 15 minutes, shaking occasionally. Add mixed herbs, sugar, salt and pepper, cover vegetables with stock and simmer until quite tender. Rub through a sieve, rinse the pan and melt the remaining margarine in it. When hot, gradually stir in flour, then milk and add the sieved purée. Cook until rich and creamy.

Potato soup

900 g (2 lb) potatoes, diced
2 onions, sliced
50 g (2 oz) margarine or butter
salt and pepper to taste

5 cups water
bunch of herbs
½ cup milk

Fry the potatoes and onions with the melted fat lightly for 10 minutes, shaking pan constantly. Add the water and cook the vegetables with the herbs until very soft. Remove the herbs and press the vegetables through a fine sieve. Mix the liquid with the purée, season to taste and heat while stirring. Carrots or pumpkin may replace some of the potatoes for a mixed purée.

Ground nut or peanut soup

450 g (1 lb) roasted peanuts
4 cups water
chicken carcass
1 tablespoon vinegar

½ cup evaporated milk
salt and pepper
1 onion

Break the carcass in pieces, and with salt, vinegar and pepper, simmer slowly in water for 1 hour. Add the finely pounded or crushed peanuts to the strained liquid (about 2½ cups). Add the finely chopped onion and season with salt to taste. Simmer for ½ hour and strain. Finally add milk and heat before serving.

Lentil soup

1 cup lentils
100 g (¼ lb) salt meat or bacon rinds
5 cups water
chopped parsley
salt and pepper to taste

1 cup diced carrots
1 sliced onion
25 g (1 oz) fat
piece of thyme and chive
1 cup milk

Heat the fat and fry the onion and carrots for a few minutes. Add the rest of the ingredients and cook until lentils are tender. Sieve, reheat, add milk last and stir well before serving.

Mutton soup

675 g (1½ lb) mutton neck or bones
5 cups water
50 g (2 oz) rice
100 g (¼ lb) carrots or turnips
1 large onion (chopped)

salt and pepper to taste
few blades eschalot or chives
1 sprig parsley
1 bay leaf

Chop bones and cut off meat, discarding fat and skin. Put into saucepan with water, add onion and seasonings and simmer for 1 hour. Strain, then add the rice and diced vegetables with the pieces of meat, and cook until tender. Serve hot.

Chicken broth

1 old fowl
1 tablespoon vinegar *or* lime juice
1 chopped onion
6 cups water
1 teaspoon chopped parsley
25 g (1 oz) rice
salt and pepper to taste

Cut the meat from the fowl and chop this and the bones into small pieces. Simmer in the water with vinegar, onion, salt and pepper for at least 2 hours. Add rice and, when tender, serve sprinkled with parsley.

Beef soup with vegetables

675 g (1½ lb) beef
6 cups water
1 cup tomato juice
1 large onion (chopped)
1 dessertspoon salt
1 teaspoon Worcestershire sauce
1 tablespoon oil *or* fat
small piece fresh pepper
1 bay leaf
100 g (¼ lb) diced carrots
1 cup chopped cabbage *or* chocho
bunch of mixed herbs
225 g (½ lb) yam or sweet potato
 (sliced)

Remove meat from bone and sauté in hot fat. Add bones, water, tomato juice, onions and seasonings. Cover and simmer for 2 hours. Add vegetables, cover and simmer for another hour. Remove bones and bay leaf before serving.

Mixed vegetable soup

1½ cups diced vegetables (chocho,
 carrot, potato, celery, green peas
 or green gunga peas)
1 sliced onion
1 cup water
2 tablespoons butter
1 cup milk
salt and pepper

Cook vegetables in melted butter for about 3 minutes, stirring constantly. Add water, cover and cook vegetables until tender (for about 15 minutes). Slowly stir in milk. Season to taste. Reheat and serve.

Callaloo soup

4 bunches eddoe/dasheen leaves
675 g (1½ lb) fresh meat
100 g (¼ lb) shrimps
225 g (½ lb) salt meat
1 sliced onion
450 g (1 lb) ground provisions
 (yams, potatoes, cassava, etc.)
salt to taste
few blades eschalot and thyme

Cut up salt meat, soak for 1 hour and put to boil with fresh meat. Cut up leaves with seasonings and add to meat after 1 hour's boiling. Add prepared shrimps, vegetables and simmer until tender. Salt to taste. Dumplings may be added (see p33).

Okra soup

1 dozen okras (ladies' fingers)
1 small bunch Indian kale or
   callaloo
salt and pepper

225 g (½ lb) salt beef
4 cups water
garnishings (tomatoes, escallion,
   thyme, red peppers)

Wash salt beef and soak overnight. Cut up the okras, and put them in water along with the beef, and simmer gently for about 2 hours. Chop finely some kale or callaloo and add to the soup. Simmer until the okras are tender. Add garnishings.

Skirt soup

450 g (1 lb) goose neck
225 g (½ lb) pigtail or salt beef
6 cups water

8 green bananas (cooked)
onion, chives, thyme and pepper
   (whole green)

Boil meat in water until tender. Cut into pieces. Add peeled and crushed bananas and seasoning to taste, and simmer until soup is of a thick consistency.

Shell fish and tomato soup

450 g (1 lb) cooked shrimps or shell
   fish
2 potatoes
4 cups water
bunch of herbs
1 bay leaf
¼ cup evaporated milk
green pepper (sweet)
lemon or lime juice

450 g (1 lb) fresh tomatoes or
1 medium-size tin
1 large onion
50 g (2 oz) rice
½ cup cooking sherry or cider
chopped parsley
salt to taste

Slice the potatoes thickly and boil them till soft in 300 ml (½ pint) water with the herbs, lemon juice and a little salt. Meanwhile cut up the tomatoes and chop the onion. Cook the tomatoes and onion without any other additions till they are quite soft. Sieve the potatoes and to them add all the water. Bring the water and potatoes to the boil, add the rice and cook till quite soft. Sieve the tomatoes and onion and add this purée to the thickened mixture. Add the wine and the chopped fish and bring the soup to boiling point. Add the chopped parsley and season well. Off the heat, stir in the milk.

Cow heel or oxtail soup

1 cow heel *or* oxtail (with skin)
8–10 cups of water
2 onions
bunch of mixed herbs
225 g (½ lb) carrots
450 g (1 lb) mixed vegetables
few cloves

few small tomatoes
1 tablespoon rice
2 tablespoons lime juice *or* vinegar
salt to taste
piece of hot pepper
1 tablespoon chopped parsley

Scald, scrape and clean cow heel or oxtail. Cut it up and put to boil in salted water, adding cloves and vinegar. Cook until almost tender. Skim and add chopped seasonings, diced vegetables. Remove large bones from soup and add rice. Simmer until vegetables are tender. Serve with chopped parsley.

Cream soups

Cream of spinach soup

450 g (1 lb) young spinach leaves
1 onion (chopped)
4 cups water

salt and pepper to taste
1 tablespoon tomato ketchup
2 cups cream sauce (1)

Wash leaves well and boil with water, salt, pepper and onion until tender. Strain and rub through a sieve. Stir in tomato ketchup. Add 2 cups of cream sauce, heat slowly without boiling and serve.

Cream of onion soup

4 medium onions (thinly sliced)
2 tablespoons butter
½ cup water

½ teaspoon salt
½ teaspoon pepper
3 cups cream sauce (1)

Fry onions lightly in butter. Add salt, pepper and water and allow to boil. Add 3 cups of cream sauce and heat.

Cream of potato soup

2 cups diced cooked potatoes
1 tablespoon chopped sweet pepper
2 cups cream sauce (1)

1 teaspoon salt
1 cup milk and water
finely chopped chives or parsley

Add 2 cups cream sauce to the ingredients. Stir well, heat and serve with finely chopped chives or parsley.

Cream or white sauce

Thin sauce for soup or vegetables (1 cup)

1 tablespoon butter *or* margarine	¼ teaspoon salt
2 tablespoons flour	1 cup milk

Medium sauce for scalloped dishes or as a sauce (1 cup)

2 tablespoons butter *or* margarine	¼ teaspoon salt
1 tablespoon flour	1 cup milk

Thick sauce for soufflés or croquettes (1 cup)

3 tablespoons butter *or* margarine	¼ teaspoon salt
4 tablespoons flour	1 cup milk

To cook the sauces, melt butter or margarine in saucepan over low heat. Blend in flour and salt. Add milk all at once. Cook, stirring constantly with a wooden spoon until the mixture thickens. Cook for 2 minutes.

For *Parsley Sauce,* add 1 tablespoon chopped parsley to 1 cup *Medium Sauce.* Serve with fish or vegetables.

For *Mustard Sauce,* add 1½ tablespoons prepared mustard to 1 cup *Medium Sauce.* Serve with fish.

For *Cheese Sauce* add 1 cup grated Cheddar cheese to 1 cup hot *Medium Sauce.* Stir until cheese is melted. Serve with omelettes or vegetables.

6 Fish

The Caribbean Sea and the Atlantic Ocean to the north and east abound in fish of many varieties available all the year round. There are two kinds of fish:

1 The oily or fatty fish with dark flesh which include species such as the jack, cavalli, tuna or bonito, herring, mullet, salmon, etc.

2 The popular white fish with lean flesh usually in large varieties, like the dolphin, king red or snapper, bream, barracuda, flying fish, grouper, shark, etc.

Fish is as nutritious as meat, both being animal protein. It has less fat and contains more water than the same weight of meat. It is easily digestible and the white varieties, especially, may be served to young and old. The rich source of gelatine in fish may be preserved by using the stock from steamed and boiled fish as gravy with the addition of butter and seasonings.

When buying fish, be on the look out for certain characteristics. Select those with bright eyes, colour and red gills, having firm flesh with the scales well fixed. They should have a fishy smell without a strong odour.

Bear in mind that fish varies greatly in price according to the state of the market, therefore the price of fish is no indication of its quality or nutritional value. The cheaper varieties of fish are often a much better buy than the more popular and usually larger ones, so flexibility in choice may be an advantage.

Flying fish frequent clear warm waters in many parts of the world and have often been seen from ship decks, leaping in and out of the water. In the Caribbean, Barbados is known as the Land of the Flying Fish, where there are large catches between December and June. These fish are delicious when boned, well seasoned and steamed or fried in fillets. Many of the islands' souvenirs are made or carved in the shape of the flying fish.

There are many flavourful ways of cooking fish. The small oily fish are generally fried, broiled or steamed. The larger fish may be boiled, fried in steaks, stuffed, baked, curried or stewed. Using either method, cooking time should be relatively short. Overcooking causes fish to break up and the flavour is also destroyed. The flesh should be flaky when finished. Vinegar, lime or lemon juice is always used in the preparation of fish and, for serving, lime or lemon slices.

Shell fish

Shell fish is plentiful in many areas. Like salt water fish, it is rich in minerals, especially phosphorus and iodine, but it is coarser in texture and not as digestible.

Shellfish may be divided into 2 classes:

1 The crustaceans, i.e. lobsters, cray fish and crabs, which frequent the clear reef waters. Black or land crabs live in swampy areas. Shrimps are harvested mainly from the banks around the northern coast of South America, and in lesser quantities in other areas.
2 The molluscs, i.e. oysters, small and large clams.

Sea eggs are a popular delicacy in Barbados. They are the roes of a sea animal which lives in a round prickly shell. The sea egg season lasts from about September to January when the roes are mature.

Turtles are caught in northern and southern waters of the Caribbean. There are several varieties but the green turtle is best for eating. The brown mottled back turtle is prized more for its tortoise-shell from which many useful articles are made and sold as souvenirs.

Tinned fish, locally processed or imported, such as salmon and sardines are very nutritious and useful when fresh fish is scarce or unavailable.
This provides extra calcium as the bones are eaten in this processed state.

Fish may be dried successfully and although some of the flavour is lost, the protein and mineral values are, however, increased.

Salted cod fish

Salted cod fish or salt fish, as it is commonly known, was imported from the early days of slavery by the colonists, and used as the main protein food for their slaves and domestic servants. Since trade between Canada and the Caribbean started early in this century, salted cod fish has been imported almost exclusively from that country up to the present day. There was much snobbery regarding salt fish before the Second World War, but as food became scarce and salt fish became more and more expensive, it was gradually accepted by all classes as a worthwhile protein substitute. Salt fish dishes are today very tastily made and widely used. Small well-seasoned fish balls made from it have long been popular cocktail snacks. Salt fish and ackee is Jamaica's most popular national dish.

Before preparation, salt fish must be washed well and soaked in cold water for several hours or overnight if necessary. The salt solution is discarded. It may be boiled up quickly and the water drained off, but the latter method reduces the flavour. The fish is then flaked or pounded and seasoned and mixed with other ingredients to make the required dishes.

Preparation of fish

Cleaning Rinse fish to remove any sand or slime. Lay it on some rough kitchen paper and scale on both sides with a dull-edged knife. Rinse off the scales. Slit the belly from just below the head to halfway down the body. Remove and discard the entrails preserving any roes or melts. The head of some fish, e.g. snapper, may be left on. In this case, remove the gills; otherwise, cut off the head around its base, also the tail. Rinse the fish well with lime juice and water.

Steaking To remove the back fin, make an incision with a sharp knife along each side of it, and from the tail end pull it firmly out. Remove the small fins likewise. The fish is now cut across in about 2.5-cm (1-in) round steaks.

Filleting The whole piece of fish from below the head to the tail is called a fillet. Fillets may be cut in pieces, i.e. fillet steaks. To cut the fillets, use a sharp knife and split the fish down the centre back to the bone. Working from the head downwards, cut the flesh cleanly all the way to the tail by keeping the knife pressed down to the bones. Remove the fillet on the other side similarly. The bones and head may be used for making soup stock.

To skin the fillets, lay them on a board with the skin side down. Holding the end of the tail skin firmly in the left hand, and using a sharp knife in the right hand, make a sawing motion between the flesh and skin of the fish from the tail end upwards pulling the skin firmly with the left hand until it is separated from the flesh.

Boiled fish

Fish is allowed to steam rather than boil, and large whole fish or large fish steaks are suitable, e.g. whole red fish, dolphin or king fish steaks (crosswise cuts). Clean the fish and marinate it in lime and salt. Place in enough boiling water to make the gravy required, add salt, pepper, sliced onion, butter and a little mixed mustard to taste. A few small garden tomatoes or tomato ketchup may also be added. Simmer together until the fish is easily removed from the bone. Serve with slices of lime.

A small quantity of fish may be seasoned similarly and steamed in a soup plate placed over a saucepan in which other food is being cooked. Cover the soup plate with the saucepan lid or plate, steam the fish, turning it once during cooking, for 20–25 minutes, or until it is finished.

Fried fish

Fish must be dried before frying and coated to prevent fat from soaking into it. Steaks and thick slices of fish should be fried in shallow fat as they require thorough cooking. Rissoles, croquettes, etc., including cooked fish are coated with batter and fried in deep fat for quick cooking. A deep saucepan with a frying basket is used. The basket should be heated in the fat before the food is fried in it, so as to maintain the temperature of the fat.

Fillets, steaks and small whole fish are best for frying. Marinate fish as for steaming. A little seasoning paste may be rubbed over the fish, if desired. Dredge the fish steaks, etc., in seasoned flour (p16). Allow steaks to stand a little, then fry in hot fat until brown. Alternatively, the fish may be dipped in beaten egg dredged in breadcrumbs and flour, and fried. Serve with slices of lime or lemon and parsley.

Grilled fish

Steaks, cutlets, fillets, small whole fish may all be satisfactorily grilled. Dry the fish, season it, brush with melted butter and score the flesh of whole fish to avoid the fish drying outside before it is finished cooking. Grease the grill rack to prevent fish from sticking to it. Cook for a short period turning fish from one side to the other. Time: about 7–15 minutes.

Brown gravy (for use with Fried fish or Rissoles)

1 medium onion, sliced
1 tablespoon butter
1 tablespoon flour
½ teaspoon salt
1 cup water *or* stock from vegetables

pepper to taste
1 teaspoon cassareep *or* burnt sugar colouring
1 tablespoon tomato sauce *or* a few sliced garden tomatoes

Melt butter, add onion. Stir in flour and salt. Cook for 5 minutes, stirring all the time. Add water and other ingredients. Stir in colouring or cassareep last.

Fish pie

450 g (1 lb) cold boiled red fish (*or* any large fish in season)
50 g (2 oz) grated cheese
450 g (1 lb) potatoes or yam
breadcrumbs
chopped parsley

1 cup cream sauce
2 large tomatoes
1 beaten egg
1 minced onion
2 tablespoons butter
pepper and salt to taste

Shred fish and arrange half on greased baking dish, sprinkle with chopped parsley, pepper, salt, onion, grated cheese and a little lime juice. Add a layer of sliced vegetables and a layer of tomatoes. Dot with butter. Repeat layers, top with vegetables, beaten egg sprinkled with breadcrumbs and dotted with butter. Garnish with parsley.

Fish soufflé

450 g (1 lb) boiled dolphin *or* red fish, etc.
1 cup soufflé cream sauce (p40)
½ teaspoon white pepper
1 tablespoon onion (finely chopped)

½ teaspoon salt
2 eggs (separated)
2 tablespoons butter
1 tablespoon lime juice

Mix beaten egg yolks with fish to which cream sauce, lime juice, onion, pepper, salt, 2 tablespoons butter are added. Fold in stiffly beaten whites. Put in greased baking dish and bake in moderately slow oven till brown. Allow space in dish for mixture to rise. Salt fish may be substituted.

Baked stuffed fish

1 whole fish (1.35 kg or 3 lb white fish, preferably)
1 tablespoon seasoning mixture poo)
1 cup bread *or* biscuit crumbs
1 onion (chopped)

salt and pepper to taste
1 tablespoon chopped herbs
1 clove garlic (minced)
2 tablespoons butter
2 tablespoons chopped pickles
water to moisten

Clean fish well, leaving on the head. Rub in a little seasoning mixture and stuff with the other ingredients mixed together to moist consistency. Skewer or sew the cut side of the fish. Baste with butter. Place it in a buttered baking dish with a cup of hot water. Bake in a moderate oven for about ¾ hour. To make gravy, add sliced onion and a little brown colouring to cooking water 20 minutes before it is finished.

Fish cakes or rissoles

1½ cups steamed or left-over fish
1 cup mashed potato or provision
½ teaspoon lime juice
1 tablespoon parsley
breadcrumbs and flour

1 tablespoon onion (chopped)
1 egg
salt and pepper to taste
oil for frying

Flake and mash the fish. Add potato, seasoning and lime juice. Beat egg and put half of it in the mixture. Shape the mixture into cakes with a spoon. Dip the cakes in the rest of the egg. Roll in breadcrumbs and flour, and fry in deep or shallow fat.

Escovitched fish

900 g (2 lb) any large fish
oil for frying
1 cup brown vinegar
piece of mace
salt

few cloves
red pepper
onions
parsley

Cut the fish into steaks and fry in oil. Lay the slices in a dish. Cover with brown vinegar that has been boiled with a piece of mace, a few cloves, salt to taste and a slice of red pepper. Let this remain until the next day. Turn the fish on the other side and place in an open dish. Strain the same vinegar and pour over the fish. Garnish with slices of raw onion, red pepper and parsley.

Curried fish steaks

3 tablespoons oil or fat
2 tablespoons chopped onion
1 clove of garlic
2 tablespoons curry powder
1 cup water or coconut milk

a little lime juice
piece of green mango
salt to taste
675 g (1½ lb) prepared fish steaks

Heat the oil, add the onion and garlic and fry them lightly but do not brown. Add the curry powder, stir and cook for 3 or 4 minutes. Add water or coconut milk, lime juice and mango, and cook until thick.

Put in fish and cook gently until tender. Do not stir fish, but to prevent it from sticking to the bottom of the pan, the pan may be moved gently backwards and forwards.

Fish, Creole style

4 or 5 fish steaks
1 small onion
1 tablespoon seasoned paste
2 medium ripe tomatoes

3 or 4 tablespoons butter *or* margarine
Vinegar *or* lime juice
salt

Marinate fish and rub with seasoned mixture (see p16). Sprinkle with a little salt. Slice onions. Melt butter in a frying pan and fry onions lightly. Remove onions from the pan. Put in fish and cover pan tightly so that the fish cooks in steam. When one side is done (4 minutes), turn carefully; arrange sliced tomatoes and onions on top, cover and steam again (4 minutes). Just before serving pour a little lime juice or vinegar over each piece of fish.

Note: Fish cooked in this way takes only 10 to 15 minutes and there is no extra sauce to be made.

Fish and vegetable mould

675 g (1½ lb) any fish
¼ cup chopped olives *or* pickles
1 cup chopped carrots
5 cups fish stock
1 large onion

celery *or* cucumber
½ cup French dressing
salt and pepper
piece of red sweet pepper
3 tablespoons gelatine

Soak gelatine in cold water. Cook fish, onion, carrots, salt and pepper until tender. Remove from heat. Take out fish and flake. Cut up onion and carrots in five cups of fish stock. Add gelatine to hot stock and stir until dissolved. Add 1 teaspoon of sugar. Add the flaked fish, allow to cool, add the chopped celery or cucumber, olives and pepper. Rinse mould in cold water, fill with mixture. Chill in refrigerator. When set, insert knife round edges and turn out on platter.

Scalloped fish

450 g (1 lb) cooked fish
½ cup soufflé sauce (p40)
pepper and salt to taste

4 tablespoons breadcrumbs
1 tablespoon butter

Grease a pie dish. Put a layer of the crumbs in the dish. Have the fish flaked, and combine with the soufflé sauce. Arrange fish and crumbs in alternate layers, finishing with breadcrumbs on top. Place the butter in small pats on the top. Bake in a moderately hot oven for about 10 to 15 minutes until crumbs are brown.

Fish pilau

450 g (1 lb) king fish
2 cups rice
3 tablespoons margarine
2 onions
1 hot green pepper with stem

tomato ketchup
chive and thyme
3 teaspoons salt
1 lime

Slice and season fish. Clean and wash rice and cook in 4 cups of boiling salted water with tomato ketchup and seasonings for 15 minutes. Place seasoned fish on top, adding margarine. Cover and cook over low heat until rice and fish are finished. Remove the pepper before it bursts.

Baked fish ring

450 g (1 lb) red salmon *or* tuna
1 cup fine dry breadcrumbs
½ cup chopped celery
½ cup chopped green pepper

2 tablespoons minced onion
1 tablespoon lemon juice
1 cup evaporated milk
1 beaten egg

Combine salmon, crumbs, vegetables and lemon juice. Combine milk and egg; add to salmon mixture, mixing gently. Turn into well-greased 5-cup ring mould. Bake in a moderate oven for about 30 to 35 minutes. Serve with salad cream and stuffed olives.

Kedgeree

450 g (1 lb) cooked fish
2 tablespoons butter
⅓ cup milk
salt and pepper to taste

1 tablespoon minced onion
3 hard boiled eggs
2 cups cooked rice

Flake the fish. Chop the egg whites and add them to the melted butter, rice, fish, salt and pepper, and onion. Add milk and stir over low heat until very hot. Serve garnished with sieved egg yolk and parsley.

Brown fish stew

900 g (2 lb) large fish (snapper,
    dolphin, etc.)
1 sliced onion
pepper and salt

fat for frying
1 tablespoon butter
water *or* stock
1 tablespoon flour

Prepare the fish cutting it crosswise in 2.5-cm (1-in) thick slices. Fry it lightly. Make a brown sauce by frying onion in butter and adding flour slowly until brown. Add water or stock to thicken and also pepper and salt to taste. Place the fish in a deep frying pan. Pour on the sauce and allow to simmer for 15 minutes, turning the fish once.

Flying fish

Method of boning Scale and clean as for any fish. Using a small pointed knife, remove the head and fins by cutting under the fins and around the base of the head. Remove the back fin by cutting with a sawing motion from the tail end upwards. Make slits on either side of the side fins and pull them out. With the point of the knife, from the head end, sharply cut downwards on either side of the centre or back bone and carefully draw it out. The fish now lies flat on the back. Holding the knife almost horizontal with the fish, then pare off the set of bones on either side; then cut out the two thin strips of fine bones situated at equal distance from the centre groove. The fish is now free from bones and may be prepared as desired.

Steamed flying fish

6 boned flying fish
2 limes
2 sliced onions
pepper and salt to taste
2 tablespoons seasoning mixture
  (p16)

1 teaspoon mustard
1 teaspoon vinegar
1 tablespoon flour
2 tablespoons butter
1 sliced tomato
1 cup water

Marinate the fish in a little salt and lime juice for 15–20 minutes. Drain and season the fish carefully with seasoning paste. Roll inwards from the tail end and arrange the rolled fish in a stewpan with mustard, vinegar, flour, butter, tomato, sliced onions and water. Add salt and pepper to taste and simmer gently until fish is cooked. Serve with lime slices and parsley.

Fried flying fish

6 boned flying fish
2 limes
breadcrumbs and flour
1–2 beaten eggs (optional)

oil for frying
2 tablespoons seasoning mixture
  (p16)
1 teaspoon salt

Marinate in lime and salt for about 15 minutes. Drain well and rub with seasoning mixture in the grooves left after boning the fish. Dip in flour, then brush with egg (if used) then flour again and fry in hot shallow fat, first on the top side then on the back of the fish fillets until brown.

Baked flying fish melts

2 cup melts
1 cup white sauce (p40)
salt and pepper to taste
breadcrumbs

50 g (2 oz) grated cheese
1 tablespoon minced onion
1 lime

Wash melts well with lime. Drain and steam for a few minutes. Add to them the white sauce, onion, salt and pepper and half the grated cheese. Divide the mixture in individual scallop shells, sprinkle with bread crumbs and the rest of the cheese. Bake in a moderate oven till golden brown. Any white fish may be flaked and baked in the same way.

Sprats

These are tiny fish resembling sardines but smaller in size. They are delicious when fried with or without batter until crisp. The bones, except perhaps the back bone may easily be eaten. They should always be cooked very fresh.

3 dozen sprats (approximately)
oil for frying
2 limes, salt and pepper to taste
seasoned flour (p16)

Wash the sprats thoroughly with lime and salt. Dry them well. Dip them in seasoned flour and fry in hot fat. Alternatively, they may be dipped in batter (p148).

Boiled dolphin's head

1.35 kg (3 lb) dolphin head
2 sliced onions
piece of hot pepper
1 sliced tomato
1 bunch herbs
4 cups water
1 dessertspoon salt

few cloves
1 tablespoon vinegar
2 tablespoons butter
2 limes
1 tablespoon flour
1 teaspoon mustard

Wash and clean head, cut in half and soak in salt and lime juice for ½ hour. Boil in water adding salt, onions, pepper, tomato, herbs, cloves, vinegar and butter. Mix together flour and mustard in a little cold water and add. Boil for 15 minutes. Serve with sliced lime.

Note: Before adding seasonings remove all bones except the skull bones.

Stewed shark

900 g (2 lb) shark	salt and pepper to taste
1 large lime	1 dessertspoon sugar
1 tablespoon rum	chives, thyme, onion and garlic to
cooking oil	taste
5 tablespoons water	vinegar

Clean shark with lime and salt and cut in thick slices. Prepare the seasoning and add to shark; put in rum and leave for about one hour. Heat the oil in a thick saucepan and add garlic and the sugar; cook until it bubbles. Remove burnt garlic. Remove fish from seasonings and fry for about 5 minutes; mix fish seasonings with Worcester sauce and 3 tablespoons water. Add to fish and cook for about 10 or 15 minutes. Add the rest of the water and cook until fish is done.

Crabs

Preparation of shells Red sea crabs are caught in some areas, but blue and black are more popular and readily available. These are usually bought one or two days before required and purged with green leaves.

To prepare them for cooking, pierce the brain, which lies on the underside of the body between the eyes, with a sharp skewer, then plunge the crab at once into boiling salted water and cook for about ½ hour. Then break the claws and pick out the meat. Discard the gall and useless tissue, retaining the meat from the body and legs. Thoroughly clean the back shell for filling.

Crab backs

12 cooked crabs	2 teaspoons vinegar
4 tablespoons browned crumbs	1 teaspoon minced pepper
salt	1 tablespoon minced onion
2 tablespoons butter	½ teaspoon curry powder

Shell crabs and mince the meat. Mix the breadcrumbs, black pepper, salt, butter, vinegar, minced pepper, onion and curry powder all with the crab meat. Fill the backs, topping with breadcrumbs and dots of butter. Bake for 15 to 20 minutes till brown.

Crab pilau

2 large crabs	2 cups rice
½ teaspoon pepper	salt to taste
2 blades chives	2 tablespoons curry powder
1 tablespoon butter	1 lime
4 tablespoons oil	1 or 2 onions
3½ cups coconut milk (1 large coconut)	few small tomatoes

Grate coconut and soak in warm water for ½ hour to extract the milk. Strain. Wash and clean crabs with lime. Put oil and butter in saucepan to heat, adding curry powder and seasonings. Add coconut milk, rice, salt and pepper. Cook over low heat until rice is cooked.

Crab gumbo

6 cooked crabs	½ red pepper
3 large tomatoes	sprig parsley and thyme
1 onion	bay leaf
1–2 blades chives	6–7 okras
water	2 tablespoons butter

Prepare crabs, extracting meat. Skin tomatoes. Wash and cut up seasonings and slice okras. Melt butter and brown crab meat. Add seasonings and put in okras. Brown all and add bay leaf and water to cover (about 4 cups). Cover and simmer for 1 hour. Consistency should be like that of thick soup. Serve with rice.

Lobsters

Preparation of shells The most humane way to kill a lobster is to pass a sharp knife through the spinal cord at the joint between the body and the tail shells. Once the spinal cord is severed, no pain can be felt. Put lobsters, head first in boiling salted water and cook for 20–45 minutes according to size. Put cooked lobster in cold water. Pull off the claws and legs and take out the flesh. Remove the craw near the head and the black vein that runs down the back to the tail. Split the body lengthways and remove the flesh carefully. The shell may be used for filling.

Baked lobster

2 cups lobster meat	pepper and salt to taste
4 tablespoons butter	lime juice *or* vinegar
1 medium onion minced	1 tablespoon Worcestershire sauce
breadcrumbs	

Sprinkle shredded lobster with a little salt and lime juice. Allow it to stand 15–20 minutes. Add 3 tablespoons butter, onion, pepper and Worcestershire sauce. Sprinkle with breadcrumbs, dot with the rest of the butter and bake in a moderate oven for about 40 minutes.

Lobster backs

The same recipe as for Crab Backs with the addition of a little cooking sherry. Use medium sized lobsters and fill the two parts of the shell; the middle section and the tail end.

Lobster salad

Flake the boiled lobster meat, mix with mayonnaise or salad dressing and lay on a bed of lettuce. Garnish with sliced olives or sweet pickles, sliced sweet pepper, onion and parsley as desired.

Creamed lobster

⅓ cup butter *or* margarine	1½ cups cooked lobster meat
2 tablespoons flour	¼ cup cooking sherry
1 cup light cream *or* evaporated milk	2 teaspoons lemon juice
2 beaten egg yolks	½ teaspoon salt

Melt butter in saucepan; blend in flour; gradually stir in cream. Cook slowly, stirring constantly till thick. Stir small amount of sauce into egg yolks; return to hot mixture and cook till blended, stirring constantly about 1 minute. Do not overcook. Add lobster, cooking sherry, lemon juice, and salt. Heat before serving in pastry shells made of plain pastry (p133).

Curried shrimps

2 cups fresh shrimps	2 tablespoons curry powder
1 teaspoon salt	2 tablespoons butter
½ teaspoon pepper	1 large tomato
1 cup water	1 onion (chopped)
fat for frying	2–3 blades eschalot

Scald shrimps in salted water for 15 minutes. Peel off heads and shells. Cut open backs and remove black vein. Wash in lime juice and salt water. Lightly brown seasonings in fat, add curry and cook 5 minutes. Add 1 cup of water and the shrimps. Cook for 15 minutes, add butter. Serve hot with boiled rice.

Shrimps in tomato sauce

4 tablespoons butter
4 cups shrimps
1 sprig parsley
2 teaspoons salt
1 sprig thyme
1 lime

1 clove garlic
1 cup diced celery
2 tablespoons sherry
2 tablespoons mixed onion
1 teaspoon vinegar
450 g (1 lb) tomatoes (peeled and sliced)

Shell, clean and wash shrimps well and soak in lime juice for 10 minutes. Season with all ingredients. Stew over a low heat in four tablespoons butter for about 20 minutes. Serve with fluffy rice.

Steamed or fried sea-egg

3 shells sea-egg
3 tablespoons margarine *or* butter
2 limes

pepper and salt to taste
1 large onion (chopped finely)

Empty the shells and carefully pick out any bits of shell. Shake in a dish with salt and water to remove any sand particles. Put in lime and salt water for about 10 minutes. Drain well in a sieve or large strainer. Either steam all ingredients in the top of a double boiler for 30 minutes, or melt margarine with onion in a frying pan, add sea-egg and seasonings, and stir lightly for a few minutes. Before serving squeeze a little lime juice over it and garnish with parsley.

Stewed turtle

900 g (2 lb) turtle
salt and pepper to taste
2–3 blades chives
1 medium sized onion
2 tablespoons butter
2 medium sized tomatoes
2 teaspoons Worcestershire sauce

1 tablespoon vinegar *or* lime juice
½ teaspoon ground spice and clove
3 tablespoons cooking oil
1 wine glass sherry *or* 2 tablespoons rum
1 tablespoon sugar

Boil a few bay leaves in 3 cups of water. Pour over turtle and soak for 10 minutes. Clean and wash turtle in this water. Sprinkle with vinegar or lime juice, and season with salt, pepper, chives, tomatoes, onions, spice and clove, wine and Worcestershire sauce. Allow to stand for 15 minutes. Heat oil and butter, brown the sugar and add meat without the seasonings. Allow to cook slowly for 45 minutes. Then add all the seasonings. Simmer gently till turtle is soft.

Boiled salt fish

225 g (½ lb) thick salt fish
few small tomatoes (cut up in
    pieces)
1 onion
piece red pepper
1 teaspoon mustard
1 dessertspoon flour

2 hard boiled eggs
1 teaspoon Worcestershire sauce
sweet marjoram
2 tablespoons butter
1 dessertspoon vinegar
1 cup water
parsley

Soak fish until flaky and free of salt. Put water in saucepan and all
ingredients except fish. Par-cook these; then squeeze flaked fish and
stir in, cooking for only about 5 minutes. Salt to taste. Add the
Worcestershire sauce and a squeeze of lime juice. A tablespoon of
curry powder may be added. Serve with sliced boiled eggs. Garnish
with parsley. Flaked fish may be browned in fat before cooking.

Frizzled salt fish

225 g (½ lb) salt fish
2 rashers bacon or slices of ham
piece red pepper
1–2 eggs
white pepper
1 teaspoon Vetsin powder (optional)
75 g (3 oz) chopped cabbage

few blades of eschalot
1 chopped onion
sprig sweet marjoram
1 large tomato or
2 tablespoons tomato ketchup
2 tablespoons butter
fat for frying
1 tablespoon parsley (chopped)

Soak salt fish, squeeze dry and pound fine in a mortar. If fish is hard,
boil first. Cut up bacon or ham, also cabbage, seasonings and mix
with fish. Melt the fat in frying pan, stir in fish and seasonings. Just
before removing from heat, stir in one or two beaten eggs, and
remove as egg is cooked. Garnish with parsley and serve with split
peas and rice.

Salt fish cakes

225 g (½ lb) fish
100 g (¼ lb) pumpkin
100 g (¼ lb) flour
2 eggs
milk to mix
1 tablespoon butter

fat for frying
breadcrumbs and flour
salt and pepper
1 tablespoon chopped onion and
herbs

Boil and mince fish finely. Add pumpkin grated raw. Beat eggs. Add
milk, butter, seasonings, and salt and pepper to taste and mix together. Add to the fish and mix well with the flour and make into
cakes or balls. Dip in breadcrumbs and flour and fry in fat till golden
brown.

Creole salt fish

100 g (¼ lb) sliced onion
1 large tomato
1 sweet pepper
1 dessertspoon lard

1 dessertspoon margarine
225 g (½ lb) salt fish
225 g (½ lb) yam
½ cup of milk

Boil and flake salt fish. Boil and slice yam. Fry onions, tomato and sweet pepper. Put ingredients in layers in a casserole and pour milk over. Simmer for twenty minutes. Garnish with sliced hard-boiled egg.

Salt fish in chemise

225 g (½ lb) salt fish
2 tablespoons oil *or* margarine
¼ teaspoon pepper
salt to taste
thyme
1 or 2 blades chives

1 small sliced tomato
½ tablespoon flour
½ onion (sliced)
2 eggs
½ cup water

Scald fish, clean and flake finely. Heat oil and sauté fish and seasonings. Add flour, water and simmer for 10 minutes. Place in buttered fireproof dish and break eggs over. Bake until eggs set. Serve at once.

Salt fish and melongenes

225 g (½ lb) salt fish
450 g (1 lb) melongenes
2 tablespoons butter *or* margarine
grated cheese *or* breadcrumbs

2 blades chives
1 tomato
2 tablespoons onion (sliced)

Scald and clean fish. Peel, slice and boil melongenes, drain and crush. Mix with fish. Sauté seasonings, mix in butter and add to mixture. Top with butter, grated cheese or breadcrumbs. Grill or bake until brown before serving.

7 Spicy meat dishes

Meat available in the Caribbean includes beef, pork, veal, lamb, mutton, offal and poultry. Wild meat or game such as agouti, lappe and wild duck and rabbit is available in some areas. Chickens, turkeys, ducks and geese are the main poultry meats used in local cookery. Meat and poultry are high quality protein foods and are also the most expensive. However, economical cuts like stewing beef, breast of lamb, pork shoulder provide the same food value as the more expensive cuts. Variety meats (offal) liver, heart, kidney, etc., are especially good value for money and should be used at least once a week.

Minced meat is economical and useful for making pies, rissoles and hamburgers. Dried peas and beans may be mixed with it in dishes and thus improve their nutritional value.

Pork is very popular in meat cookery in the area, even the head and feet (trotters) are used for making souse. Mutton and goat meat are used in curries, also chicken, especially by sections of the population who, for religious and other reasons, do not eat pork and beef.

Fresh meat should be of a good colour and without an unpleasant odour. Pork flesh should be pale with firm fat. It should always be thoroughly cooked. Beef should be deep red streaked with fat, but veal should be pale and leaner with less fat. Lamb and mutton should be paler than beef with solid white fat.

If there is no refrigeration, meat should be used as soon as possible, especially offal and minced meats. Avoid par-cooking meat for later use. It may become a source of food poisoning. Cook it thoroughly, cover and keep it in a cool place, and reheat before using. Unwrap frozen meat before storing in a refrigerator. After refrigerated meat is thawed out, it should never be re-frozen.

Methods of cooking meat

Oven roasting, grilling, frying, stewing and braising are the popular ways of cooking meat. In whichever way it is prepared, the temperature should be low to moderate heat. Better cuts are roasted, grilled, fried; cheaper and tougher cuts are stewed and braised, thus being allowed to simmer until tender.

Large cuts of fresh meat to be served cold are put in hot water with seasonings, simmered and sliced when cool. Salt meat is soaked beforehand and cooked in cold water.

When doing pressure or rotisserie cooking, follow the instructions given with the equipment.

Whenever a meat thermometer is used in roasting meat, be sure that it is pushed into the meat so that the tip of it reaches the centre of the thickest muscle and not in the fat.

Roasting Season meat, place in oven at 170°C, 325°F or Gas 3 with fat side up. Leave meat uncovered. It is unnecessary to baste it or to put water in the pan. The meat will brown as it cooks. Roasting time for beef is 25–40 minutes per 450 g (1 lb) depending on how well done it is required. Pork needs to be well done, about 45 minutes to 450 g (1 lb). Veal requires 30 minutes and lamb 35–40 minutes to 450 g (1 lb).

Broiling (grilling) Follow directions for your cooker. Turn meat once only. Time varies according to the thickness of the steaks being cooked.

Frying A heavy frying pan is useful for thin beef steaks, veal cutlets, pork chops and liver which are usually fried in a small amount of fat.

Stewing Tougher joints are cut in serving pieces, seasoned, browned in hot fat, covered with water and allowed to simmer. Vegetables are added towards the end of the cooking period.

Braising and Pot Roasting Pieces of meat are seasoned with salt and pepper and browned on all sides in hot fat. Water is added in small amounts as required. Keep the saucepan covered and cook very slowly until tender.

Roast tenderloin, sirloin or rib

1.8–2.7 kg (4–6 lb) meat
2 cloves garlic (sliced)
butter
salt and pepper

Rub salt and pepper on meat and place fat side up in roasting pan. Cut gashes in meat between fat streaks and insert garlic. Baste with butter.

For *Tenderloin* roast in hot oven for about 1 hour. Cover with aluminium foil.

For *Sirloin*, cover and cook in a moderate oven for about 2 hours until tender.

For *Standing Rib Roast*, place on roasting pan without water in a slow oven. Leave it uncovered and allow 20 minutes per 450 g (1 lb) for rare, 25 minutes per 450 g (1 lb) for medium and 30 minutes per 450 g (1 lb) for well done roast.

For *Rolled Rib Roast*, cook in the same way as for Standing Rib Roast, allowing 10 minutes more per 450 g (1 lb) for rare, medium or well done meat.

For *Pot Roast*, chuck or rump steak are good cuts. Take off any excess fat. Heat fat in heavy saucepan or Dutch pot. When melted to about 2 tablespoons of liquid, remove pieces of fat. Season roast with pepper, salt and garlic slices. Sprinkle with flour. Brown on all sides. Add ½ cup of water, cover tightly and cook 2–3 hours adding more water when necessary to prevent it from burning. Whole onions or carrots may be added during the last 45 minutes of cooking. Add enough water to make gravy.

Beef stew and vegetables

450 g (1 lb) stewing steak
pepper and salt to taste
100 g (¼ lb) carrots *or* turnips
25 g (1 oz) fat for frying

15 g (½ oz) flour
1 large onion
2 cups water
few garden tomatoes

Cut meat into serving pieces. Slice onion. When fat is smoking hot, fry meat on both sides till brown. Lift out and keep hot. Fry the onion, stir in flour, and fry slowly to a rich brown. Add the water, boil up, add salt and skim. Return meat to pan. Add diced vegetables to the stew and allow to simmer for 2 hours. Lift meat on to a hot dish, arrange vegetables at each end, and pour the sauce over.

Beef loaf

450 g (1 lb) minced meat
¾ cup breadcrumbs
1 beaten egg
1 small can tomato soup
½ cup finely chopped onion

2 tablespoons chopped sweet
    pepper
1½ teaspoons salt
1 teaspoon chopped mixed herbs

Combine all ingredients and mix well. Shape mixture into a loaf in shallow baking dish. Garnish with sweet pepper slices after baking in a moderate oven for about 1 hour.

Meat balls

325 g (¾ lb) cooked minced beef   1 tablespoon chopped onion
¼ cup cooked potatoes   salt and pepper to taste
½ teaspoon chopped herbs   flour and breadcrumbs
1 beaten egg

Mash the potatoes, add meat and mix in other ingredients thoroughly. Shape into balls, roll in breadcrumbs and flour, and fry in hot fat until brown.

Grilled steak

Choose porterhouse, T-bone or tenderloin steak, cut 2.5 cm (1 in) thick. Score the fat in places, but not the meat. Place steaks on pre-heated grill rack, near the heat for thin steaks – farther from heat for thicker ones. Brown the top side, sprinkle lightly with salt and pepper, then the other side; season, and serve very hot. For 2.5-cm (1-in) steaks, allow 5–8 minutes each side for *rare*, 6–10 minutes for *medium*; for 3.5-cm (1½-in) steaks, allow 8–10 minutes each side for *rare*, 10–15 minutes for *medium*, and longer in each case for well done, when meat should look grey.

Minute steaks

These steaks are thin cuts of meat from round steak. They are scored all over with a sharp knife or special machine to break the tissues and so tenderize them. Cook them quickly on a heavy greased pan for 1 or 2 minutes on each side. Sprinkle with salt and pepper before serving hot.

Baked pork

2.7–3.5 kg (6–8 lb) pork loin   1 teaspoon white pepper
2 teaspoons salt   2 teaspoons sugar
seasoning mixture (p16)   25 g (1 oz) butter

Wash the meat and dry thoroughly. With a sharp knife, make deep gashes in the meat in several places. Rub the joint *thoroughly* with the salt and white pepper. Cover and put it aside for 15–20 minutes. Rub some seasoning mixture into the gashes made in the meat. Baste the joint with the butter and put into a roasting pan, uncovered, in a moderate oven allowing it to bake 25 minutes for each pound and 25 minutes extra, turning and basting occasionally with the dripping from the pan. During the last half hour of baking, sprinkle the skin side with the sugar, and raise the oven temperature to 200°C, 400°F or Gas 6 to allow the skin to become crisp and brown. Serve the roast with Mock Apple Sauce and Brown Gravy (see below).

Mock apple sauce

450 g (1 lb) green pawpaw
¼ cup hot water
50 g (2 oz) sugar
1 tablespoon lime juice

Peel and cut the pawpaw in pieces. Place in a saucepan with water to cover and bring it to the boil. Throw off this water, drain and add ¼ cup of water and the sugar, allowing the pawpaw to simmer until it is very soft. Remove it from the heat; add one tablespoon of lime juice and beat it with a wooden spoon until smooth. Serve one to two tablespoons with each serving of baked pork.

Brown gravy

2 onions
2 tablespoons dripping
few slices tomato *or*
1 teaspoon tomato paste

pepper and salt to taste
sediment from baked pork
1 cup hot water *or* stock

Wash and slice the onions into the hot dripping in the frying pan, sprinkling over the flour to brown well. Skim off the fat and add the sediment from the meat, also one cup of hot water with the tomato. Stir well and simmer until it thickens. Add salt and pepper to taste.

Stuffed pork shoulder

Bone a shoulder or hand of pork. Rub over with salt and pepper. Fill with *stuffing*. Tie up firmly and bake slowly in moderate oven until brown, turning over and basting with some of its dripping. Raise the heat for the last 15–20 minutes to brown the skin, and allow to become crisp.

Stuffing
1 cup bread *or* biscuit crumbs
2 tablespoons fat for frying
1 chopped onion
2 rashers of bacon cut in pieces
1 clove garlic (chopped)
milk or water to moisten

1 tablespoon raisins *or* sweet
  pickles
black pepper and salt to taste
1 beaten egg
2 teaspoons dried sage *or* mixed
  herbs

Mix all ingredients and fry lightly in 2 tablespoons of fat. Cool a little and stuff joint carefully.

Grilled pork chops

6 pork chops
white pepper
garlic salt

Season chops well, rubbing over with garlic salt and pepper or season with some basic marinade (p15). Put under grill with medium flame allowing about 25 minutes for cooking; turn up the flame during the last 5–6 minutes for browning. Put them in a covered dish in a moderate oven to cook through for about 20 minutes. Serve with caramel sweet potatoes.

Fried pork chops

6 chops
white pepper
garlic salt
fat for frying

Rub salt and pepper on chops. Brown on both sides in hot fat. Pour off any excess fat. Add a little water and cook over low heat covering the pan tightly, *or* bake the chops in a moderate oven for about 45 minutes in a covered pan.

Picnic shoulder of ham

one 2.25 kg (5 lb) picnic shoulder
¾ cup vinegar
few whole cloves
thin garlic slices

Cut slits here and there in the meat about 1 cm (½ in) deep and insert the slices of garlic. Place it in a saucepan and cover with cold water. Add the vinegar and whole cloves. Cover and simmer for about 3 hours. Skin the meat, remove from liquid and bake at 180°C, 350°F or Gas 4 for about 15–20 minutes. Use the following glaze:

Mustard glaze
Mix together 1 cup brown sugar, 1 teaspoon dry mustard, 2 or 3 tablespoons ham fat or dripping. Baste this on the meat before baking.

Baked ham

Place the ham, fat side up, on a rack in the shallow oven pan. Bake in a slow oven for 2–3½ hours allowing 15–20 minutes per 450 g (1 lb). Half an hour before it is finished, remove the ham from the oven, skin it, pour off the dripping, score the ham fat in diamond shapes. Stick in whole cloves and pour over it some *mustard glaze* as used for Picnic Shoulder. *Canned* cooked hams may be baked and glazed as for Baked Ham allowing about 20–35 minutes in the oven at 180°C, 350°F or Gas 4.

Veal and ham croquettes

3 tablespoons butter	1 cup milk
⅓ cup flour	1 cup minced ham
½ teaspoon salt	1 cup minced veal
2 tablespoons prepared mustard	1 tablespoon chopped onion

Melt butter, add flour and salt. Blend well and stir in milk gradually over low heat. When cool add the meat, onion and mustard. Shape into croquettes (cork shape), dredge them over with breadcrumbs and flour, brush with beaten egg, dredge again in crumbs and flour. Allow to stand a little before frying in deep hot fat until brown. Drain on absorbent paper. Makes 12 croquettes.

Veal roast

A leg or loin roast with bone may be chosen or a boned rolled rump or shoulder roast may be used with the same filling as for stuffed pork shoulder (p61).

Place the roast, fat side up, on rack in the roasting pan. Lay slices of bacon on the top and bake at 170°C, 325°F or Gas 3, allowing 35–40 minutes per 450 g (1 lb). For boned rolled roasts, allow 40–50 minutes. Before slicing to serve, allow roast to stand about 20 minutes to become firm.

Veal chops or cutlets

Cut piece of veal 2.5-cm (1-in) thick in chops. Season with garlic salt and pepper, dip in flour *or* in beaten egg and breadcrumbs, and fry in hot fat. Add a little water, cover and cook until tender, for about 45 minutes.

Lamb roast

Leg of lamb is the popular cut for roasting. Trim off excess fat. Rub with garlic salt and pepper. Make gashes in the flesh and put in some seasoning mixture *or* slices of garlic as desired. Roast at 170°C, 325°F or Gas 3 for about 30–35 minutes per 450 g (1 lb). Allow it to stand before serving.

Lamb chops

Rib, loin or shoulder chops are equally good. Cut them 2-cm (¾-in) thick, season with basic marinade and drain (see p15). Grill them under medium heat for about 10 minutes on each side. Sprinkle on a little Italian Dressing (p17).

Curried mutton or goat

900 g (2 lb) mutton	225 g (½ lb) carrots
3 onions	2 tablespoons curry powder
1 bunch herbs	1 teaspoon sugar
1 clove garlic	2 tablespoons tomato ketchup
1 dessertspoon salt *or* to taste	1 tablespoon fat
water to cover	

Cut meat in pieces, fry lightly in fat, add curry powder and simmer in water to cover with seasonings until meat is nearly tender (about 1½ hours). Dice carrots and add. Continue cooking until meat and carrots are tender.

Variety meats (offal)

Variety meats or offal are not usually as popular as carcass meat although they are of high nutritional value, especially liver, and may be prepared in many tasty ways. These meats also include heart, kidney, tongue, sweetbread, tripe, oxtail, pig's feet, pig's head and cow-heel.

Calves' liver is more expensive than ox liver, but is equally good. That of the lamb and pig are sometimes used.

Fried liver slices

675 g (1½ lb) thinly sliced liver (1-cm or ½-in)
flour
oil for frying
1 tablespoon vinegar

Remove the skin and membrane from the liver and rinse in cold water. Marinate slices in some basic marinade (p15) and allow them to stand a little. Drain them and dredge in plain or seasoned flour (p16). Fry in hot shallow fat on both sides until brown. Alternatively, liver may be floured, placed in a greased baking dish with about 8 rashers of bacon arranged on top and allowed to bake in a moderate oven until bacon is crisp.

Fried kidneys

6 lamb or sheep kidneys
salt and pepper
butter or dripping
tomato ketchup

Split the kidneys lengthwise without separating them. Remove the fat in the centre and marinate them using basic marinade (p15) for about 15 minutes. Drain them.

Use a skewer to hold the kidneys open and flat. Melt the fat and fry them quickly. Do not overcook them. Sprinkle them with a little salt and pepper. Brush with tomato ketchup and serve hot. Alternatively, brush the kidneys with the fat or melted butter. Grill under hot grill, cooking the cut side first and turning when necessary. Serve with butter or bacon.

Mixed grill

2 lamb kidneys   4 bacon rashers
4 lamb chops   4 tomatoes
100 g (4 oz) mushrooms   salt and pepper
½ teaspoon celery salt   ½ teaspoon garlic salt

Rub lamb chops and kidneys with basic marinade mixture (p15). Drain and brown lamb chops on one side under hot grill. Lightly fry kidneys and mushrooms with bacon rashers. Brown other side of chops. Arrange kidneys, mushrooms and halved tomatoes around them. Sprinkle with salt and pepper. Arrange bacon rashers on top and cook under medium heat until chops are finished.

Braised sweetbreads

2 calves' sweetbreads   1 small onion
bacon fat or butter   1 carrot
salt and pepper   piece of celery
½ teaspoon mixed herbs   1½ cups water

Soak sweetbreads in cold water for about ½ hour. Cook in boiling salted water for 5 minutes. Then place in cold water for 20 minutes. Cook and leave for about 1 hour between two plates to hold the shape.

Fry vegetables for about 10 minutes and add the seasonings. Put in a baking dish and cover with 1½ cups water. Place the sweetbreads on top, baste with fat or butter, cover and cook in a moderate oven for about 1 hour. Add more water, if necessary, during cooking time.

Boiled ox tongue

900 g (2 lb) ox tongue

1 large onion

2 tablespoons vinegar

bunch of herbs

salt and pepper

Wash and scrape tongue thoroughly and soak for about an hour or more. Soak longer if it is pickled. Put the tongue in a saucepan of cold water and cover it. Skin it as it boils, add onion, vinegar, salt, pepper and herbs and cook over medium heat, 30 minutes for 450g (1 lb) or until tender. When cold, slice thinly and serve with sliced ham, or serve hot in a butter sauce using some of the cooking stock and mixing about 2 tablespoons butter, $\frac{1}{2}$ teaspoon mustard and a few garden tomatoes cut in pieces.

Tripe with onions

675 g (1½ lb) tripe

1 cup milk

2 large onions

25 g (1 oz) flour

salt and pepper

25 g (1 oz) butter

Blanch the tripe by pouring boiling water over it, and cut it into serving pieces. Put it in a saucepan with the milk, 1 cup of water and allow it to boil. Add sliced onions sautéd in butter, and simmer for about 2 hours. Mix the flour to a smooth paste with a little cold milk and add. Stir until it boils. Simmer for about 10 minutes longer, season to taste and serve.

Chicken

Nowadays, chickens may be bought frozen or almost oven-ready, but many people in the Caribbean area prefer to buy them live, hence they must be plucked and drawn at home.

Drawing a chicken To draw a chicken, the feathers must first be plucked, pulling them downwards from the neck; singe away the hairy feathers with a taper. Cut off the head half-way along the length of the neck. Fold the skin over and cut the neck close to the body. Wipe the neck skin clean, and loosen the crop and gizzard from the neck cavity. With a sharp knife, make a slit about 7 cm (3 in) above the vent. Draw out the entrails carefully taking care not to break the gall bladder which is dark green in colour and attached to the liver. Carefully remove all the organs taking the gall bladder from the liver. Cut open the gizzard, remove the contents and coarse lining skin. Wash the giblets (gizzard, neck, liver and heart) which may be used in the stuffing or to make stock for gravy.

Trussing a chicken for roasting A bird may or may not be trussed before roasting, but trussing makes it more attractive when finished. To do this, first cut off the feet at the first leg joint, and draw out the tendons; peel the skin off the legs. With the bird on its breast, fold the neck over the opening on to the back and fold wing tips under shoulder joints to keep the loose skin in place. Turn bird upwards. Push the legs close to the sides, then with a large packing needle and a long piece of string, pass the needle through one wing joint, then through the leg joint near the thigh bone, through the body and over to the other leg and wing. Draw through the string and tie the legs with the tail (parson's nose) firmly together. If the bird is to be stuffed, fill it through neck and vent ends and sew up the opening before trussing.

Before cooking a frozen bird, untie the string around it after it has been thawed out and clean thoroughly before cooking. Season chicken using the basic marinade mixture (p15) before stuffing.

Stuffing for chicken 1.3–1.8 kg (3–4 lb)

2 cups coarse breadcrumbs	1 medium onion
giblets (liver, gizzard, heart)	1 sprig thyme *or* marjoram
1 bacon rasher	hot pepper and salt to taste
fat from chicken *or* oil	few raisins *or* capers
few garden tomatoes (small)	1 teaspoon soy sauce (optional)
1 tablespoon butter	

Moisten the crumbs with water to soften, but do not make into a paste. Fry the chicken fat with the giblets and bacon cut in pieces. Cook for about 5 minutes. Add the chopped onion, tomatoes and other seasonings. Stir in the damp crumbs mixing in well; add butter and cook for about 5 minutes more. Cool the mixture and stuff the chicken sewing or skewering to close the opening. Brush with butter or bacon fat. Place in roasting pan, breast upwards. Allow ½ hour per 450 g (1 lb) at 200 °C, 400 °F or Gas 6.

Stewed chicken

1.35 kg (3 lb) chicken
1 clove garlic
1 teaspoon sugar
2 medium sliced onions
2 teaspoons soy sauce
about 2 cups water

salt and pepper to taste
1 tablespoon vinegar
2 tablespoons tomato sauce
3 tablespoons fat
½ cup diced carrot
few whole cloves

Cut the chicken limbs and breast into 12 pieces, and the bony residue of carcass in 4. Marinate these in vinegar and salt for about 15 minutes. Fry the crushed garlic and sugar in the oil until very brown, then remove garlic. Brown the chicken pieces in the hot fat. Drain off excess fat, add water and other ingredients and allow to simmer for about 1 hour.

Chicken à la King

¼ cup melted butter or chicken fat
3 tablespoons flour
2 cups cooked diced chicken
1 cup chicken broth

1 cup milk
1 teaspoon salt
75 g (3 oz) sliced mushrooms
½ cup chopped pimento

Blend together the fat, flour, broth and milk. Cook stirring over low heat until mixture is thick. Add the other ingredients and heat well. Serve on toast.

Fried chicken

Cut up and marinate chicken using the basic marinade (p15). Drain and dredge in seasoned flour and allow to stand a little. Fry in hot fat, on both sides until brown. Add a little water, cover and steam for about 30 minutes till tender, or cover and finish the cooking in the oven.

Chicken salad

4 cups cooked diced chicken
1 cup chopped celery
1 cup chopped sweet pepper
2 tablespoons grated onion
lettuce leaves, parsley, etc.

½ cup French dressing
½ cup mayonnaise or salad
   dressing
½ cup chicken stock
salt and pepper to taste

Combine the first four ingredients. Mix together dressings, stock and seasonings and pour over the chicken mixture, blending thoroughly. Chill in refrigerator until required; then serve on a bed of lettuce. Garnish with parsley or as desired.

Turkey (roast)

Prepare turkey for roasting in the same manner as for chicken. Allow about ¾ cup of stuffing to pound of net weight of bird. Rub with some basic marinade (p15) and allow to stand. Before filling, drain well. Stuff turkey and skewer or sew the vent end securely; also sew down the skin flat at the neck end after filling. Bacon rashers may be placed across the breast to baste as it cooks. A cover of aluminium foil may be used to cover the bird lightly. Roast it at 170°C, 325°F or Gas 3, 3½–4 hours for 2.7–5.4 kg (6–12 lb) birds, 4½–7 hours for 5.4–9 kg (12–20 lb) birds. To test for finish, press the thick part of the leg; the meat should feel very soft. Before carving, allow the turkey to stand for about 20 minutes when the flesh will have become set and easier to slice.

Salmi or duck

1 duck, 1.8–2 kg (4–5 lb)
3 tablespoons cooking oil
1 tablespoon margarine
1 onion, sliced
2 tablespoons wine *or* rum
salt and pepper to taste
1 tablespoon vinegar

2 teaspoons sugar
1 tablespoon flour
thyme and chives
⅛ teaspoon ground cloves
2 tomatoes and 1 clove garlic
¼ cup olives
2 to 3 cups water and few capers

Cut the duck into serving pieces and mix seasonings well into it. Set aside for 30 minutes. Heat oil and add the meat, leaving the seasonings in the bowl. Add water gradually until meat is tender. Then add seasonings and margarine. Cook until seasonings are done. Thicken gravy with flour mixed into a paste. Add olives, capers and wine or rum last.

Roast duckling

Prepare for roasting the same way as for chicken, adding a little rum and orange juice to the stuffing. Baste well while roasting in a fairly hot oven for about ¾ hour. Drain off any fat, add water, sliced onions, brown colouring and a little butter to make a gravy. Allow to cook in a slow oven until tender, 30–40 minutes or longer. It may be garnished with slices of orange heated in a little wine.

Roast Goose may be prepared in the same way as for duckling. Roast at 170°C, 325°F or Gas 3 for about 30 minutes per 450 g (1 lb). Prick the legs and wings with a fork or skewer to allow the fat to run out while baking.

Rabbit stew

900 g (2 lb) rabbit
2 large onions
3–4 rashers bacon
2 tablespoons rum *or* wine
seasoned flour (p16)
2 cups water

salt and white pepper to taste
few cloves
2 tablespoons butter
bouquet garni
1 tablespoon vinegar

Cut the rabbit meat in pieces. Rub in salt, vinegar and pepper and set aside. In the meantime, dice the bacon, slice the onions, melt the butter in a saucepan, fry the onions and bacon until brown, and remove from the pan. Drain pieces of meat, dredge in seasoned flour and fry in same fat until very brown. Replace onions, add water and other seasonings. Cover tightly and simmer until meat is tender, an hour or more. About 15 minutes before serving, add rum or wine. Garnish with bacon pieces and onions.

8 Energy foods

There is a great variety of these foods from which to choose. Root crops, cereal foods, other starchy fruits, fresh and dried peas and beans (pulses) all contribute to our wealth of energy foods. They are a valuable source of calories as they contain a high percentage of starch.

Yams, sweet potatoes, tannia, eddoes, dasheen, cassava are among the commonly used root crops. Plantains, green bananas and bread-fruit are other favourites. Dried peas and beans not only supply calories but supplement the animal proteins which are scarce and expensive. Imported English potatoes are still used widely and assist with the diet especially when root crops are in short supply.

Rice, a cereal food, is, however, the basic starchy food eaten throughout the Caribbean area. It is cheap and always available as it is grown in the area, chiefly in Guyana. Rice is also rich in calcium and has good supplies of iron and protein and B vitamins. To maintain this nutritive value, rice is being produced parboiled and lightly milled in increasing quantities. Brown or unpolished rice is superior nutritionally, but white rice is in greater demand and is now fortified in some countries. Pulses are used regularly in rice dishes and, with small amounts of meat or fish added, they provide excellent dishes.

Green corn or maize is boiled and served on the cob as a vegetable, and dried corn is ground into meal and cooked in porridge and other dishes. The yellow corn contains carotene and is better than the white variety. The protein in corn is not a useful food supplement.

Macaroni products or pasta are used in dishes to add variety to meals.

All starchy vegetables may be boiled in salted water and served in slices or mashed and buttered. Cook them in a covered saucepan to save vitamin loss and, whenever possible, cook them in the skins, e.g. sweet potatoes.

Broiled yam

Peel and boil vegetable in salted water until tender. Baste with butter, and place in dish on toast rack over heat to brown, under broiler or grill flame, or on a greased gridiron over a red hot coal fire. Brown on both sides, spread with more butter before serving. Tannias and other root vegetables may be cooked likewise.

Sweet potato balls

450 g (1 lb) mashed vegetable
1 tablespoon butter
1 beaten egg
1 chopped onion

¼ teaspoon salt
1 tablespoon flour
½ teaspoon chopped parsley
milk to bind

Mix together all ingredients. Shape into balls and fry in hot fat after dredging them in breadcrumbs and flour. Yam may be served in the same way.

Scalloped sweet potato and onions

900 g (2 lb) medium sized potatoes
100 g (¼ lb) onions
¾ cup milk
50 g (2 oz) flour

½ teaspoon salt
½ teaspoon white pepper
1 tablespoon grated cheese
25 g (1 oz) butter

Parboil sweet potatoes, peel and slice thinly. Also slice onions. Grease a baking dish with butter. Put the potatoes and onions in it in alternate layers. Sprinkle between layers with a mixture of flour, salt and white pepper. Dot with butter and grated cheese and almost cover the vegetables with milk. Bake in moderate oven. Yams and English potatoes may be cooked in the same way.

Caramel sweet potato

4 cups cooked and mashed sweet
    potatoes
3 tablespoons butter
¼ cup sugar (brown)

marshmallows
½ cup orange or pineapple juice
1 teaspoon peanut butter

Dissolve sugar in butter over low heat. Add mashed potatoes to juice and peanut butter. Put into a greased baking dish and arrange marshmallows on top of mixture. Bake in a moderate oven until marshmallows are spread and light brown.

White eddoes (Pulped)

Boil eddoes in skins until soft. Make a pickle of hot water, salt, pepper and lime juice. When soft, pulp (i.e. cut off tops and squeeze out) eddoes into the pickle and keep hot until ready to serve. Place in another dish, spread with butter and serve with salt meat, salmon or any salted fish.

Baked stuffed breadfruit

1 breadfruit (not over-ripe)
225 g (½ lb) fresh meat
100 g (¼ lb) salt meat
1 onion

1 tomato
salt and pepper to taste
2 tablespoons butter
2–3 blades eschalot or chive

Peel breadfruit and parboil whole in salted water. Lightly fry meat in some fat and seasonings. Cut up meat and mince. Cut off stem of breadfruit, peel and core it well. Fill it with meat mixture mixed with butter. Bake in a greased dish in a moderate oven for about 45 minutes. Baste fruit with butter and serve hot.

Pickled breadfruit

Peel, core and cut an under-ripe breadfruit in 1-cm (½-in) slices. Boil in salt water. Prepare pickle of lime juice, chopped onion, salt and pepper. Pour this over breadfruit slices in a dish. Keep warm and when ready to serve, spread with butter. Salt fish or meat is a good accompaniment for this dish. Green bananas may also be pickled.

Foo Foo (Pounded Plantain)

Boil 4 plantains (3 green, 1 ripe, but firm) and when soft, pound them in a large mortar. Dip pestle in cold water in between pounding to prevent sticking. When smooth, mix with 2 tablespoons of butter and salt to taste. Keep warm.

Breadfruit pudding

1 breadfruit, 1–1.3 kg (2½–3 lb)
100 g (¼ lb) salt meat
2 teaspoons or less salt
1 bunch herbs

about 2 cups stock
2 tablespoons butter
1 chopped onion

Cut breadfruit in slices and boil with salt meat cut in pieces, herbs and onion, in water just covering the fruit. When soft, take from heat and mash well with a potato masher, then with a heavy wooden spatula until it is a very smooth and stiff paste, adding stock when necessary. Stir in some of the butter, put in a dish and spread with remainder of the butter.

Fried plantain

plantains
oil for frying
sugar

Thinly slice some very ripe plantains crosswise or lengthwise in
⅛-inch slices. Fry in hot oil until golden brown. Drain on absorbent
paper. Sprinkle with fine sugar if desired.

Tannia fritters

450 g (1 lb) tannias
1 teaspoon chopped onion
chives *or* eschalot
milk to mix

salt and pepper to taste
1 teaspoon butter
1 tablespoon flour

Parboil tannias, allowing them to cook for about 10 minutes. Cool
and grate them. Add seasonings, butter and flour, and moisten with
a little milk. Drop by spoonfuls into hot shallow fat. Brown on both
sides and serve hot.

Creole bananas

6 green bananas
6 tablespoons flour
1 dry coconut
1 large onion
100 g (¼ lb) mackerel (salted)
100 g (¼ lb) corned pork

100 g (¼ lb) carrots
100 g (¼ lb) tomatoes
50 g (2 oz) margarine
½ hot pepper
1 sprig parsley

Wash mackerel and pork. Soak for 30 minutes in cold water. Place
pork in saucepan, cover with cold water and bring to boil. Pour off
water. Cut pork in pieces and brown lightly. Cover and steam until
meat is tender. Remove bone and skin from mackerel and cut in
pieces. Add to pork. Add onions, tomatoes and pepper. Grate
coconut and add water to make 900 ml (1½ pints) milk. Peel and
grate bananas and add flour. Pour coconut milk over meat and bring
to boil. Add banana by spoonfuls and cook for 25 minutes. Add
carrots and cook for 15 minutes more. Decorate with parsley and
sweet pepper.

Curried green bananas

8 green bananas (medium)
1 cup coconut milk
2 tablespoons curry powder
25 g (1 oz) margarine

1 teaspoon hot sauce
salt and pepper to taste
1 beaten egg
boiled rice

Fry curry in margarine for 2 minutes. Peel and slice bananas, place in margarine and curry and brown lightly. Add pepper, salt and coconut milk and simmer gently for $\frac{1}{2}$ hour. Stir in beaten egg. Serve with boiled rice.

Rice dishes

Preparation of rice Wash rice thoroughly, but do not rub it vigorously. Use a heavy saucepan for cooking it and use just enough water to swell the grains and make them soft, without being soggy. 2 cups of water to 1 cup of rice is normally adequate. Avoid straining water from rice, as in doing this the thiamine (Vitamin B1), which is water soluble, will be lost. Cook rice over low heat.

Boiled rice

2 cups rice
4 cups water
1 dessertspoon salt
1 dessertspoon butter

1 small onion
few blades of eschalot (optional)
1 tablespoon lime juice *or* vinegar

Put water to boil with salt. Sprinkle in cleaned, washed rice. Add chopped onion, lime juice and butter. Cover saucepan and boil over moderate heat at first, then allow to steam over low heat until all the water is absorbed and grains are soft (about $\frac{1}{2}$ hour). Serve hot.

Pigeon peas and rice

2 cups rice
salt to taste
1 tablespoon butter
2 cups pigeon peas
1 large tomato

4 cups water
bunch of herbs
100 g ($\frac{1}{4}$ lb) salt meat (optional) cut
  in pieces
1 tablespoon lime juice

Boil peas with seasonings and salt meat, if used, for 20 minutes. Then sprinkle in rice, lime juice and crushed tomato. Add butter and cook same as for boiled rice. Any fresh green peas or beans may be substituted.

Split peas and rice

Use $\frac{1}{2}$ to 1 cup dry split peas to 2 cups rice. Soak beforehand and boil split peas until half cooked before putting in rice. Dried lentils may also be used and put in just before the rice. No soaking is necessary.

For *Whole Peas and Rice*, soak peas several hours or overnight, remove husks and cook like split peas.

Curried rice

2 cups rice	2 onions
4 cups water	2 tablespoons curry powder
3 tablespoons fat	1 dessertspoon salt
2 large tomatoes	1 tablespoon butter

Brown onion in frying pan with fat. Add tomato, salt, curry and cook for 5 minutes. Boil the water, add the curried mixture, then sprinkle in rice and cook as usual.

Calypso rice

2 cups rice	$\frac{1}{2}$ cup chopped ham *or* salt meat
4 cups water	piece red pepper
20 g (1$\frac{1}{2}$ oz) butter	1 small red sweet pepper (sliced)
1 large onion	1 tablespoon grated cheese
2 teaspoons salt	chopped parsley

Wash rice and add to boiling salted water. Cook gently until rice grains are almost soft, then add butter, onion, ham and pepper. Stir gently with a fork, cover and steam 10 minutes to finish. Serve hot with chopped parsley, sweet pepper and grated cheese.

Legumes and pulses

Among the varieties of legumes (green peas and beans) used in the diet are red peas, gunga or pigeon, black eye, cow peas, kidney, white and lima beans, string and pole beans. These supply valuable minerals and vitamins. When these foods are dried, they are known as pulses.

The legumes should be cooked covered in a small amount of boiling salted water for 20 to 30 minutes. Avoid overcooking.

Pulses must be picked over, washed and soaked in boiling water. (1 cup of peas yields about 2 cups after soaking.) Soak them for several hours or overnight to swell the grains. Use the same water for cooking. Add 1 teaspoon salt per cup towards the end of cooking.

Peanuts may be considered with these foods. They supply protein and fat to the diet and should be used more often.

Corn on the cob should be covered in salted water, and boiled until it is tender. A little sugar may be added to the water.

Green peas (Pigeon) stewed

2 cups green peas (1 cup dried)
50–100 g (2–4 oz) salt meat
red pepper and salt to taste
1 dessertspoon minced onion

1 bunch herbs
1 tablespoon butter
water to cover

Boil peas in water with seasonings (except onion and butter) until soft and water is almost dried out. Add butter and onion and cook until all the water is absorbed. Drain if necessary and serve hot, with boiled rice and steamed fish.

Doved peas

2 cups green peas (1 cup dried)
1 teaspoon salt
2 bacon rashers or piece salt meat
1 tablespoon minced onion

piece sweet red pepper
sprig each of thyme and sweet
 marjoram or
½ teaspoon dried herbs

Boil green peas in salted water until soft. Drain. Cut up the bacon rashers or pieces of salt meat with minced onion, red pepper and herbs. Mix seasonings together with peas and fry in hot fat until dry. Remove from heat and stir in a little butter.

Red pea loaf

2 cups red peas
flour to bind
1 tablespoon grated cheese

1 egg
1 tablespoon butter
salt to taste

Boil peas, strain, mash and rub through a sieve. Mix with flour, butter, and egg to bind until it holds shape. Place in greased baking dish, sprinkle with grated cheese and bake in moderate oven. Serve with gravy if liked.

Buttered string beans

450 g (1 lb) string or green beans
salt
25 g (1 oz) butter

Trim the beans, top and bottom, and string them if necessary. If young, cook them whole, if older slice them in a slanting direction. Put in just enough fast boiling salted water to cover them and cook in a covered saucepan. When tender, after about 10–15 minutes, drain, add butter and serve immediately.

White beans with cream sauce

900 g (2 lb) broad beans
1 cup water
bouquet garni
salt and pepper to taste

1 teaspoon sugar
1 egg yolk
½ cup evaporated milk or cream

Shell the beans and cook them in the water with sugar and herbs. When the beans are tender, lift out the herbs. Beat the egg yolk with the cream and stir it carefully into the saucepan. Reheat, stirring all the time until almost simmering. Season and serve at once.

Corn pudding

3 slightly beaten eggs
2 cups drained cooked or canned
    whole kernel corn
2 cups milk

¼ cup finely chopped onion
1 tablespoon butter, melted
1 teaspoon sugar
1 teaspoon salt

Combine ingredients; pour into greased casserole. Place in shallow pan and fill pan to 1 inch with hot water. Bake at 180°C, 350°F or Gas 4 for 40 to 45 minutes or till knife inserted in centre comes out clean.

Split pea pudding

1½ cups split peas
1 medium onion
salt and pepper to taste
¼ cup chopped ham or bacon

1 teaspoon minced fresh herbs
50 g (2 oz) butter
1 egg

Wash, pick and soak the peas overnight. Put in saucepan with same water and extra to cover. Bring slowly to the boil, stirring occasionally and cook until tender and water has almost evaporated. Rub through a coarse sieve. Add butter, beaten egg, meat, pepper and salt to taste. Beat well, put into a covered oven dish and bake in a moderate oven for 20 to 25 minutes.

Peanut butter

2 cups shelled roasted peanuts
½ teaspoon salt

1 tablespoon oil

Peanuts must be freshly roasted. Cover them with boiling water for 2 minutes and drain well. Grind them in a hand mill, pound in a mortar very fine or pulverize in a mincing machine or electric mixer. Add oil, salt and mix well. Keep the butter in covered glass jars.

Mock chicken

1 cup roasted peanuts
1 whole egg
1 egg yolk

1 egg white
breadcrumbs
about 225 g ($\frac{1}{2}$ lb) sweet potatoes

Grind the roasted peanuts until they are oily. Stir in the whole egg
and yolk beaten well. Add breadcrumbs to thicken. Parboil potatoes
and cut into thin slices. Spread tops thickly with peanut mixture,
dip in beaten egg white. Fry in deep fat to golden brown and serve
hot.

9 Salad vegetables and fruit

These embrace the green and yellow vegetables which are of special importance because they provide carotene (pro Vitamin A) and Vitamin C and some calcium. Carrots, pumpkins, red sweet peppers, avocados, okras also the *dark green* leaves of spinach, cabbage, lettuce, kale, sweet potato, beet and turnip, watercress and parsley are all good sources of carotene. Vitamin C is present in *all* green vegetables but is very quickly lost from the vegetable after it is picked or cut from the garden. Storing, especially in warm climates, causes further reduction or loss of Vitamin C.

All fresh fruits, especially the yellow varieties such as mango, banana, pawpaw, pineapple, citrus varieties, avocado pear, plums, garden cherries, golden apple, monkey apple, cashew, guavas, etc. are rich in carotene, iron and Vitamin C in varying proportions. They are usually eaten raw, but are also used in drinks, cooked in jams and jellies and used in many ways in desserts. Raw fruit should always be carefully washed before use. Storing of fruits, like vegetables, reduces the flavour and vitamin content.

It is very necessary, therefore, to obtain vegetables and fruits which are garden fresh and young. If they must be stored for a few days, keep them in plastic bags in a refrigerator or cool place.

Cooking and preparing vegetables

Rinse all vegetables quickly in cold water. Cook them in the minimum of fast boiling salted water. Any residue of water after cooking should be used for gravies to save the soluble Vitamin C content. Plan the meal preparation so that green vegetables are cooked just before the meal is to be served, as exposure to air and heating over a long period cause further deterioration. Cooking of vegetables in a steamer or pressure cooker helps to preserve their nutritive qualities. The use of bicarbonate of soda in cooking water must also be strictly avoided.

Take great care in the preparation of leafy green vegetables for raw salads. They should be rinsed leaf by leaf to remove any sand particles, or grubs, but no vegetables should be left soaking in water. Drain the salad greens in a colander or salad shaker, and dry carefully on a clean towel. All greens for salad must be young and in perfect condition. A salad cream or French dressing may be used for seasoning just before serving.

Vegetables may be cut or shredded, but avoid grating them as they lose crispness as well as vitamins. Use lettuce leaves whole or tear them apart. After preparing salads, cover them until they are to be served.

Green vegetables are also important in the diet for their cellulose content which is not digestible, but acts as roughage, stimulates the digestive tract and therefore has a laxative effect.

Dehydrated, frozen and canned vegetables and fruits

Dehydrated produce available nowadays surpasses any of the old methods of drying. By this quick drying process, the Vitamin C and carotene content are scarcely affected, and the flavour and quality are very good. They compare favourably with fresh produce, but are more expensive.

Frozen vegetables are very carefully selected from sound produce. They are cooked very quickly by a special method, and quickly frozen to retain the vitamin content. They are therefore specially favoured for their superior quality to the average market vegetables. There is little labour in their preparation and they are an excellent substitute for home grown vegetables. Be sure to cook them quickly before they are thawed out.

Canned vegetables and fruit are also as valuable as those freshly cooked. During the process of canning, some of the vitamin content is drawn into the liquid in the can, so it should also be used when cooking. After cans are opened, use the contents as quickly as possible.

Cooked vegetable dishes

Fried egg plant (Melongene)

450 g (1 lb) egg plant
salt and pepper to taste
flour and breadcrumbs
oil for frying

Peel, wash and cut egg plant in 1-cm (½-in) thick slices. Cover slices thoroughly in a mixture of salt, black pepper, flour and breadcrumbs. Let stand for about 10 minutes. Shake off excess flour and fry in hot fat till golden brown. Serve with fried fish and sliced tomatoes.

Baked stuffed egg plant (Melongene)

450 g (1 lb) egg plant
2 tablespoons butter
salt and pepper to taste

1 small onion (chopped)
breadcrumbs
1 tablespoon tomato ketchup

Boil the egg plant in skin until tender. Skin, and crush to pulp with the butter, salt and pepper to taste, 1 chopped onion and a little tomato. Sprinkle with breadcrumbs and dot with butter. Bake in moderate oven until brown in an earthenware dish.

Boiled spinach

225 g (½ lb) spinach
15 g (½ oz) margarine
1 tablespoon chopped sweet pepper

1 medium onion (chopped)
pepper and salt to taste
½ cup water

Carefully wash spinach leaves and tear in pieces. Put into fast boiling salted water, add onions, sweet pepper. Cover saucepan and cook quickly until leaves are tender. Sprinkle with white pepper and stir in margarine to serve. Carrots, beet, sweet potatoes and turnip leaves may all be prepared in the same way.

Fried cabbage

225 g (½ lb) cabbage
salt and pepper to taste
3 rashers bacon

1 tablespoon butter
1 tablespoon fat

Wash and shred cabbage and sprinkle with a little salt and pepper. Cut up bacon and fry in fat. Put in cabbage turning it over during cooking until finished. Remove from heat, stir in butter and serve with fried rice (p183).

Fried okras

1 dozen okras (ladies' fingers)
about ½ cup milk
1 beaten egg
salt and white pepper

fat for frying
breadcrumbs and flour *or*
seasoned flour (p16)

Wash okras, dry them and cut in half, lengthwise. Brush them with egg and milk, dip in crumb mixture, brush and dip again. Let them stand for about 10 minutes. Fry in hot shallow fat. Drain on kitchen paper and serve hot.

Stuffed sweet peppers

4 sweet peppers
1 stalk celery *or* 225 g (½ lb) chocho
325 g (¾ lb) cooked minced meat
2 tablespoons onion

2 teaspoons tomato sauce
1 teaspoon cornflour
breadcrumbs
salt and pepper

Cut the peppers in half and remove the seeds. Chop the vegetables and mix with the minced meat. Add the tomato sauce, cornflour and salt to taste, and mix well. Stuff the peppers with this filling, and bake them for ½ hour.

Green vegetable salads

Stuffed avocado salad

2 avocado pears
1 tomato
1 head lettuce
pepper and salt to taste
100 g (4 oz) peas *or* cooked beans
50 g (2 oz) grated cheese

salad cream
2 hard boiled eggs
1 medium cucumber
2 tablespoons sour *or* sweet pickle
2 tablespoons lime juice
2 tablespoons chopped nuts

Wash lettuce and put in covered bowl in refrigerator to chill. Strain peas from stock. Wash and slice cucumber and add salt to taste. Cut avocado pears lengthwise and peel off skin. Place avocados in bowl and sprinkle with lime juice. Cover. Mix together pickle, cheese, peas and season for stuffing. Fill hollows of avocados. Place 2 wedges of tomatoes in each half. Arrange on a bed of lettuce. Lay cucumber slices, slices of hard boiled eggs on dish around avocados. Dot with salad cream and sprinkle with chopped nuts.

Tossed green salad

1 large head lettuce
1 cucumber
2 or 3 tomatoes
1 sweet pepper
1 stalk celery
sprig of escallion *or* chives
French dressing

Wash the lettuce and dry on a towel. Place in salad bowl. Mix with pared and sliced cucumber, tomatoes and sweet pepper. Cut in rings the escallion, celery and chives. Toss well with French dressing. Serve chilled.

Carrot salad

3 large carrots
1 lettuce
French dressing
finely chopped parsley

Grate the carrots finely and serve on a bed of lettuce leaves. Sprinkle with the French dressing. Garnish with chopped parsley.

Stuffed cucumber salad

1 large cucumber
2 or 3 large tomatoes
any mixture of vegetables, cooked
    and cold
salad cream
parsley
watercress

Cut the cucumber into 2.5-cm (1-in) rings and scoop out the centres with a teaspoon. Peel the tomatoes and cut into slices, one for each ring of cucumber. Mix the vegetables with salad cream and chopped parsley. Place the tomato slices on a flat dish; put a cucumber ring on each; fill with the vegetable mixture. Decorate with watercress.

Stuffed tomato salad

6 large firm tomatoes
lettuce leaves

For *stuffing* use any mixture of vegetables (diced), with meat, fish, shrimp or crab meat, chopped hard boiled eggs, sweet pickles – mixed with salad cream.

Cut off the tops of the tomatoes, take out the centres and the pulp. Use a little of the pulp with the stuffing. Mix the chosen stuffing and fill the tomatoes. Replace the tops. Garnish with tiny sprigs of parsley or with a suitable ingredient of the filling. Serve on crisp lettuce leaves on individual dishes or plates.

Cucumber and avocado salad

1 avocado pear	1 tablespoon lime juice
1 cucumber	salt and pepper to taste
slices of sweet pepper	1 teaspoon minced onion
lettuce and parsley	

Peel and slice the cucumber; season with salt, pepper, lime juice, minced onion and pieces of red pepper to taste. Pile the slices in the middle of a salad dish on a bed of crisp lettuce and arrange the avocado slices around. Garnish with slices of sweet pepper and pieces of parsley.

Potato salad

6 large English potatoes	1 tablespoon chopped radishes
French dressing	1 tablespoon chopped chives
2 tablespoons chopped parsley	salt and pepper to taste

Cook the potatoes in their skins until soft. Peel and dice while still hot and mix with French dressing and other seasonings. Serve cold.

Moulded vegetable salad

2 tablespoons powdered gelatine	¾ cup chopped sweet pepper
½ cup sugar	½ cup vinegar
1 teaspoon salt	2 tablespoons lime juice
1½ cups boiling water	2 cups finely shredded cabbage
1½ cups cold water	1 cup chopped celery or cucumber
few stuffed green olives	lettuce leaves

Mix gelatine, sugar and salt. Add boiling water and stir till gelatine dissolves. Add cold water, vinegar and lime juice; chill till partially set.

Add vegetables, pour into ring mould. Chill till firm. Unmould on lettuce leaves. If desired, fill ring with tiny whole cooked carrots marinated in French or Italian dressing.

Alternatively, chill gelatine till partially set; pour ½ cup of gelatine into mould. Arrange trios of stuffed green olive slices in mould and chill till firm. Add vegetables to remaining gelatine and pour over. Chill till set.

Salad plates

Cold salads, accompanied by cold drinks, are often preferred at lunch time to a large meal. Salad plates with cold meat, fish and vegetables may be arranged on lettuce leaves as desired, and served with bread or rolls and butter, *or* cream crackers.

Suggestions for salad plates

Sliced ham and stuffed tomatoes (p84)
Lobster or shrimp mayonnaise with cucumber and avocado (p85)
Moulded vegetable and fish mayonnaise (p85)
Chicken salad with carrots and sweet pepper (p84)
Salmon mayonnaise and potato salad (p85)
Stuffed avocado (p83) *with cold meat slices*

Vegetable and fruit salads

Sunshine salad

2 seedless oranges
2 or 3 large bananas (just under-
   ripe)
2 tablespoons French dressing
few cherry halves

salad cream
watercress
sugar
1 otaheite apple *or*
2 thick slices pineapple

Peel the oranges thickly, removing all the pith. Take out the orange sections and sprinkle them with 1 teaspoon of sugar. Slice the bananas with a stainless steel knife and marinate them in French dressing. Mix in the orange sections and other fruit (diced), and pile mixture in centre of a salad bowl. Garnish with cherry halves and watercress. Put the salad cream over the salad.

Grapefruit-avocado salad

3 pink (Texan) grapefruit
1 large avocado pear
watercress

sugar
French dressing

Pare and section grapefruit; drain, and reserve juice. Peel and slice avocado; brush with grapefruit juice.

Arrange grapefruit sections and avocado slices on small plates. Decorate with watercress and sprinkle with sugar and French dressing.

Banana-nut butter salad

3 bananas (just under ripe)
1 tablespoon peanut butter
1 tablespoon sugar or honey

lemon juice
lettuce leaves
¼ cup salad cream

Split bananas in half, lengthwise. Cut out dark centres, sprinkle lemon juice over them. Arrange them on a plate of lettuce. Blend together the peanut butter, sugar and salad cream and spread it on the bananas. Garnish with broken peanuts.

Fruit

Like green and yellow vegetables, fresh fruits are rich in Vitamin C (ascorbic acid) and carotene in varying amounts. Citrus fruits, pineapples, guavas and pawpaws are the best sources. Avocado pears and bananas are rich in iron, so are dried fruits, e.g. prunes, raisins. Avocados are also rich in fat.

The Caribbean area has an abundance of fruit of many varieties which are useful in the diet at every meal eaten raw, as fruit juices, stewed and baked. Fruits add variety, attraction to meals and are popular with everyone. They are excellent as snacks in between meals, also in desserts and salads.

Fruit should be used just ripe and should always be washed before being eaten raw. Chilling in a refrigerator improves the flavour and retains the sound condition of most fruit, bananas being the exception. After slicing bananas, mangoes, avocados or apples for salad, sprinkle them with citrus fruit juice or French dressing to retain their bright colour.

Dried fruits for stewing should be washed, soaked in water and cooked in the same water.

Fresh fruit salad

1 grapefruit
few slices of pineapple
1 dessert mango (Bombay or Julie)
1½ cups water

1 seedless orange
few garden cherries
1 cup sugar
1 tablespoon sherry

Boil sugar and water together till syrup is formed. Set aside to cool. Wash and peel fruit, discard seeds, and cut all into neat pieces. Mix fruit in a glass dish. Pour the syrup over the fruit. Chill and add sherry just before serving.

Shaddock bowl

1 medium sized pink shaddock
2 tablespoons rum
a few cherries

½ cup sugar (or more)
Bitters

Cut fruit from centre top to centre bottom in sections and peel off thick rind and pith. Divide into sections. Remove fruit in pieces. Place in a bowl and mix with enough fine sugar to sweeten, and set aside. Add the rum and bitters, chill and serve garnished with cherries.

Melon wedges

1 medium sized water melon
   (chilled)
French dressing

grapes
sugar

Cut 7.5-cm (3-in) wedges from the melon. Scoop out melon balls from each wedge with a ball cutter. Sprinkle lightly with sugar and marinate balls with French dressing. Add some green grapes and toss them lightly together. Refill the wedges piling them up. Garnish as desired.

Grapefruit halves

grapefruit
cherries
sugar

Wash grapefruit, cut in halves. Core with corer or sharp knife to remove seeds. Cut along the circumference of the fruit just inside the pith, cutting downwards. Cut across to loosen the pulp in each section. Sprinkle with sugar and place a cherry in the centre. Chill before serving.

Citrus bowl

1 grapefruit
1 seedless orange
2 tangerines or portugals
2 tablespoons grenadine syrup

Peel and skin fruit sections. Cut the fruit in pieces and lightly mix them together in a bowl with the grenadine syrup. Chill before serving.

Ambrosia

3 oranges
2 ripe bananas
2 tablespoons dates (cut up)

2 tablespoons sugar
½ cup grated coconut

Peel the oranges and cut them in pieces in a dish. Slice the bananas crosswise and stir them with the oranges, adding the sugar and dates. Sprinkle over it the grated coconut and chill before serving.

Grapefruit or orange baskets

1 grapefruit *or* large orange
1 slice fresh pineapple
1 slice dessert mango
few slices of banana

3–4 garden cherries
1 tablespoon lime juice
50 g (2 oz) granulated sugar
⅛ cup water *or* fruit juice

To prepare a grapefruit or orange basket, wash the fruit and cut it from both sides almost in half leaving about 2 cm (¾ in) uncut towards the centre. Cut the two top quarters downwards leaving the uncut 2 cm (¾ in) now about halfway around the circumference and remove the quarters. With a fruit knife cut the fruit from the semi-circle thus forming a handle. Core and remove the fruit from the basket which is now cleaned by scraping out all the pith well. Dice the pineapple and mango; add banana slices and some of the grapefruit sections, squeezing the lime juice over and mixing together in a dish. Now pour over the mixture a light cool syrup previously made by boiling the sugar and water together until it is slightly thick. Fill the basket with the mixture and garnish it with sliced cherries. Chill before serving and if desired, tie a coloured ribbon to the handle for decoration.

Pineapple slices

To prepare pineapple slices, twist off the top leaves to remove the crown. Wash the stem thoroughly, then with a long sharp knife, cut off the skin thickly beginning at the top. Remove the eyes with a pointed knife and cut it in 1.5-cm (½-in) slices. Remove the hard core from each slice and sprinkle with sugar, if necessary.
Note: Fresh pineapple should not be used in recipes with gelatine, as the fruit contains pectin which prevents the gelatine from setting. It may be used if it is first stewed, or tinned pineapple may be substituted.

Stewed fruit

Many fruits may be stewed and used with custard sauce, in iced desserts, etc. Guavas, garden cherries, gooseberries, golden apples, etc., are the most commonly used. Fruit should be firm and just under ripe. Use 1 cup water and 1 cup sugar to 450 g (1 lb) of fruit. Acid fruit will need more sugar. Allow the sugar to boil in the water about 5 minutes. Add the fruit and continue simmering until it is soft. A stick of cinnamon (spice) or grated nutmeg may be added during cooking.

Dried fruit

Wash fruit, soak in cold water to cover until fruit is swollen. Cover and simmer in the same water until fruit is soft, about 20 minutes. Add sugar to taste, stir and simmer until sugar is dissolved. Serve cold with custard, etc.

10 Desserts

A variety of desserts are used to accompany the spicy and often highly seasoned local dishes. Cold desserts are most popular and provide contrast for hot meals in a warm climate. Choose a refrigerator dessert, a gelatine mixture, a frozen dessert or a chilled fruit salad. Fancy cakes and pies are often favoured and sometimes hot desserts are suitable with some menus.

Floating island

600 ml (1 pint) milk (2 cups)
3 eggs (separated)
1 teaspoon vanilla essence

sugar to taste
2–3 tablespoons soft guava jelly

Make a custard with the milk and egg yolks adding sugar to taste and essence. Cool and pour into a glass dish. Beat the egg whites stiffly and lightly fold in the jelly a little at a time. Drop spoons of mixture on to the custard to make rough shapes. Serve very cold.

Fruit and rice mould

1 cup fresh or canned crushed
    pineapple
⅔ cup parboiled rice
⅔ cup water
½ teaspoon salt

1 cup diced marshmallows
1 large ripe banana (diced)
2 teaspoons lime juice
1 cup whipping cream, whipped or
    evaporated milk (whipped)

Drain pineapple and keep syrup. In saucepan, combine rice, water, syrup and salt. Mix just to moisten rice. Bring quickly to boil; cover and simmer for 5 minutes. Remove from heat; let stand for 5 minutes. Add marshmallows, pineapple, banana and juice. Cool, fold in whipped cream, pour into a wet mould and chill.

Garden cherry cheesecake

1 cup flour
¼ cup sugar
1 teaspoon grated lemon or lime
   peel (rind)

½ cup butter
1 slightly beaten egg yolk
¼ teaspoon vanilla

Blend together flour, sugar and peel. Cut in butter until mixture is crumbly. Add egg yolk and vanilla and mix well. Pat dough on bottom and sides of greased 22-cm (9-in) pan. Bake in a moderate oven for 8 to 10 minutes until light brown. Put aside to cool.

Filling

225 g (8-oz) creamed cheese
¼ teaspoon vanilla
½ teaspoon grated peel (rind)
1 cup sugar
3 tablespoons flour
¼ teaspoon salt

2 large eggs
1 egg yolk
¼ cup whipping cream
1 cup stewed garden cherries
pineapple pieces

Soften cream cheese, add vanilla and lemon peel, then sugar, flour and salt. Add eggs and yolk, one at a time, beating after each just to blend. Gently stir in whipping cream. Put into the crust-lined pan, bake in hot oven for 12 minutes. Reduce heat to moderate and bake until cake is firm. Cool in pan for about ½ hour. Loosen crust in pan and remove when cold. Top with pineapple pieces and stewed cherries.

Orange or pineapple trifle

1 Swiss roll *or*
small sponge cake (sliced thinly)
1½ cups custard sauce
few stewed cherries
peanuts (crushed)

1 cup fresh orange *or*
pineapple pieces
wineglass of sherry *or* rum
fruit syrup
jam

Spread some jam on the sponge slices and arrange them in alternate layers with the fruit and nuts in a glass dish. Moisten each layer with sherry and fruit juice, adding some custard sauce. Finish with a layer of custard. Decorate top with cherries and pieces of fruit. Alternatively, a meringue may be used on top before decorating.

Meringue

To 2 stiffly beaten egg whites, add 4 tablespoons granulated sugar gradually with 1 teaspoon of lime juice. Whip until mixture makes stiff peaks and add to top of trifle.

Gelatine desserts

Guava whip

¾ cup sugar
1 tablespoon powdered gelatine
¾ cup water
1 tablespoon lemon *or* lime juice
¼ teaspoon salt

1 cup fresh guava pulp
2 egg whites
1 cup coconut cream (optional)
   (p94)

Soak gelatine in ¼ cup water. Add remainder of water to sugar and heat almost to boiling point. Remove from heat, add gelatine, stir till dissolved. Cool. Press guava pulp through sieve. Add salt, lemon juice and gradually beat in cooled syrup. Chill and when it begins to thicken, fold in coconut (if used) and stiffly beaten egg whites. Mould and chill. Decorate with shredded coconut and cherries. Other fruit purées may be used for whips.

Sea moss jelly

50 g (2 oz) dried sea moss
½ cup evaporated milk
1 tablespoon lime juice
sugar to taste

food colouring
essence
fruit as desired

Soak the sea moss overnight washing it thoroughly to remove grit and sand. Clean it well and cover with boiling water and allow it to simmer, replacing boiling water if necessary. Squeeze a little lime juice in the saucepan during the cooking period to soften the moss and make the jelly clear. When the mixture is very thick, cool it and strain through a piece of muslin, then sugar to taste. Add the milk and flavouring and colour as desired. Pour it into wet moulds and allow it to chill. Serve with fruit.

Coconut cream mould

2 cups coconut milk
2 tablespoons sugar
stewed cherries

whites of two eggs
25 g (1 oz) powdered gelatine
2 tablespoons cold water

Soak the gelatine in cold water until soft, then dissolve over low heat. When cool add it to the already sweetened coconut milk. Put to set; when beginning to thicken, fold in the stiffly beaten white of eggs, pour all into wet mould and chill until firm. Serve with stewed cherries.

Prune mould

450 g (1 lb) prunes
3 cups water
1 tablespoon lemon *or* lime juice
little red colouring (optional)

3 oz sugar
1 piece of cinnamon (spice)
20 g (¾ oz) powdered gelatine

Wash prunes, and soak overnight in the measured water. Cook with sugar and cinnamon until quite soft. Remove stones and chop prunes to a pulp. Soak the gelatine in 2 tablespoons cold water for a few minutes, then heat until dissolved. Add to prune mixture and flavour with lemon juice. Colour if necessary. Stir thoroughly and pour into a wet mould. When set, unmould and serve with custard sauce.

Mango cream mould

1 cup mango purée
⅓ cup sugar
1 cup cream

1 tablespoon lime juice
15 g (½ oz) powdered gelatine
¼ cup warm water

Whip cream, add purée, sugar and lime juice. Dissolve gelatine in warm water and add to mixture. Whip until creamy. Pour into ring mould and allow to set. Unmould and fill centre of mould with mango slices and cherries. Pawpaws, guavas or any soft fruit may be used.

Garden cherry jelly

900 g (2 lb) garden cherries
2 cups water
150–200 g (6–8 oz) sugar

40 g (1½ oz) powdered gelatine
¼ cup cold water

Clean and wash fresh ripe cherries. Cook them in water and sugar until soft. Soak gelatine in water for 5 minutes, then heat until it is dissolved. Rub cherries through a fine sieve. Add more sugar if required. Strain gelatine into fruit purée and stir well. Pour into a wet mould and chill. Serve with Coconut Cream. Other berries may be used as well.

Coconut cream

Grate a coconut, add 1 cup of hot milk and stir well. Let it stand for about ½ hour. Squeeze coconut through a muslin cloth in a bowl. Place bowl in the refrigerator or cool place until cream settles on the top, then carefully skim it off. Beat a little icing sugar into it to taste and keep it in a cool place. Serve with fruit jellies.

Whipped cream (1)

Using evaporated unsweetened milk

Boil the unopened tin of milk in water for about 20 minutes, then cool it quickly. Pour into a bowl and chill in the refrigerator overnight. Whip with a chilled egg beater until double in bulk.

Whipped cream (2)

Chill heavy cream thoroughly. Whip in a chilled bowl with a chilled beater until cream becomes double in bulk.

To unmould jellies

When the jelly is set firm, dip the mould quickly in *very* hot water up to the rim. Allow it to remain in the water for about 2 *seconds*, then carefully ease around the edges with a knife and turn mould upside down on a serving dish to unmould

Syrup for fruit salads

1 cup water
½ cup sugar (granulated)
1 tablespoon lime juice

1 tablespoon sherry *or* rum (optional)

Boil sugar and water together to make a light syrup. Cool the liquid and stir in lime juice and sherry. Serve with fruit to sweeten. Fruit juice may be added to the syrup.

Frozen desserts

To freeze ice cream

Freezer method

The old method of freezing ice cream in the crank freezer is more laborious but still very popular because it makes a creamier and lighter ice cream, and large quantities can be made at once. The freezer can should be filled not more than two thirds full of cooled mixture to allow for expansion while churning, and six parts ice to one of salt should be used around it in alternate layers. Keep the wooden bucket well packed with ice and salt during the freezing period. Turn the handle slowly at first, then more quickly until the mixture stiffens. Remove the handle. Wipe the cover carefully with a clean towel before removing it and take out the dasher. Cork the hole in the cover, replace it, pour off excess brine through the side hole of the bucket, pack lightly with ice and salt, then place layers of newspapers on top covered with a heavy piece of sacking. Leave ice cream for 3–4 hours before serving.

Follow manufacturers' directions for using an electric freezer.

Refrigerator method

Smaller quantities of ice cream for dessert may be made satisfactorily in refrigerator ice trays. Directions for freezing are usually provided with electrical equipment, but before freezing desserts, remember to set the refrigerator at the maximum temperature about ½ hour before mixture is put in. Wet the surface of the freezing unit so that the trays will adhere to the surface immediately. When the mixture begins to thicken (it looks solid all round the edge of the tray), take out the trays, empty the mixture in a chilled bowl, beat quickly but thoroughly and return it to the freezing tray. Beat mixture once again after semi-freezing to improve the texture. When it is firm, the refrigerator may then be set to half the maximum temperature which will maintain the firmness of the ice cream mixture.

Note: Remember to make ice cream mixtures sweeter and more strongly flavoured than those to be served chilled.

Coconut ice cream

1 large coconut (grated)
sugar to taste
2 beaten egg whites
recipe for Custard Sauce (p28) using almond essence

Cover the grated coconut with 1½ cups warm water and allow it to stand for ½ hour. Then squeeze out the coconut milk, mix it well with the custard and sugar to taste. Fold in beaten egg whites before freezing.

Soursop ice cream

1 large ripe soursop
2 cups hot water
sugar to taste

1 tin condensed milk
¼ tin (150 g or 6 oz) evaporated milk

Peel the fruit, crush it in a bowl, pour hot water over it, stir, and allow to stand for about ½ hour. Then press the pulp through a colander to extract the juice, sugar to taste after adding milk and freeze.

Guava ice cream

About 2 dozen ripe guavas
2 cups milk
2 cups water
sugar to taste

Peel the guavas and cut in half, removing the seeds. Tie the seeds up in a piece of muslin and put them in a saucepan with the water. Bring to the boil and add 1 cup of sugar and the guavas. Boil again until guavas are soft, then take out the bag of seeds and rub the guavas through a sieve. Add cold milk and sugar to taste, blending well. Allow to cool and freeze.

Vanilla ice cream

one recipe for Custard Sauce *or* Economical Custard (p102)
1 cup evaporated milk
sugar to taste
2 teaspoons vanilla essence

Mix all ingredients together and freeze. Either custard base may be used with other flavourings as a basic recipe.

Cherry ice cream

900 g (2 lb) cherries *or* other berries
1 cup milk
1 cup condensed milk
sugar to taste

Crush cherries to pulp in a bowl, remove stones and mix with the milk. Sugar to taste and freeze.

Coconut water ice

2 water coconuts
sugar to taste
1 dry coconut

Grate the dry coconut in a bowl and pour over it water from the dry coconut and the water coconuts. Allow to stand for ½ hour and squeeze to extract the cream. Cut up the coconut jelly in small pieces and add. Sweeten to taste and freeze.

Pineapple or orange sherbet

2 cups water
225 g (8 oz) caster *or* granulated sugar
2 egg whites
1 cup fresh *or* canned pineapple *or* orange juice

Dissolve the sugar in water, and boil it for 10 minutes. Cool and add pineapple juice and stiffly beaten egg whites. Freeze.

Lime sherbet may be made similarly using: ½ cup fresh lime juice, ½ cup water, 1 cup pineapple juice.

Pawpaw water ice

pawpaw
sugar
water
lime *or* orange juice

Crush some pawpaw to make a pulp. Add a little water to make the mixture the consistency of thick cream; add sugar to taste and flavour with the fruit juice. Freeze.

Fruit desserts

Coconut and orange or pineapple salad

1 small grated coconut
3 seedless oranges (sliced) *or*
1 medium sized pineapple (sliced)
2 tablespoons caster sugar
cherries

fruit juice
recipe for Syrup for Fruit Salads
 (p95)
1 wineglass sherry *or* rum

Put alternate layers of coconut fruit and sugar in a glass dish. Add sherry to liquid and sprinkle between layers. Finish with a layer of coconut. Decorate with cherry halves and chill.

Stewed cashew

8 cashew fruits (fresh)
1 cup brown sugar
1 tablespoon lime juice
water

1½ cups water
recipe for Coconut Cream (p94)

Peel cashews and cut in quarters. Put in bowl with water to cover and add lime juice. Allow to stand for ½ hour. Remove cashews and cook in 1½ cups water with sugar added, until tender. Cool and serve with coconut cream.

Stewed guavas and custard

See recipes for Stewed Fruit and Custard Sauce (pp89 and 102).

Fruit cup

1 ripe banana
1 grapefruit (medium size)
1 tangerine
1 slice pawpaw

25 g (1 oz) granulated sugar
2 teaspoons lime *or* lemon juice
¼ teaspoon grated nutmeg
2 tablespoons grated coconut

Prepare fruits in medium sized segments. Drain off juice and add to it sugar, lime juice and grated nutmeg. Mix well together, top with grated coconut and chill before serving.

Pineapple delight

3 small pineapples
2 oz castor sugar

2 tablespoons rum
300 ml (½ pint) vanilla ice cream

Cut the pineapples in half lengthwise. Scoop out the pulp and cut into chunks. Mix it with sugar and rum. Pile it back into the pineapple halves and chill. Just before serving place a spoonful of vanilla ice cream on top.

Banana split

6 bananas
2 cups vanilla ice cream
1 cup Melba Sauce (p102)

½ cup whipped sweetened cream
50 g (2 oz) chopped peanuts
8 stewed cherries

Peel bananas, split in half lengthwise and place in small oval dishes. Place two small scoops or slices of ice cream between the halves of bananas. Coat the ice cream with Melba Sauce; sprinkle with chopped nuts. Decorate with piped cream and cherries.

Puddings and hot desserts

Vanilla pudding

⅓ cup sugar
3 tablespoons cornstarch
¼ teaspoon salt

2¼ cups milk
1½ teaspoons vanilla

Mix sugar, cornstarch and salt; gradually blend in milk. Cook over medium heat, stirring constantly, till mixture thickens. Cook for 2 or 3 minutes more. Add vanilla.

Pour into 5 or 6 individual moulds and chill; or pour into large mould and chill until firm. Unmould and serve with Chocolate Sauce.

Chocolate pudding

Follow directions for Vanilla Pudding, but increase sugar to ½ cup and mix ⅓ cup cocoa with sugar and cornstarch. Serve with cream or Custard Sauce (p102).

Caramel pudding

Syrup
¼ cup sugar (brown)
½ cup boiling water

Custard
¼ cup sugar
3 tablespoons cornstarch
2 cups milk
¼ teaspoon salt
1½ teaspoons vanilla

Melt brown sugar in heavy saucepan over low heat, stirring, till rich medium brown.

Remove from heat. Slowly add the boiling water, return to heat and stir till lumps dissolve. Set aside syrup.

For the custard, combine the sugar, cornstarch, and salt in saucepan; blend in 2 cups milk. Stir in caramel syrup. Cook and stir over medium heat till thick. Cook for 2 minutes more. Add 1½ teaspoons vanilla. Pour into a mould, chill and serve with Caramel Sauce (p103).

Raisin bread pudding

2¼ cups milk
2 slightly beaten eggs
2 cups stale bread cut in 2.5-cm (1-in)
  cubes (buttered)
¼ cup brown sugar

½ teaspoon cinnamon (spice)
1 teaspoon vanilla
¼ teaspoon salt
½ cup seedless raisins

Combine milk and eggs; pour over bread cubes. Stir in remaining ingredients. Pour mixture in a round baking dish. Place in shallow pan on oven rack; pour hot water around it 2.5 cm (1 in) deep. Bake at 180°C, 350°F or Gas 4 for about 45 minutes or till knife inserted halfway between centre and outside comes out clean.

Banana coconut custard

2 cups milk
2 eggs
¼ teaspoon salt
¾ cup grated coconut

¼ teaspoon vanilla
2 tablespoons sugar
1 cup sliced ripe bananas

Beat eggs slightly with essence. Add milk, sugar and salt, then coconut, folding in bananas last. Pour into greased baking dish. Bake in slow oven.

Carrot pudding with rum sauce

½ cup butter
¾ cup raisins
1½ cups grated raw carrot
1 egg
½ teaspoon cinnamon
¼ cup rum and water

1 cup flour
⅔ cup sugar
1 teaspoon baking powder
½ teaspoon salt
½ teaspoon nutmeg

Cream butter, add beaten egg, raisins, grated carrot and mix well. Sift dry ingredients and add to first mixture. Stir in rum last; mix well and pour into greased, floured pan. Bake in moderate oven for 40 minutes. Serve with Rum Sauce (p104).

Mango Brown Betty

2 cups under ripe mango slices
¾ cup brown sugar
3 tablespoons water (if necessary)

3 tablespoons butter
⅔ cup breadcrumbs
½ teaspoon nutmeg

Melt fat and add breadcrumbs and nutmeg. Place layer of buttered crumbs in oiled baking dish. Add layer of mangoes. Sprinkle with sugar and cinnamon. Finish with crumbs on top layer. Bake for 1 hour in a moderate oven.

Baked grapefruit pudding

2½ cups grapefruit sections, free
    from skin and membrane
¾ cup light brown sugar
1 tablespoon flour
1 tablespoon melted butter
½ cup milk

1½ cups flour
1 teaspoon baking powder
¼ teaspoon salt
3 tablespoons butter
1 egg

Put grapefruit into a shallow buttered baking pan. Mix brown sugar and 1 tablespoon of flour and add melted butter. Sprinkle this mixture over grapefruit.

Sift together flour, baking powder and salt. Add butter, mixing in well with fork. Beat egg slightly in measuring cup; add milk to make ½ cup; add to pan mixture. Turn out on floured board and toss lightly until outside looks smooth. Roll out about ¼ inch thick to fit pan. Place on top of grapefruit and bake in hot oven (220°C, 425°F or Gas 7) for about 24 minutes. Cut into pieces and serve bottom side up.

Baked rice pudding

4 cups milk
1 cup raw white rice
⅓ cup sugar or to taste

¼ cup raisins
rind of lime (grated)
salt to taste

Wash rice and mix with other ingredients in a buttered baking dish with cover. Bake in slow oven until rice is soft, for about 2 hours. Remove cover during cooking and stir a little, but not during last ½ hour; allow crust to form. Serve hot or cold with raisins, caramel or fruit sauce.

Coconut steamed pudding

150 g (6 oz) flour
¼ teaspoon salt
1 rounded teaspoon baking powder
50 g (2 oz) butter *or* margarine

50 g (2 oz) sugar
50 g (2 oz) grated coconut
1 egg
milk to mix

Grease a 1-litre (1½-pint) pudding bowl. Sift together the flour, salt and baking powder. Rub in the fat and add the sugar and coconut. Mix to a soft dropping consistency with the beaten egg and milk. Put the pudding mixture into the bowl and cover with a piece of greased paper. Steam for 1½–2 hours.

Sweet sauces

Custard sauce

1 See recipe on p28
2 *Economical Custard Sauce* (Using Cornflour)

25 g (1 oz) cornstarch
600 ml (1 pint) milk
1½ tablespoons sugar

piece of lemon rind *or*
½ teaspoon essence

Blend the cornflour with a little of the cold milk. Boil the rest of the milk with the thinly cut lemon rind if used. Remove rind and stir the boiling liquid into the blended cornflour. Rinse the pan and return the sauce to it. Bring to boiling point and boil for 3 minutes. Sweeten and flavour the sauce, unless lemon rind has been used for flavouring.

Melba sauce

15 g (½ oz) arrowroot
300 ml (½ pint) water (1 cup)
¼ cup cherry jam
2 tablespoons lime juice and water

Blend the arrowroot with a little of the water. Boil remaining water with the jam and lime juice. Strain it on to the blended mixture, return to the pan and boil up stirring all the time. Cool before using.

Chocolate sauce

1 tablespoon cornflour
2 tablespoons cocoa
3 tablespoons sugar

1¼ cups water
¼ teaspoon vanilla essence
2 tablespoons butter

Blend together the cornflour, cocoa and sugar with a little of the water. Boil remaining water and pour on to blended mixture. Return to pan and boil for 2 minutes, stirring all the time. Add vanilla and butter. Serve hot or cold.

Coffee sauce

⅓ cup very strong coffee
⅓ cup milk
1 heaped teaspoon cornflour *or*
    custard powder

1 egg yolk
sugar to taste
vanilla essence
1 teaspoon rum (optional)

Thicken the coffee and milk with the cornflour or custard powder (as for *Custard Sauce 2*). Cool the sauce, add the egg yolk and cook it without boiling. Sweeten and flavour to taste.

Caramel sauce

50 g (2 oz) brown sugar
⅓ cup water
cup of Custard Sauce
vanilla essence

Put the sugar and 2 tablespoons water in a small pan; dissolve the sugar over gentle heat, then boil the syrup so made until it is a deep golden brown. Add to the caramel the rest of the water and leave it in a warm place to dissolve. Add the dissolved caramel to the custard sauce and flavour to taste.

Hard sauce

75 g (3 oz) butter
150 g (6 oz) icing sugar *or* 110 g
    (4½ oz) icing sugar and 25 g (1 oz)
    ground almonds

1 teaspoon–1 tablespoon rum
1 whipped egg white (optional)

Cream the butter till soft. Sift the icing sugar and cream it with the butter till white and light in texture. Mix in the almonds if used.

Work the rum carefully into the mixture. Fold the stiffly-whipped egg white into the sauce.

Serve with Christmas or other steamed puddings. Store in an airtight jar.

Rum sauce

100 g (4 oz) butter
200 g (8 oz) soft brown sugar
1 sherry glass rum

Beat the butter to a cream and beat in the sugar. When light and creamy, add the rum gradually. Transfer to a serving dish and chill thoroughly before using.

11 Cooling thirst quenchers

What can be most refreshing after a hot morning's shopping, an energetic game or a long swim in the sea ? A cold icy drink is always the popular choice. In the Caribbean there is a wide variety of local beverages made chiefly from common garden fruits with simple flavourings which are much more delectable, nourishing and economical than the more expensive imported varieties.

As snacks between meals, or served with meals, hosts and visitors alike never cease to enjoy our Caribbean citrus squashes, fruit punches, chilled coconut water, etc. Most home-made drinks take some time to prepare but many housewives will agree that the effort is worth the praise received from those who enjoy them.

Lemonade, the commonest and perhaps most refreshing drink, is made from fresh garden limes, rarely from lemons, as these when locally grown tend to be coarse skinned, seedy and not as juicy and pleasantly flavoured as Mediterranean species.

Use the following methods for mixing your favourite drinks and vary them for greater enjoyment on all occasions.

Pineapple drink

peelings from 1 pineapple plus
   2 slices fruit
6 cups boiling water
sugar to taste

small piece dried orange peel
½ teaspoon grated nutmeg
few cloves

Put peelings, cloves, and orange peel in a jug and pour on boiling water. Cover and leave for one day. Strain and sweeten. Sprinkle in nutmeg and stir. Use at once or bottle and keep for 1 or 2 days. Serve with ice.

Soursop squash

1 medium sized soursop
sugar to taste
1 cup milk (optional)

4 cups hot water
little grated nutmeg

Wash and peel the fruit. Remove the heart and seeds. Crush with a fork and pour over the hot water. Allow it to stand until cool. Strain off liquid, sugar to taste, add milk if desired, stir in nutmeg and serve with ice or chilled. Granadilla fruit may be served similarly.

Lemonade (1)

Juice of 2–3 large fresh green limes (strained) (about ½ cup)
4 cups water
1 cup granulated sugar

½ teaspoon aromatic bitters (optional)
1 lime rind

Stir sugar with lime rind in water until sugar dissolves, add lime juice and bitters and stir well. Serve at once in glasses with cracked ice.

Lemonade (2)

Cook 1 cup sugar and 1 cup water for 5 minutes to make a thin syrup; store in refrigerator. For each serving, mix 3 to 4 tablespoons syrup, 1½ tablespoons lemon or lime juice, and 1 cup water. Pour into ice-filled glasses.

Tamarind drink

450 g (1 lb) shelled tamarinds
4 cups hot water
2 cups brown sugar (or more)
grated nutmeg

Soak tamarinds in hot water for 1 hour and scrape off pulp with a spoon. Add sugar, stir well and strain off liquid. Serve very cold with grated nutmeg. Aerated soda water may be added to make a more refreshing drink.

Pawpaw drink

1 medium sized ripe pawpaw
150 g (6 oz) sugar
1 teaspoon grated ginger *or*
1 or 2 fresh limes

Slice, peel and crush a medium sized ripe pawpaw. To every pint of crushed fruit add 2 pints water, stir thoroughly and strain. Sweeten to taste and chill or add cracked ice. A small bit of ginger, grated, or a dessertspoon of juice from fresh green limes will improve the flavour.

Mango Drink may be made similarly.

Cherry or gooseberry drink

2 cups fruit
2 cups water (warm)
1½ cups sugar

Wash fruit and crush. Add water and allow it to stand for 1 hour. Strain through a coarse sieve, sugar and serve cold.

Coconut refresher

4 cups coconut water
2 cups grapefruit juice
½ cup sugar
2 tablespoons rum (optional)

Combine all ingredients and serve with ice.

Guava drink

¼ teaspoon nutmeg
2 cups guava purée (fresh ripe)
1 cup sugar
1½ cups water
¼ teaspoon salt

Combine all ingredients. Strain and chill thoroughly. Serve with cracked ice. Ginger ale may be added at the last for variation.

Mauby

50 g (2 oz) mauby bark
12 cups water
piece of mace
brown sugar (about 900 g or 2 lb)
large piece cinnamon (spice)
few cloves
piece dried orange peel

Boil mauby bark in water (about 4 cups) with spice, cloves, mace and orange peel until liquid is very bitter (about ½ hour). Strain it off, add the rest of water and sugar until very sweet. Bottle the cooled liquid, leaving neck of bottle unfilled for froth. Cover and leave for 3 days. Serve very cold.

Iced tea

Use recipe for hot tea (p109), using 1½ teaspoons tea per cup. Strain hot tea into tall glasses filled with cracked ice and serve with lemon slices and sugar.

Ginger beer (1)

100 g (¼ lb) green ginger
1 gallon water
1 large green lime
900 g (2 lb) granulated sugar

Scrape ginger, wash and pound it. Put it in a large bowl and pour boiling water over. Stir in the sugar until dissolved. Peel the lime and add both lime and rind to the liquid. Cool and pour in a glass or earthenware jar. Cover and let it stand for 6 days, stirring with a wooden spoon every other day. When ripe, strain, pour off into bottles which may be placed in the refrigerator to chill. Bottles may be kept at room temperature and allowed to ripen for a further 2 or 3 days before using.

Ginger beer (2)

5 litres (1 gallon) water
675 g (1½ lb) sugar
76 g (¼ oz) cream of tartar

25 g (1 oz) green ginger
½ lemon
25 g (1 oz) dry yeast

Bruise the ginger, put in the water, add the sugar and boil for 1 hour. Skim and pour on to the sliced lemon and cream of tartar. When almost cold add the yeast. After 2 days strain and bottle. Use in a day or two.

Sorrel (1)

100 g (¼ lb) dried sorrel sepals
piece of dried orange peel
piece of cinnamon (spice)
few whole cloves
100 ml (1 gill) rum

5 litres (1 gallon) boiling water
900 g–1.3 kg (2–3 lb) sugar
1 teaspoon powdered cinnamon
½ teaspoon powdered cloves

Put the dried sorrel, orange peel, stick of cinnamon and whole cloves in a jar, pour the boiling water over. When cool, cover and leave the mixture to steep for two days. Then strain off the liquid, sugar rather sweetly, add rum, powdered spices and let it stand for another 2 days before serving chilled or with crushed ice. This is a popular drink at Christmas time when sorrel is in season. The dried sorrel will last for months if stored in a dry place.

Sorrel (2)

4 cups sorrel sepals
15 g (½ oz) green ginger (crushed)
few cloves

8 cups boiling water
450–900 g (1–2 lb) sugar
piece of dried orange peel

Wash the sorrel and put into a jar with the ginger, cloves and peel. Pour over the boiling water and allow to stand for one day or overnight. Strain, sugar and serve with ice.

12 Hot beverages

Tea and coffee are both favourite drinks at the main meals of the day, and they are enjoyed as in-between refreshing snacks, because of their stimulating effects.

Cocoa and chocolate are also widely used especially as hot drinks for children. They have good food value being rich in iron. Chocolate contains about 50% fat and is sold in sticks or cakes. Cocoa is sold in powder form and contains very little fat. The addition of at least half milk or sometimes all milk in making these beverages, makes them even more nutritious, and an excellent way of serving milk to children and adults when they tire of plain milk which is undoubtedly the best of all food drinks.

Some people enjoy hot mocha which is a mixture of coffee and cocoa. It is a sophisticated drink and delicious in flavour.

Hot tea

There are numerous varieties of tea which differ only in the manner of processing, but are brewed in the same way.

1 teaspoon tea *or*   1 cup water per person
1 tea bag (if used) per person   cold milk *or* lemon
sugar (granulated)

Water must be freshly drawn, brought to the boil and immediately poured into a teapot previously heated by rinsing with boiling water. Steep or draw the tea for 3–5 minutes. Pour and serve at once. Hot water may be added to make a weaker brew.

Instant tea is time saving and economical and is sometimes used for a quick brew.

Coffee

A good cup of coffee is more difficult to make than one of tea, but success will be ensured if a few simple rules are followed:

1 Be sure that the coffee maker is quite clean.

2 Always use fresh cold water.

3 Keep coffee always fresh by storing it in a dry container.

4 Use 1 rounded tablespoon coffee per person to 1 cup water, or more coffee if desired.

5 Allow the water to boil before pouring it on to the coffee and let it draw for 8–10 minutes in a warm place. Boiling coffee causes loss of flavour and bitterness. Timing is also important.

There are also many different kinds of coffee makers. Among them are automatic, percolator and vacuum types.

Automatic Manufacturers' directions should be followed when using the automatic.

Percolator The percolator is most commonly used. Percolated coffee has a rich flavour. Put in the required amount of cold water, boil, measure the coffee in the strainer at top. Allow the coffee to 'perk' very gently, 6–8 minutes. Remove the strainer and serve.

Vacuum This type has an upper and a lower bowl. Put the amount of cold water in the lower bowl. Insert the filter and measure the coffee in the upper bowl. When the water boils, fix the upper bowl into the lower one. As the water rises to the top bowl, stir it, lower the heat and remove from the heat after three minutes. Lift off the upper bowl as coffee returns to lower bowl, from which it is served. Vacuum coffee has a clear amber colour.

Hot coffee

1 rounded tablespoon freshly ground coffee per cup
hot milk

brown sugar
boiling water
salt (optional)

Make coffee according to the type of coffee maker.

Demitasse (after-dinner coffee)

Use 2 rounded tablespoons of ground coffee per measuring cup of boiling water. Serve in small cups, black, or white with cream, with or without brown sugar. 1 measuring cupful = 3 demitasse cupfuls.

Instant coffee

Measure 1 teaspoon instant coffee in each cup and pour boiling water over, or mix larger amounts in the same proportion in coffee pot. Heat gently for 5 minutes and serve. For *demitasse*, use twice the amount of instant coffee.

Café au Lait

1 cup milk
1 cup thin cream *or* evaporated milk
brown sugar

4 rounded teaspoons instant coffee
2 cups boiling water

Heat milk mixture over low heat until it is hot. Pour into a jug. Whisk until foamy. Dissolve coffee in boiling water and pour it into another jug. Pour into serving cups simultaneously from both jugs. Sugar to taste.

Breakfast cocoa

6 rounded teaspoons cocoa
2 cups water
2 cups milk

$\frac{1}{4}$ teaspoon salt (optional)
4–6 tablespoons brown sugar

Bring water to the boil, mix cocoa, sugar and salt with a little of the water and stir in the cocoa mixture. Boil for 3 minutes; stir in milk and heat just to boiling point. More milk than water may be used. Makes 6 breakfast cup servings.

Hot chocolate

2 25-g (1-oz) sticks chocolate
2 cups hot water
4 tablespoons brown sugar

$\frac{1}{4}$ teaspoon salt
2 cups milk

Cut chocolate sticks in pieces and heat in water over low heat until the chocolate is dissolved. Add sugar and salt, and cook for 4–5 minutes. Stir in milk, heat slowly to boiling point and serve.

Mocha (or cocoa plus coffee)

4 rounded teaspoons cocoa
4 teaspoons instant coffee
1 cup water
3 cups milk

$\frac{1}{4}$ teaspoon salt
4–6 tablespoons brown sugar
whipped cream *or*
whipped evaporated milk

Add cocoa, coffee, sugar and salt to water. Stir and cook 3–4 minutes over low heat. Gradually add milk until it is very hot. Remove from heat, whisk until it is frothy. Pour into serving cups and top with spoonfuls of whipped cream.

13 Party drinks and punches

On all festive occasions there is a great demand for cold drinks and punches especially at dances, sporting functions, or similar events.

Weekend parties are a regular feature in many homes and public places of entertainment where friends meet together for social intercourse. Fruit and rum punches are among the most popular to be served, but many varieties of the luscious fruits of the area serve as a base for some of the most delectable drinks enjoyed by residents and visitors alike. Milk, tea and coffee mixtures also contribute to the variety from which to choose. Alcoholic and non-alcoholic beverages are equally popular.

Iced tea

4 tablespoons tea
6 cups boiling water
sugar to taste

6 cups cold water
lime or lemon slices

Measure the tea in a teapot, pour boiling water over, cover and allow tea to infuse for about 5 minutes. Stir and strain it off. Add the cold water immediately and allow tea to cool. Pour into tall glasses filled with ice cubes or cracked ice. Serve with lime or lemon slices. Makes 12 servings.

Tea punch

3 cups fresh boiling water
3 teaspoons tea
½ cup lemon juice
½ cup orange juice

sugar to taste
600 ml (1 pint) ginger ale
6 mint sprigs
6 slices orange

Pour boiling water over tea, cover and let steep for 5 minutes. Strain and cool quickly by pouring over cracked ice or ice cubes. Stir in lemon and orange juice, and sugar, if desired. When ready to serve, add ginger ale. Serve with ice in tall glasses with a sprig of mint and a slice of orange in each glass.

Iced coffee

Make the required amount of coffee as for hot coffee. Put it in covered containers and chill in the refrigerator for about 3 hours. Chill the milk separately using evaporated milk. When ready to serve, sweeten to taste, add a little salt, if liked, whisk and pour into glasses.

Iced mocha

Combine equal quantities of breakfast cocoa and hot coffee. Cool and chill thoroughly in the refrigerator. Flavour with vanilla essence – 1 teaspoon to 2 cups. Pour into tall glasses and serve with a whipped cream topping.

Chocolate soda

1 cup chocolate syrup
½ cup evaporated milk
4 small bottles soda water

about 2 cups vanilla ice cream
4–6 chilled tall glasses

Mix chocolate syrup with the milk and pour equal quantities in the glasses. Add soda water to fill glasses ¾ full. Stir well and add a scoop of ice cream. Fill with soda water and serve with long spoons.

Chocolate syrup

1½ cups brown sugar
½ cup cocoa
2 teaspoons vanilla essence

¼ teaspoon salt
1 cup water

Mix together and cook for about 8 minutes. Cool, add essence, and store in refrigerator. Makes about 2 cups.

Milk punch

4 cups milk
4 tablespoons granulated sugar
nutmeg

2 tablespoons rum
½ cup cream *or* evaporated milk
    (whipped)

Boil the milk, dissolve the sugar in it, cool and chill. Add the rum and whipped cream. Mix well and semi-freeze. Serve in sherbet cups with a little grated nutmeg.

Egg-nog

¾ cup sugar
4 egg yolks
piece of lime rind
½ teaspoon salt
1 cup cream (whipped)

4 egg whites
⅓ cup sugar
2 teaspoonfuls vanilla essence
¼ cup rum

Beat the egg yolks with the ¾ cup sugar and rind. Add salt and stir in the milk. Cook over low heat until mixture coats the spoon. Remove rind and cool. Beat egg whites until frothy. Gradually add ⅓ cup sugar, beating to soft peaks. Add to custard and mix well. Add flavourings. Chill several hours. Pour into a punch bowl. Dot whipped cream on top of punch and sprinkle grated nutmeg over. Makes 10–12 servings.

Pawpaw and mango punch

1 cup mango pulp
1 cup pawpaw pulp
1 cup fresh orange juice
1 teaspoon grated orange rind
¼ cup lime juice
4 cups water
sugar to taste

Crush slices of mango and pawpaw to make pulp. Add other ingredients blending well. Sugar to taste and serve chilled or with cracked ice.

Pawpaw and grapefruit punch

2 cups pawpaw pulp
½ cup condensed milk
½ teaspoon nutmeg
1 cup grapefruit juice
2 cups water
sugar to taste

Prepare pawpaw pulp by crushing pawpaw with fork until smooth. Pour into jug and add milk, fruit juice, water and stir. Sugar to taste, add nutmeg and ice or chill. Swizzle and serve.

Mixed fruit punch

2 cups orange juice
1 cup lime juice
8 large bottles ginger ale
2 cups grenadine syrup
1 cup pineapple juice
sliced fruit

Mix together juices and grenadine syrup. Chill. Before serving, stir in ginger ale chilled. Garnish with seasonal fruit pieces in each glass. Makes 20 servings.

Caribbean cocktail

¼ cup rum
1 cup fresh pineapple juice
1 tablespoon caster sugar
2 tablespoons lime juice
1 teaspoon bitters
soda water

Shake all ingredients well together, put some ice into tall glasses and fill halfway with mixture. Finally pour on soda water to fill glasses. Stir and serve. Four servings.

Guava nectar

ripe guavas
lime juice
granulated sugar
nutmeg

Crush some ripe guavas and to every cup of pulp use 1½ cups sugar, one teaspoon lime juice and ⅛ teaspoon nutmeg. Mix pulp with sugar, stir and bring to the boil. Simmer for 15 minutes or longer until guava is cooked. Cool, add lime juice. Chill and serve with ice and grated nutmeg.

Alcoholic drinks (using rum)

Rum punch (Cold)

¼ cup lime juice
½ cup sugar
bitters or nutmeg

¾ cup rum
1 cup water

Dissolve sugar in water, add rum and lime juice. Blend well. Chill and serve with bitters or nutmeg. Makes 4 servings.

Rum punch (Hot)

2 cups hot strong tea
rind of ½ lime
juice of 2 lemons
2 cups rum

2 tablespoons brandy
1 teaspoon bitters
150 g (6 oz) caster sugar

Mix sugar, lime juice and rind in bowl. Add hot strained tea and leave to draw. When cold, add rum and brandy. Add bitters. Serve warm, keeping it over mild heat. About 16 cocktail glass servings.

Rum flip

½ glass finely cracked ice
1 teaspoon sugar syrup
dash of bitters

1 egg (whisked)
1 wineglass rum

Mix well together and grate nutmeg on top. Chill and serve in tall glass. One serving.

Rum cocktail

2 wineglasses rum
¼ cup honey *or* granulated sugar
½ cup lime juice
½ teaspoon bitters

Combine ingredients and whisk until well blended. Pour into cocktail glasses half filled with finely crushed ice. Serves 4.

Rum sour

2 tablespoons rum
1 teaspoon sugar
½ slice orange

1 tablespoon lime juice
bitter lemon soda
cracked ice

Swizzle rum, sugar, lime juice and ice or shake in a cocktail shaker. Pour into a tall glass, fill up with bitter lemon and put ½ slice orange in glass. Makes one serving.

Scorpion

1 tablespoon bitters
100 g (¼ lb) sugar
¼ cup water

¼ cup lime juice
1 wineglass rum

Boil a syrup with water and sugar (about 8 minutes). Cool and add lime juice and bitters. Mix together, add rum and blend well. Serve with or without ice in cocktail glasses. Makes 8 servings.

14 Appetizers and cocktail delicacies

Appetizers are the tasty savoury snacks served before a meal to stimulate the appetite. They may take the form of hors d'oeuvres, spreads, dips used with small crackers, seasoned vegetable juices or shell fish cocktails. Small glasses of alcoholic beverages may also accompany them as desired. The snacks are usually served on trays and passed around, or guests may help themselves from a buffet. Some appetizers are served on small plates as a first course at the dinner table. Fruit cups are popular appetizer courses and may take the place of soup.

A variety of these savouries and canapés are ideal snacks for formal cocktail parties. Serve them more informally at home when friends arrive at short notice or serve as late night snacks during television shows. It is a good plan to keep small squares of buttered toast in an airtight tin for quick use, and spread with some of these quickly-made mixtures.

Cheese and ham spread

225 g (½ lb) chopped ham *or* 1 small
    tin
1 medium sized tomato (chopped)
1 tablespoon prepared mustard

pepper and salt to taste
50 g (2 oz) cream cheese
1 tablespoon milk
15 g (½ oz) butter

Mix together all ingredients and spread on squares of toast. To serve, garnish with parsley.

Cheese dip

2 cups grated Cheddar cheese
75 g (3 oz) cream cheese
salt and pepper to taste

1 tablespoon milk
1 tablespoon minced onion

Blend well together and use on toast or small crackers.

Tomato-cheese filling

2 large tomatoes
50 g (2 oz) cheese
2 tablespoons butter
1 beaten egg

1 large onion
1 teaspoon chopped parsley
pepper and salt to taste
breadcrumbs

Mix together crushed tomato, chopped onion, salt and pepper and chopped parsley. Add butter and beaten egg. Mix well. Cook in saucepan over heat until egg is cooked. Take off and stir in grated cheese and sufficient breadcrumbs to make a smooth paste. Used for sandwiches, bouchées, and on toast.

Savoury eggs

Cook some eggs until hard-boiled (15 minutes). Place in cold water for ½ hour. Then shell eggs and divide in halves or quarters. Pick out yolks, crush them and mix with enough butter and salad cream to make a paste, add salt, white pepper and mix well. Pipe mixture into egg white pieces or refill with a knife. Garnish with parsley and pieces of sweet pepper.

Cheese straws

100 g (4 oz) flour
¼ teaspoon salt
½ teaspoon white pepper
¼ teaspoon dry mustard

3 oz butter
3 oz grated cheese
1 beaten egg yolk
2 teaspoons cold water

Rub butter into dry ingredients with cheese. Add beaten egg and mix in ice water to make a stiff dough. Roll and cut in lengths 1-cm × 7-cm (½-in × 3-in) long for straws, which may be twisted in shapes for variety.

Shrimp or crab meat canapés

1 cup shredded shrimp or crab
  meat
1 tablespoon salad cream

1 teaspoon minced onion
pepper and salt to taste
1 teaspoon chopped parsley

Blend well together ingredients and serve on toast. Any fried cooked fish may be substituted.

Serve the following snacks hot on cocktail sticks or toothpicks:

Sausage and bacon

cocktail sausages
streaky bacon strips
toothpicks or cocktail sticks

prepared mustard
tomato sauce
salt

Cut and wrap bacon strips around sausages. Fasten each with a toothpick. Put on pan in moderate oven until bacon is crisp. Mix equal quantities of mustard and tomato sauce. Add salt to taste. Serve hot dipped in the sauce.

Curried salt fish cakes

1½ cups prepared salt fish
½ cup mashed yam or potato
2 tablespoons flour
1 tablespoon curry powder
oil for frying
1 tablespoon butter

1 tablespoon minced onion and herbs
1 egg
salt and pepper to taste
breadcrumbs and flour *or* seasoned flour

Shred fish finely. Mix in dry ingredients, mashed potato and beaten egg. Make into small balls, roll in seasoned flour or breadcrumbs and flour. Allow to stand for about 15 minutes. Fry in deep fat until golden brown. Serve hot on toothpicks. Dip in cocktail sauce.

Cocktail sauce

½ cup tomato sauce
1 teaspoon Worcestershire sauce
1 tablespoon minced onion
1 teaspoon paprika

1 teaspoon salt
½ teaspoon white pepper
1 tablespoon lime juice

Blend well together and use for fish and seafood snacks.

Ham-pineapple rolls

fresh or tinned 2-cm (¾-in) pineapple chunks
ham slices

Cut ham in inch wide strips. Wrap around pineapple chunks. Fasten with toothpicks. Serve with prepared mustard.

Tomato juice cocktail

1 large tin tomato juice (2½ cups)
1 teaspoon sugar
½ teaspoon celery salt

1 teaspoon Worcestershire sauce
¼ teaspoon white pepper

Combine ingredients and chill before serving. Makes 4 servings.

Oyster cocktail

Allow 6 oysters per person
cocktail sauce

Have oysters opened beforehand. Loosen oysters. Drain and chill. Serve in small cocktail glasses with Cocktail Sauce.

Shrimp cocktail

1 cup cooked shrimps
Cocktail Sauce
½ cup finely chopped celery
lettuce

Mix together shredded shrimps and celery. Serve 2 tablespoons on small plates with lettuce leaves and Cocktail Sauce.

15 Tea and coffee occasions

Mid-morning coffee parties are informal occasions for relaxing between household chores, when housewives get together to exchange experiences or club members introduce new friends or visitors from overseas. A choice of dainty sandwiches with coffee cakes and biscuits may be passed around with hot or cold coffee.

Afternoon tea parties may be formal or informal. Small parties at home are usually informal, but larger club room parties, held in honour of special guests, are often formal. In either case, the hostess or hostesses will want to prepare a variety of sandwiches, cakes and snacks.

Scones and cakes

Scones (Basic recipe)

2 cups flour
4 teaspoons baking powder
⅜ cup milk

¼ teaspoon salt
2 teaspoons sugar
4 tablespoons shortening

Sift together flour, baking powder, salt and sugar. Cut in shortening until mixture resembles coarse crumbs. Add cold milk *all at once*. Stir quickly with a fork until dough leaves the bowl cleanly. Turn dough (which should be soft but not sticky) on to a lightly floured board. Toss lightly to make dough into a ball, roll out 1.5 cm (½ in) thick. Cut with biscuit cutter, brush with milk or egg and bake in a hot oven for 15–20 minutes.

For *Tea Scones*, add 2 tablespoons sugar, 1 beaten egg, ½ teaspoon vanilla essence, using ½ cup milk.

For *Girdle Scones*, use basic recipe cutting dough 6 mm (¼ in) thick and bake on both sides on a greased hot baking iron (tawa), electric hot plate or heavy frying pan.

Muffins

1¾ cups sifted flour
2 tablespoons sugar
2½ teaspoons baking powder
¾ teaspoon salt

1 well-beaten egg
¾ cup milk
⅓ cup melted shortening

Sift dry ingredients into mixing bowl; make well in centre. Combine egg, milk and shortening. Add all at once to dry ingredients. Stir quickly only till dry ingredients are moistened. Fill greased muffin pans or paper baking cups ⅔ full. Bake at 200°C, 400°F or Gas 6 for about 25 minutes. Makes about 12.

For *Fruit Muffins*, add ½ cup coarse cut dried fruit or peanuts. Stir in lightly.

Rock buns

225 g (8 oz) flour
75 g (3 oz) butter
100 g (4 oz) granulated sugar
100 g (4 oz) raisins *or*
1 cup grated coconut plus 2 oz flour

1 teaspoon baking powder
1 egg
1 teaspoon vanilla essence *or* lemon

Rub together butter and sugar with fork. Add beaten egg and essence. Stir in flour, baking powder and raisins or coconut. Roll into buns and bake in a moderate oven.

Coconut cake

2½ cups flour
1½ teaspoons baking powder
2 eggs
1 cup granulated sugar

½ cup milk
1½ cups grated coconut
½ teaspoon vanilla essence
½ cup shortening

Cream shortening and sugar. Add beaten eggs and essence, then grated coconut. Lastly, fold in flour sifted with baking powder alternately with milk. Bake in moderate oven.

Two-egg cake

¾ cup shortening
1¼ cups sugar (granulated)
1 teaspoon vanilla
2 eggs

2¼ cups sifted cake flour
2½ teaspoons baking powder
1 teaspoon salt
1 cup milk

Cream shortening to soften. Gradually add sugar and cream thoroughly. Add vanilla. Add eggs, one at a time, beating well after each. Sift flour with baking powder and salt; add to creamed mixture alternately with milk, beating after each addition. Bake in moderate oven 190°C, 375°F or Gas 5 for about 45 minutes.

This is a good basic recipe for *Plain* or *Fruit Cake*. Add 1 cup raisins or mixed fruit or ½ cup floured glacé cherries. Bake in square shallow pans and cut in pieces. Use for small tea cakes also. Top with glacé icing or fluffy frosting and decorate.

Butter sponge

Use any number of eggs, their weight in granulated sugar, butter and flour. Cream butter and sugar, add well-beaten egg yolks with a little vanilla essence, grated lime rind and a little water. Mix in sifted flour lightly. Fold in egg whites last. Bake in moderate oven. Spread over with icing and decorate with peanuts or cherries.

Jam layers or sandwich

8 oz flour
6 oz granulated sugar
4 oz butter
2 or 3 eggs
2 tablespoons water

½ teaspoon vanilla
1 teaspoon cream of tartar and
½ teaspoon baking soda *or*
1½ teaspoons baking powder

Cream butter and sugar. Add beaten eggs and water mixed with cream of tartar, then essence and lastly flour mixed with baking soda. Put mixture in two layer cake pans or sandwich. Bake in moderate oven and when cool, sandwich together with jam, guava jelly or butter icing.

Butter icing

200 g (8 oz) icing sugar
75 g (3 oz) butter
½ teaspoon vanilla
2 teaspoons boiling water

Beat butter, sugar and boiling water till creamy. Add vanilla. When cold spread over cake. Use also as a filling for layer cakes.

Glacé icing

200 g (8 oz) icing sugar
2 tablespoons warm water
flavouring
colouring

Roll lumps out of sugar. Sieve in a bowl and place over hot water. Add warm water gradually. Beat until icing is smooth and warm. Remove from heat. Add flavouring and colouring gradually. The icing should coat the back of a spoon. Cool and use on cakes.

For *Coffee Icing*, add 1 teaspoon coffee essence, reducing water by same amount.

For *Lemon Icing*, substitute lime, orange juice for ½ water in recipe. Use lemon or orange colouring.

Chocolate cake

1 cup shortening
2 cups sugar
2 teaspoons vanilla
2 2.5-cm (1-oz) squares unsweetened chocolate, melted *or*
6 tablespoons cocoa

5 eggs
2¼ cups sifted flour
1 teaspoon soda
1 teaspoon salt
1 cup sour milk *or* buttermilk

Stir shortening to soften. Gradually add sugar, creaming till light and fluffy. Blend in vanilla and cooled chocolate. Add eggs, 1 at a time, beating well after each.

Sift together, flour, soda and salt; add to creamed mixture alternately with milk, beating after each addition. Bake in moderate oven for 20 to 25 minutes. When cold ice with Chocolate Icing.

Chocolate icing

50 g (2 oz) cocoa
200 g (8 oz) icing sugar
3–4 tablespoons warm water

Blend sieved icing sugar with cocoa. Mix well with water until smooth.

Orange cake

150 g (6 oz) butter *or* margarine
150 g (6 oz) caster sugar
3 eggs
225 g (8 oz) plain flour

¼ teaspoon salt
1½ level teaspoons baking powder
1 orange

Line cake-tin with greaseproof paper. Cream the fat and sugar until light; add the beaten eggs gradually, beating well between each addition. Sift flour, salt and baking powder and add with the grated rind and juice of the orange to the creamed fat; mix well. Place in the cake-tin and bake in a moderate oven for 1–1¼ hours. Ice with Orange Frosting, when cold.

Orange frosting

grated rind of 1 orange
½ teaspoon lemon or lime juice
icing sugar

1 tablespoon orange juice
1 egg yolk

124

Add rind to fruit juices and let stand for 15 minutes. Strain. Add gradually to egg yolk. Stir in sugar until of very thick consistency. Beat until very smooth.

Fluffy frosting

1 cup sugar	dash of salt
⅓ cup water	1 egg white
¼ teaspoon cream of tartar	¼ teaspoon vanilla

Bring sugar, water, cream of tartar, and salt to boil; cook until sugar dissolves.

Slowly add to unbeaten egg white, beating constantly with electric or rotary beater till of spreading consistency. Add vanilla.

Coffee cake

100 g (4 oz) butter or margarine	1 teaspoon baking powder
100 g (4 oz) caster sugar	2 teaspoons instant coffee
2 eggs	3 tablespoons milk
200 g (8 oz) plain flour	

Cream the fat and sugar until very light and add the eggs one at a time with a dessertspoon of flour. Beat well. Sift the flour, baking powder and coffee and fold lightly into the mixture with the milk. Pour into greased cake-tin and spread evenly. Bake in a fairly hot oven, for 35–40 minutes until firm. Cool. Use Coffee Icing (see Glacê Icing) and top with peanut halves.

Banana cake

¼ cup butter	½ teaspoon salt
¼ cup sugar	1 cup milk
1 egg	1½ bananas, sliced
2 cups flour	½ cup sugar
2½ teaspoons baking powder	2 teaspoons powdered cinnamon

Cream butter; add sugar slowly, beating in well. Add egg and beat well. Sift together dry ingredients and add alternately with milk to first mixture. Fold in banana slices carefully until well mixed. Pour into two greased layer pans or pie tins. Mix ½ cup sugar and cinnamon and sprinkle over the top. Bake in moderate oven for about 30 minutes. Makes 2 17-cm (7-in) cakes.

Jam or swiss roll

1½ cups flour
2 teaspoons baking powder
¼ teaspoon salt
⅔ cup milk
jam for spreading

4 eggs
1½ cups caster sugar
1½ teaspoons vanilla
2 tablespoons margarine

Sift dry ingredients. Heat milk and melt margarine in it. Beat eggs in bowl until frothy. Gradually add sugar continuing to beat until light. Add essence. Fold in dry ingredients. Fold in liquid last until just blended. Pour thinly into prepared shallow pan greased and then lined with greaseproof paper. Bake in hot oven (200°C, 400°F or Gas 6) for 8–10 minutes.

To roll: Spread a tea towel on table. Cover with a sheet of greaseproof paper liberally sprinkled with caster sugar. Trim ¼ inch from edges all round cake. Turn cake on to sugared paper, quickly peel off greaseproof paper, spread quickly with warmed jam or jelly, roll up tightly with aid of paper, and leave to cool wrapped in paper and cloth to hold its shape. Butter icing may be used to spread instead of jam. When cold, slice and serve.

For *Lady Fingers*, use same mixture, fill greased Lady Finger pans ⅔ full, sprinkle top with sugar and flour and bake.

Sponge cake

6 egg yolks
½ cup cold water
1½ cups sugar
½ teaspoon vanilla
½ teaspoon orange or lemon juice

1½ cups flour
¼ teaspoon salt
6 egg whites
¾ teaspoon cream of tartar

Beat egg yolks till thick and lemon-coloured; add water; continue beating till very thick. Gradually beat in sugar, then vanilla and orange extract. Sift flour with salt three times; fold into egg-yolk mixture a little at a time.

Beat egg whites with cream of tartar till stiff peaks form. Fold into first mixture, turning bowl gradually.

Bake in greased and lightly floured pan in slow oven for about 1 hour. Invert pan to cool.

Crust for Sponge Cake

1½ tablespoons sugar
1 tablespoon flour

Mix sugar and flour together. Dust insides of greased pans and sprinkle on top of cake before baking, in tube or round pans.

Marble cake

150 g (6 oz) sugar
200 g (8 oz) plain flour
1½ teaspoons baking powder
1½ dessertspoons cocoa
100 g (4 oz) butter or margarine
2 eggs

½ cup milk
1 teaspoon lime juice
grated lime peel
cochineal (red colouring)
vanilla essence

Cream the butter or margarine and sugar and add the eggs alternately with the milk. Sift in together the flour and baking powder and mix well. Divide the mixture into 3 parts. Flavour one part with the cocoa, one with a little grated lime peel and the third part with vanilla essence and a few drops of cochineal. Grease a cake pan and drop in alternate spoonfuls of the 3 mixtures until all is used. Bake in a moderate oven.

Breadcrumb cake

1 cup flour
1½ cups breadcrumbs
1 egg
100 g (4 oz) currants or sultanas
¾ cup sugar

100 g (4 oz) shortening
1 teaspoon baking powder
1 teaspoon mixed spices
about 1 cup milk

Sieve the flour, baking powder and spices into a bowl and rub in the shortening until well mixed. Mix in the sugar, breadcrumbs and currants, add the beaten egg and enough milk to make a soft dough. Grease a cake pan and pour in the mixture and bake in a moderate oven.

Biscuits and cookies

Basic cookie recipe

⅔ cup shortening
¾ cup sugar
½ teaspoon grated orange peel
½ teaspoon essence
1 egg

4 teaspoons milk
2 cups sifted flour
1½ teaspoons baking powder
¼ teaspoon salt

Thoroughly cream shortening, sugar, orange peel and essence. Add egg; beat till light. Stir in milk. Sift together dry ingredients; blend in creamed mixture.

On floured board, roll to 3 mm ($\frac{1}{8}$ in). Cut in desired shapes with cutters. Bake on greased shallow pan at 190°C, 375°F or Gas 5 for about 6 to 8 minutes. Cool slightly; remove from pan. Cool on rack. Makes 2 dozen.

Cherries, raisins and any desired flavouring may be added.

Peanut cookies

$\frac{1}{2}$ cup shortening	2 cups flour
1 cup sugar	1 teaspoon baking powder
2 eggs	1 cup chopped peanuts
2 tablespoons milk	$\frac{1}{2}$ teaspoon salt

Cream together butter and sugar. Add eggs one at a time beating well. Sift flour, baking powder and salt, blending in peanuts. Add alternately with the milk to first mixture to make a soft dough. Roll out on floured board and cut with a cookie cutter. Bake in moderate oven for about 15 minutes. Makes 3 dozen cookies.

Press cookies

2 cups flour	1 egg
100 g (4 oz) margarine	1 teaspoon baking powder
100 g (4 oz) sugar	cherries to decorate
1 teaspoon vanilla	

Cream together margarine and sugar. Add beaten egg and essence and mix in flour sifted with baking powder. Mix to a soft dough. Place dough in cookie press or forcing bag and pipe into shapes, adding dough to the press until all is used up. Decorate with cherries or nuts.

Corn biscuits

150 g (6 oz) fresh cornmeal	1 teaspoon bicarbonate soda
100 g (4 oz) flour	1 beaten egg
100 g (4 oz) margarine	$\frac{1}{2}$ teaspoon essence
75 g (3 oz) sugar	milk

Stir cool melted margarine into flour, cornmeal and soda sifted together. Beat egg slightly with essence and add with a little milk to make a stiff dough. Roll on floured board and cut into shapes. Bake for 15 minutes in a moderate oven.

Coconut wafers

1 coconut, grated (about 2 cups)
6 tablespoons shortening
1 cup sugar

1 teaspoon baking powder
2 cups flour
1 beaten egg

Cream shortening and sugar. Add coconut and mix well. Stir in beaten egg and add sifted flour and baking powder. Blend well. Drop spoonfuls on floured board. Press with a floured fork to make thin wafers. Bake on a greased shallow pan in a moderate oven.

Frosted ginger biscuits

¼ cup shortening
½ cup sugar
1 egg
⅓ cup cane syrup (molasses)
2 cups sifted flour
½ teaspoon baking soda

½ teaspoon salt
1 teaspoon powdered ginger
½ teaspoon spice (cinnamon)
½ teaspoon cloves
½ cup water

Cream together shortening and sugar; beat in egg. Stir in cane syrup. Sift dry ingredients; add alternately with water. Drop from teaspoon on to greased shallow pan. Bake at 200°C, 400°F or Gas 6 for about 8 minutes and while still warm, spread with glacé icing. Makes 3 dozen.

Chocolate biscuits

100 g (4 oz) margarine
100 g (4 oz) sugar
1 egg
¼ teaspoon vanilla

2 cups flour
1 teaspoon baking powder
1 heaped tablespoon cocoa
milk

Cream margarine and sugar, add the well beaten egg and vanilla. Sift the flour and cocoa, and stir into the creamed mixture, and if necessary add a little milk to make a fairly stiff but not sticky consistency. Pipe mixture from a cookie press or forcing bag on to a greased baking sheet. Bake in a moderate oven. These may be sandwiched in pairs with butter icing.

Sponge kisses

4 eggs
1½ cups flour
100 g (4 oz) sugar

1 teaspoon baking powder
few drops of vanilla
1 teaspoon melted butter

Mix as for Sponge Cake. Fold in cool melted butter last. Drop on greased baking sheet by spoonfuls leaving a space between each. Bake in a moderate oven. When cool, sandwich together with jam.

Sandwiches

Always use sandwich bread for best results when cutting, rolling and spreading. Trim off crusts. Spread filling as desired between 2 slices of bread, and cut in 4 squares or triangles.

Experiment with filling mixtures, making them tasty. Cover sandwiches with a damp towel or aluminium foil and chill to keep them fresh before serving.

Use brown or white bread preferably one-day old and make different shapes for variety.

Open sandwiches may be made from 6-mm ($\frac{1}{4}$-in) thick bread, cut in attractive shapes with biscuit cutters and spread with butter, peanut butter or salad cream with cucumber, tomato, ham and meat slices and garnished with parsley, watercress, sweet pepper slices etc.

Pinwheel sandwiches

Sandwich bread should be fresh and not brittle. Cut lengthwise and trim crusts. Spread alternately with these contrasting spreads, e.g vegetable, peanut butter, meat or fish, then roll up as for Jam Roll. Seal end firmly. Arrange sandwich rolls in a flat dish. Cover with a damp tea towel and put in the refrigerator. Cut crosswise to make pinwheels before serving.

Neapolitan sandwiches

Butter three or four slices of bread with the inner slices buttered on both sides. Spread two or three varieties of filling between. Fix neatly together. A mixture of white and brown bread may be used. Tint the fillings in pastel shades with food colouring if desired. Use such fillings as crushed pineapple with butter and cheese, peanut butter, fish and shrimp with salad cream. Use parsley, sweet pepper and watercress mixed in the fillings. Wrap the sandwiches in aluminium foil. Chill and cut in thin slices for serving.

Fillings

Tomato-cheese Filling (p118)

Sardine and Egg

1 tin sardines	2 hard boiled eggs
1 tablespoon butter	pepper and salt to taste
1 teaspoon lime juice	1 teaspoon chopped parsley

Crush sardines and eggs with butter. Add pepper and salt to taste, then lime juice and chopped parsley. Blend well. Fish may be substituted for sardines.

Sweet Pepper and Cheese
1 large sweet pepper   ½ teaspoon white pepper
100 g (4 oz) cream cheese   salt
1 tablespoon butter

Chop pepper finely and blend in butter and cream cheese. Season with pepper and salt to taste.

Chicken with Chutney
1 cup minced chicken   ¼ cup diced celery
2 tablespoons mango chutney   salad cream
salt to taste

Blend together ingredients using enough salad cream to moisten.

16 Sweet and savoury pastries

Many good cooks are timid about making pastry admitting that it is one of their weaknesses. If, however, a few basic facts are clearly understood, a little practice will make perfect.

1 Use cold ingredients and utensils.
2 Handle as little and lightly as possible.
3 Lift the flour while rubbing the fat into the flour to introduce cold air into the mixture.
4 Use cold or ice water for mixing.
5 Lemon juice also helps to lighten mixture.
6 Dough should be pliable but not sticky.
7 Handle as little as possible and roll thinly and quickly with a rolling pin, lifting it between the strokes away from the body.
8 Use very little flour while rolling. Always turn dough after rolling before cutting in shapes.
9 Pastry needs a very hot oven for baking to expand the dough and so make it light.

Short Pastry is a good everyday pastry and if well made is adequate for most requirements. For *Rich Short Pastry*, use 50 g (2 oz) extra shortening and $\frac{1}{2}$ teaspoon of lime juice in the water to 200 g (8 oz) flour. Cover in greaseproof paper and put ball of dough to chill before rolling it out.

Flaky and *Puff Pastry* are richer pastries but more difficult to make. *Hot Water* and *Suet Pastries* are seldom used.

Cheese Pastry is used for making cheese straws and biscuits and *Choux Pastry* for crème puffs and éclairs.

To Finish Tops of Pies
For a one-crust pie, trim pastry 1 cm ($\frac{1}{2}$ in) beyond the rim of the dish and fold under to make a double edge. Use the index finger to make scallops, with the thumb and index finger of the other hand used as a wedge, or use a pastry edger.

For a two-crust pie, *lattice strips* may be used for the top. Cut strips of dough 1 cm (½ in) wide, twist half the number and lay over pie 2.5 cm (1 in) apart. Twist the other half in the opposite direction. Moisten the ends of the strips and stick to the edges of the bottom crust.

To cover the top of the pie make both edges 1 cm (½ in) wider than the dish. Damp the edges of the bottom crust. Place the top crust on it and pinch the edges together. Crimp with a fork. Cut slits on top to make a design to prevent the pastry from puffing. Brush with beaten egg before baking.

Short pastry

200 g (8 oz) flour
75 g (3 oz) lard
25 g (1 oz) margarine
5–6 tablespoons iced water

½ teaspoon salt
½ teaspoon sugar (for sweet dishes only)

Sift the dry ingredients in a bowl and cut in the fat lightly with two knives or a fork until the mixture resembles fine breadcrumbs. Add the water gradually, tossing the mixture with a fork until a ball is formed which does not stick to the bowl. Roll on a lightly floured board to 3 mm (⅛ in) thick, turning the dough before cutting it into the desired shapes. This quantity makes a double 22–25-cm (9–10-in) pie or 2 single shells.

Meat patties

200 g (8 oz) short pastry
100 g (4 oz) beef
100 g (4 oz) pork
25 g (1 oz) bacon
piece of red pepper
1 onion

few sprigs thyme and marjoram
1 tablespoon butter
½ teaspoon Worcestershire Sauce
2 tablespoons flour
½ cup stock

Cut the meat into pieces and boil with salt to taste in water until it is soft enough for mincing. Cool and mince with the bacon, pepper and other herbs. Make a binding sauce by melting the margarine in the saucepan, adding the flour gradually then the stock slowly until it is smooth. Add this to the minced mixture and stir in the Worcestershire Sauce making a soft paste. Cut the rolled dough in 5-cm (2-in) rounds with a pastry cutter and place a small teaspoon of the mixture on each round. Cover with another round of dough, damping the inner edges. Press the edges together with a fork, and with a skewer, make a hole in the centre of each patty on the top and brush with beaten egg. When finished, bake the patties in a greased shallow baking tin at 230°C, 450°F or Gas 8 for about 20 minutes or until very light brown. Makes about 3 dozen patties.

Bouchées

For making bouchées roll out some rich short pastry very thinly. Cut in rounds 5 cm (2 in) in diameter and fit neatly into special bouchée tins. Prick dough in the tins and bake until crisp, in a moderate oven. Any sandwich fillings may be used. Garnish as desired.

Cheese biscuits and straws

100 g (4 oz) flour
¼ teaspoon salt
75 g (3 oz) margarine
iced water

½ teaspoon white pepper
100 g (4 oz) grated cheese
1 egg yolk

Mix flour, grated cheese, salt and pepper together. Rub in margarine and mix to a smooth paste with yolk of egg. Pipe out with cookie press or forcing bag or cut into straws or thin strips and twist. For *biscuits*, use 40 g (1½ oz) margarine, 50 g (2 oz) cheese and a little beaten yolk to make a stiff rolling dough. Cut strips 6 cm × 1 cm (2½ in × ½ in) and bake in a moderate oven for about 20 minutes.

Choux pastry

100 g (4 oz) flour
1 cup water
¼ teaspoon salt
50 g (2 oz) butter *or* margarine

½ teaspoon vanilla essence
1 egg yolk
2 eggs

Sift and warm the flour. Place water, salt and fat in a pan, and bring to boiling-point. Remove from heat, add flour all at once and beat well (using a wooden spoon) over the heat again, until it becomes a smooth soft paste and leaves the sides of the pan clean. Remove from the heat, add vanilla and egg yolk immediately and beat well. Add the other two eggs one at a time, beating thoroughly between each addition. Bake in a fairly hot oven for about 30 minutes.

Éclairs and cream puffs

Use the same mixture as for choux pastry. Put mixture in teaspoonfuls on greased shallow pan leaving space between each to allow for rising, when making Cream Puffs. Split and fill with cream.

For Éclairs, pipe the mixture through a piping bag with a 1 cm (½-in) pipe in 7.5 cm (3-in) lengths. When cool, coat with chocolate icing.

For *Chicken Puffs*, use the same method as for Cream Puffs, but instead of filling with cream, split and fill with a seasoned chicken mixture.

Sausage rolls

150 g (6 oz) rich short pastry
225 g (½ lb) sausages (skinless chipolatas)
Egg or milk for brushing

Make the pastry and roll out thinly to a rectangle. Cut the sausages into 8 pieces. Place these on the pastry in two rows. Wet between each sausage and round the edges. Fold the pastry from the top and bottom into the centre and press lightly to form rolls. Cut each roll separately and flake the edges and mark the top with a knife. Brush with egg or milk and bake in a hot oven for 25–30 minutes. Makes 8 sausage rolls.

Sweet pastries

Guava or Otaheite apple pie

2 dozen stewed guavas *or*
½ dozen fresh apples
325 g (¾ lb) granulated sugar
225 g (½ lb) flour

100 g (4 oz) shortening
milk *or* water to mix
½ teaspoon powdered cinnamon
¼ teaspoon salt

Trim apples, removing seed and stem ends. Slice lengthwise in very thin strips. Place in saucepan. Add enough water to cover and sugar. Cook uncovered until tender and red in colour. Make pastry of flour, water, shortening and salt. Roll out thinly and line the pie-dish. Fill with prepared apples or guavas and decorate with remaining pastry or Crumb Topping.

Crumb topping

½ cup sugar
¾ cup enriched flour
⅓ cup butter or margarine

Mix sugar with flour and cut in butter till crumbly. Sprinkle over fruit and bake in a hot oven for 40 minutes, or till done.

Pumpkin pie

1½ cups cooked pumpkin
¾ cup sugar
½ teaspoon salt
1 to 1¼ teaspoons cinnamon
1 cup milk
150 g (6 oz) rich short pastry

½ to 1 teaspoon ginger
¼ to ½ teaspoon nutmeg
¼ to ½ teaspoon cloves
3 slightly beaten eggs
¾ cup evaporated milk

Make a 22-cm (9-in) pastry shell. Thoroughly combine the pumpkin, sugar, salt and spices. Blend in eggs, milk and evaporated milk. Pour into unbaked pastry shell. Bake in hot oven for 50 minutes or until inserted knife comes out clean. Cool.

Garden cherry pie

1 cup sugar
¼ cup flour
¼ cup juice from cherries
3 cups stewed cherries

¼ teaspoon salt
¼ tablespoon softened butter
¼ teaspoon almond essence
8 oz rich short crust pastry

Combine sugar, flour and salt; stir in juice. Cook and stir over medium heat till thick; cook 1 minute longer. Add cherries, butter, essence and ¼ teaspoon red colouring. Let it stand; make pastry.

Line 22-cm (9-in) pie plate with pastry; fill. Top with lattice crust. Crimp edges. Bake in very hot oven for 10 minutes. Reduce heat to moderate and bake about 45 minutes more.

Gooseberries and other berries may be used similarly.

Caribbean pie

1 cup sugar
⅓ cup cornstarch
¼ teaspoon salt
1 cup pineapple juice
½ cup orange juice
1 tablespoon lime juice
4 slightly beaten egg yolks

1 tablespoon butter
1 teaspoon vanilla
2 stiffly beaten egg whites
1 baked 22-cm (9-in) pastry shell
(See p133)
1 recipe Meringue (p137)

In saucepan combine sugar, cornstarch, and salt. Blend in fruit juices. Bring to boil over medium heat stirring constantly. Cook and stir 2 minutes. Remove from heat.

Stir small amount of hot mixture into egg yolks; return to hot mixture. Bring to boiling point and cook for 1 minute, stirring constantly. Remove from heat. Add butter and vanilla. Cool till just slightly warm.

Fold in stiffly beaten egg whites. Pour into cooled shell. Spread meringue over filling, sealing to edges of pastry. Bake in moderate oven for 12 to 15 minutes or till meringue is golden brown. Cool pie thoroughly.

Meringue
Beat 2 egg whites, $\frac{1}{4}$ teaspoon cream of tartar, and $\frac{1}{2}$ teaspoon vanilla till soft peaks form. Gradually add 4 tablespoons sugar, beating until stiff peaks form and all sugar is dissolved.

Raisin pie

1 cup brown sugar	1 tablespoon mixed peel
3 tablespoons cornstarch	$\frac{1}{3}$ cup orange juice
1$\frac{1}{3}$ cups water	3 tablespoons lime juice
2 cups seedless raisins	225 g (8 oz) rich shortcrust pastry

Combine all ingredients in saucepan. Cook, stirring constantly, over medium heat until thick. Add $\frac{1}{2}$ cup chopped peanuts (optional). Pour into pastry-lined 22-cm (9-in) pie plate. Moisten edge of plate, top with lattice crust brushed with milk. Sprinkle with sugar and bake in a hot oven for about 40 minutes.

Vanilla cream pie

$\frac{3}{4}$ cup sugar	2 tablespoons butter
$\frac{1}{4}$ cup flour	1 teaspoon vanilla
$\frac{1}{4}$ teaspoon salt	225 g (8 oz) rich short crust pastry
2 cups milk	1 recipe Meringue (p137)
2 slightly beaten egg yolks	

In saucepan, combine sugar, flour and salt; gradually stir in milk. Cook and stir over medium heat till mixture boils and thickens. Cook for 2 minutes longer. Remove from heat.

Stir small amount hot mixture into yolks; return to hot mixture; cook for 2 minutes, stirring constantly. Remove from heat. Add butter and vanilla; cool. Make pastry shell and cool then pour in mixture. Top with Meringue and bake as for Caribbean Pie.

Banana cream pie

Use same mixture as for Vanilla Cream Pie. Slice 3 large bananas and put them on the pastry shell. Pour over mixture. Top with meringue and bake.

Jam tarts

450 g (1 lb) guava, mango, garden cherry *or* pineapple jam
225 g (8 oz) short crust pastry
beaten egg *or* sugar syrup

Cut the rolled dough in rounds with a 7-cm (3-in) pastry cutter and place in shallow greased tart pans. With a skewer prick each round well and place a teaspoon of jam in each. Cut 1-cm ($\frac{3}{8}$-in) strips from some of the dough and twist them damping the edges, across the tarts in lattice fashion. Brush them with egg or thick sugar syrup and bake in a hot oven. Makes about 3 dozen tarts.

Coconut custard tarts

Cut rounds of dough as for Jam Tarts and place in pans. Prick well all over and bake them blind or empty, in a hot oven until creamy brown. Cool.

Filling

4 tablespoons custard powder	1 cup grated coconut
2 cups milk	1 teaspoon vanilla essence
4 tablespoons sugar	1 tablespoon margarine
pinch of salt	caster sugar

Bring the milk to the boil and remove from the heat. Add the custard powder, sugar and salt mixed with about $\frac{1}{4}$ cup of the milk. Stir until the mixture thickens. Return to the heat and cook for 3 minutes until it is very thick. Cool and add vanilla essence and margarine. Lastly, stir in $\frac{2}{3}$ of the grated coconut. Fill each tart shell with some of the mixture and garnish them with the rest of the grated coconut to which a little caster sugar may be added.

Note: To bake a large pie shell blind or empty, cut a round of grease-proof paper and fit it into the unbaked pie shell. Place some dried peas on it, and bake. This prevents the shell from rising.

Fruit flan

225 g (8 oz) rich short pastry
1 slice ripe pawpaw
2 slices ripe mango
few cherries
1¼ cups water and fruit juice

1 seedless orange
1 banana
1 tablespoon caster sugar
½ package lemon *or* orange jelly
  crystals

Make a pie shell to fit a 22-cm (9-in) pie pan. Scallop the edges with the fingers or with a special edge cutter. Prick it well and bake blind in a hot oven. Cool. Arrange in it a mixture of diced pawpaw and mango, orange sections and banana slices. Sprinkle sugar over. Add boiling water to jelly crystals; stir and cool. Pour over the fruit and chill in refrigerator until jelly is set.

17 Home-baked breads

The art of bread-making is very old. Bread was once made exclusively in the home but nowadays most of it is baked in commercial bakeries. White bread flour is even enriched to improve its quality, but home-made bread is preferred by many busy housewives who still find time to bake once or twice a week. Home-made bread is usually made from wheat flour, but cornmeal, cassava, banana, breadfruit flours, when available, can all be used quite satisfactorily mixed with wheat flour.

Quick breads are very popular, easy to mix and make, and the raising agents used in them are baking powder, baking soda and cream of tartar. They may contain dried or fresh fruit, nuts, coconut, molasses, sugar, milk, butter, or eggs, etc., and make nourishing additions to meals. They may also be used as snacks.

Quick breads

Coconut bread

4 cups flour
100 g ($\frac{1}{4}$ lb) shortening
$\frac{3}{4}$ cup milk and coconut water
150 g (6 oz) sugar
1 egg

2 cups grated coconut
1 teaspoon vanilla essence
2 teaspoons baking powder
150 g (6 oz) raisins (optional)
$\frac{1}{2}$ teaspoon salt

Sift dry ingredients. Add sugar, then beaten egg with milk, melted shortening and essence. Stir in grated coconut, raisins (floured) if used. Blend ingredients well. Knead slightly on floured board. Shape into loaves and put in greased loaf pan, filling only two thirds of each pan. Dust with fine sugar. Bake in moderate oven. Makes 2 loaves.

For heavier Coconut Bread, use only 1 teaspoon baking powder, and $\frac{1}{2}$ cup milk. Knead well on board, using extra flour, until dough is very firm. Shape into loaves. Score the tops, and brush with sugar and water.

Raisin bread

4 cups flour
2 teaspoons baking powder
1 teaspoon salt
225 g (8 oz) sugar
100 g (4 oz) shortening
½ teaspoon spice and nutmeg

225 g (½ lb) raisins *or*
150 g (6 oz) raisins plus 50 g (2 oz)
  mixed peel
2 eggs
1 teaspoon vanilla
1½ cups milk

Sift dry ingredients in bowl. Add sugar. Melt shortening, and add to it the milk, beaten eggs and essence. Make a hole in centre of the flour and mix. Add floured fruit and blend well. Put in greased loaf pan filling only two-thirds of the pan. Sprinkle top with granulated sugar. Bake in moderate oven (180°C, 350°F or Gas 4).

Cassava bread (Bammie)

4 cups finely grated cassava
1 teaspoon salt
butter or margarine

Peel and wash some cassava sticks. Grate very finely. Wring out all the juice in a strong cloth. Add salt and mix well. Spread out and leave exposed to air overnight. While still damp, put about ½ cup cassava meal inside greased tin rings on a greased baking sheet or tawa over moderate heat. After a few minutes, as the steam rises, remove the rings, then flatten and press the bread into shape with a knife or wooden palette. Place the baking sheet in the sun or in a warm oven until the bread rounds are quite dry and stiff. Brown under grill or toast, and butter before serving.

Banana-peanut bread

2 cups flour
½ cup sugar
⅓ cup butter *or* margarine
2 ripe bananas (mashed)
1 egg
½ cup peanuts (crushed)

3 teaspoons baking powder
1 teaspoon vanilla
½ teaspoon grated nutmeg
½ cup raisins (optional)
pinch of salt

Cream butter and sugar and well-beaten egg. Sift flour, baking powder, salt and add alternately with mashed bananas. Flour and add chopped nuts and raisins if desired. Pour into greased tin. Bake in moderate oven until golden, about 30 minutes.

Gingerbread

½ cup shortening
1 cup brown sugar
2 eggs
½ cup cane syrup *or* molasses
½ teaspoon salt
½ teaspoon spice
½ teaspoon nutmeg

2 teaspoons ginger (powdered *or* freshly grated)
1 teaspoon baking powder
1 teaspoon baking soda
2 cups flour
⅔ cup hot water

Grease and line a shallow tin with waxed paper. Sift dry ingredients. Warm sugar, fat and syrup gently, and add hot water. Add beaten eggs. Combine liquids with dry ingredients and beat thoroughly. Pour thick batter in pans and bake in a slow oven (170°C, 325°F or Gas 3) for about 1 hour.

Orange bread

2¼ cups sifted flour
¾ cup sugar
2¼ teaspoons baking powder
¾ teaspoon salt
¼ teaspoon soda

¾ cup orange juice
1 tablespoon grated orange peel
1 beaten egg
2 tablespoons melted margarine

Sift together dry ingredients; stir in orange peel. Combine egg, orange juice and margarine; add to dry ingredients, stirring just until moistened.

Pour into greased loaf pan and bake in a moderate oven (180°C, 350°F or Gas 4) till done, about 55 minutes. Remove from pan; cool.

Sweet potato pudding

4 cups cooked mashed sweet potatoes
¾ cup sugar
2 eggs
2 tablespoons butter
½ cup coconut milk
grated rind of 1 lime

1 tablespoon lime juice
2 tablespoons sherry *or* rum
¼ teaspoon salt
½ teaspoon baking powder
½ teaspoon powdered cinnamon
1 tablespoon seedless raisins

To mashed potatoes, add sugar gradually and whole eggs, one at a time, mixing well after each addition. Mix in butter with a fork. Add milk. Blend well. Mix in grated rind of lime and lime juice. Add rum. Mix well. Add salt, baking powder and cinnamon, sifted together. Mix. Add raisins. Pour this mixture into a greased pan and bake in a moderate oven (180°C, 350°F or Gas 4) for about 50 minutes, until done. Makes 8 servings.

Cornmeal pone

100 g (¼ lb) grated pumpkin
2 cups grated coconut
½ cup sugar
1 cup cornmeal
½ teaspoon salt

½ cup flour
2 tablespoons shortening
1 teaspoon rice
2 oz raisins
milk or water to mix

Mix together pumpkin and coconut with dry ingredients. Melt shortening and add. Mix in liquid last. Bake in a greased shallow pan in a moderate oven.

Corn bread

1 cup flour
¼ cup sugar
2 teaspoons baking powder
¾ teaspoon salt

1 cup yellow corn meal
2 eggs
1 cup milk
¼ cup shortening

Sift flour with sugar, baking powder, and salt; stir in corn meal. Add eggs, milk and shortening. Beat until just smooth. Pour into greased loaf pan and bake in a hot oven for 20 to 25 minutes.

Yeast breads

White and brown bread loaves and rolls are made with yeast and take a much longer time than quick breads in the process of making. Yeast may be bought in compressed cakes or in active dry form. When moisture is added to yeast, it produces carbon dioxide, the bubbles thus produced expand, causing the dough to rise. Yeast thrives best in a warm temperature, 26–30°C (80–85°F). A high temperature kills the yeast and a low temperature prevents the growth, so luke-warm water is always used in mixing yeast.

For the best results follow these general rules for making yeast breads:

1 Scald milk and cool to lukewarm before adding yeast or use warm water and leave yeast to dissolve for 5–10 minutes.

2 Add sugar to increase fermentation and give flavour. Salt also adds flavour.

3 Measure the correct amount of flour to make a soft but not sticky dough.

4 Knead dough thoroughly and lightly to distribute the yeast cells and gas bubbles, to develop the gluten, and make the dough smooth. Push the dough with the base of the palm. Give the dough a quarter turn, fold over and push down again. Knead until dough is light and springy, 8–10 minutes.

5 Place dough in lightly greased bowl. Lightly grease surface. Cover and allow it to rise until double in bulk, for about 1–2 hours.

6 Punch down the dough, turn over and let it rise again. Then shape into loaves and place in pans. Leave to prove, i.e. rise again to fill the pans, about 20 minutes. When pressed lightly, dough should retain an impression. It is then ready for baking. Oven temperature should be 190–200°C, 375–400°F or Gas 5–6.

White bread

1 package dry *or* compressed yeast	6 cups sifted flour
¼ cup water	1 tablespoon shortening
2 cups hot milk	2 teaspoons salt
2 tablespoons sugar	

Soften active dry yeast in warm water or compressed yeast in luke-warm water. Combine hot milk, the sugar, salt, and shortening. Cool to lukewarm.

Stir in 2 cups of the flour; beat well. Add the softened yeast; mix. Add enough of remaining flour to make a moderately stiff dough. Turn out on lightly floured surface; knead till smooth and satiny (8 to 10 minutes). Shape in a ball; place in lightly greased bowl, turning once to grease surface. Cover; let rise in warm place till double (about 1½ hours). Punch down. Let rise again till double (about 45 minutes).

Cut dough in 2 portions. Shape each in smooth ball; cover and let rest 10 minutes. Shape in loaves; place in 2 greased loaf pans. Let rise till double (about 1 hour). Bake in a hot oven.

Whole-wheat bread

1 package dry *or* compressed yeast	3 teaspoons salt
¼ cup water	¼ cup shortening
2½ cups hot water	3 cups whole-wheat flour
½ cup brown sugar	5 cups sifted white flour

Soften active dry yeast in ¼ cup warm water or compressed yeast in ¼ cup lukewarm water. Combine hot water, sugar, salt and shortening; cool to lukewarm.

Stir in whole wheat flour and 1 cup of the white flour; beat well. Stir in softened yeast. Add enough of remaining flour to make a moderately stiff dough. Turn out on lightly floured surface; knead till smooth and satiny (10 to 12 minutes).

Shape dough in a ball; place in lightly greased bowl, turning once to grease surface. Cover; let rise in warm place till double (1½ hours). Punch down. Cut in 2 portions; shape each in smooth ball. Cover, and let rest for 10 minutes.

Shape in loaves; place in greased loaf pans. Let rise till double (1¼ hours). Bake in a moderate oven for about 45 minutes. Cover with foil last 20 minutes, if necessary. Makes 2 loaves.

Dinner rolls

450 g (1 lb) flour	2 teaspoons sugar
1 teaspoon salt	25 g (1 oz) shortening
15 g (½ oz) yeast	1 cup milk, scalded

Make as for White Bread. When well risen, form into rolls on a floured board. Prove for 15 minutes, brush with egg and bake in a hot oven for about 20 minutes.

Bun bread or raisin buns

450 g (1 lb) flour	300 ml (½ pint) scalded milk
75 g (3 oz) margarine	15 g (½ oz) dry yeast
50 g (2 oz) raisins ⎫	75 g (3 oz) sugar
50 g (2 oz) currants ⎬ optional	½ teaspoon vanilla
25 g (1 oz) mixed peel ⎭	½ teaspoon salt
1 egg	

Dissolve dry yeast in a little warm milk in bowl for about 10 minutes. Add salt, sugar and shortening to the rest of milk. Keep lukewarm and add to the yeast mixture when yeast is dissolved and stirred. Add to flour gradually and mix to a pliable dough. Knead lightly, but thoroughly for 10 minutes. Put to rise covered with a cloth, in a warm place for 1 hour or until dough is doubled in bulk. Punch down dough, cover and leave to rise again. Then shape into loaves or buns and put in greased pans, covering and leaving to prove or rise again, for about 20 minutes. Brush with sugar and water, sprinkle with granulated sugar and bake in a moderate oven until light brown.

Hot Cross buns

450 g (1 lb) flour
1 package dry yeast
½ teaspoon salt
½ teaspoon spice
50 g (2 oz) sugar

1 teaspoon ginger
50 g (2 oz) margarine
25 g (1 oz) mixed peel
50 g (2 oz) raisins
1 cup milk

Dilute yeast in a little lukewarm milk, leave for 5–10 minutes. Sift dry ingredients together (salt, spice, ginger, salt and flour). Add sugar. Rub fat into flour. Add warm milk to yeast and mix in dry ingredients gradually. Knead and sprinkle in fruit. Knead again and put to rise until double in bulk. Knead once more and shape into loaves or buns. Put to prove. Before baking, cut 2 gashes at right angles to form a cross. Gashes may be filled with Glacé Icing (p123).

Tea ring

1 package dry yeast
¼ cup warm water
½ cup milk, scalded
3 tablespoons shortening
3 tablespoons sugar

1 teaspoon salt
2½ to 2¾ cups sifted flour
1 beaten egg
½ teaspoon vanilla
fruit filling (see below)

Soften yeast in warm water. Combine milk, shortening, sugar and salt; cool to lukewarm; add 1 cup of the flour; beat well. Add softened yeast, egg and vanilla. Mix in enough flour to make soft dough. Knead lightly on floured surface. Place in greased bowl; turn once to grease surface. Cover; let rise till double (1½ to 2 hours).

Roll to 33 × 22 in (13 × 9 cm) rectangle, about 6 mm (¼-in) thick. Brush with melted butter; spread evenly with fruit filling. Roll lengthwise; seal edge. Shape in a ring on greased baking sheet. With scissors, snip almost to centre at 2.5-cm (1-in) intervals. Pull sections apart and twist slightly. Let rise till double (35 to 45 minutes). Bake at 190°C, 375°F or Gas 5 for about 20 minutes.

Fruit filling

Combine ¼ cup sugar, 1 teaspoon cinnamon, ½ cup chopped peanuts, and ½ cup raisins and mixed peel.

Doughnuts

1 package dry or compressed yeast
¼ cup water
¾ cup milk, scalded
¼ cup shortening

¼ cup sugar
1 teaspoon salt
1 egg
3½ to 3¾ cups sifted flour

Mix dough as for Bun Bread. When risen, roll out dough 6 mm ($\frac{1}{4}$ in) thick. Cut with floured doughnut cutter. Let rise till very light (30 to 40 minutes). Fry in deep hot fat till browned. Drain on paper towels. While warm, dip doughnuts in granulated sugar. Makes about $1\frac{1}{2}$ dozen.

Note: Dough for doughnuts should be as soft as can be handled. A soft dough is easier to roll when well chilled.

18 Fritters and pancakes

Fritters and pancakes may be sweet or savoury. These fried batters are enjoyable served at breakfast, lunch or as desserts. Pancakes are fried or rather pan-baked in hardly any fat, i.e. a greased hot pan or griddle. Fritters are made from a batter mixture used to coat food or to combine with it. They are fried in fat 1–2.5-cm ($\frac{1}{2}$–1-in) deep. Food dipped in a coating batter may be fried in deep fat.

Coating batter for frying

100 g (4 oz) flour
$\frac{1}{4}$ teaspoon salt
$\frac{1}{2}$ cup milk

1 egg (optional) *or*
$\frac{1}{2}$ teaspoon baking powder

Sift together flour and salt. Make a hole in centre of flour and add the egg and some of the milk. Mix well to a stiff consistency, adding the rest of the milk. Allow it to stand for 30 minutes. Then fry in hot fat as a blue haze rises from it. This batter is also used for Pancakes and Yorkshire Pudding.

Sweet fritters

Sweet potato fritters

coating batter
sweet potato slices (parboiled)
frying fat
caster sugar

Dip sweet potato slices in batter until they are well-covered. Fry in hot fat until brown, drain on absorbent paper and dredge with sugar.

Pumpkin and sweet potato fritters

1 cup grated raw pumpkin
½ cup crushed cooked potato
1 cup flour
¼ cup sugar
½ teaspoon spice

½ teaspoon baking powder
2 teaspoons melted shortening
¼ teaspoon salt
milk to mix
fat for frying

Sift flour, salt and baking powder. Add sugar, spice, crushed vegetable and shortening. Blend in milk to make a thick batter. Fry by spoonfuls in hot fat. Drain and serve hot.

Banana fritters

4 firm bananas
coating batter
fat for frying
sugar to taste

Prepare the batter. Cut each banana lengthwise and across the middle, making four portions. Coat with batter. Fry in hot fat, which is just beginning to haze.

Sprinkle well with sugar and serve immediately.

Cornmeal fritters

½ cup cornmeal (fresh Indian corn)
½ cup flour
1 teaspoon baking powder
¼ teaspoon salt
3 tablespoons sugar

1 egg
1 cup milk
2 tablespoons margarine
few drops vanilla

Sieve salt, flour and baking powder in a bowl. Put in beaten egg and milk by degrees, after rubbing the margarine into the flour mixture. Beat until smooth. Drop by spoonfuls in frying pan and fry in hot fat. Drain on absorbent paper before serving.

Pineapple fritters

coating batter (1 recipe)
12 slices pineapple (fresh or tinned)
fat for frying
caster sugar

Make the batter. Drain the pineapple well. Dip each slice into batter and then using a skewer, lower the slice into the deep fat which should be just hazing. Cook until crisp and nicely browned. Drain; dredge with caster sugar and serve at once.

If liked, serve with pineapple sauce made from the syrup. Allow 2 fritters for each helping.

Orange fritters

coating batter
4 oranges
fat for frying
caster sugar

Prepare the batter. Remove the peel and pith from the oranges; divide them into pieces of 3–4 segments. Carefully cut into the centre to remove pips. Dip into the batter and fry in hot fat until golden brown, about 3–4 minutes. Drain well.

Dredge with sugar and serve at once.

Rice fritters

1 cup cooked rice
1 cup hot milk
1 tablespoon butter
2 tablespoons sugar

2 beaten eggs
2 tablespoons flour
½ teaspoon lemon essence
oil for frying

Melt butter in hot milk, add beaten eggs, rice, sugar and essence. Mix in flour last to make thick batter. Fry by spoonfuls in hot fat until brown. Drain well.

Savoury fritters

Cucumber or chocho fritters

1 large chocho (225 g or ½ lb) *or*
1 cucumber (without seeds)
1 egg well beaten
¼ cup milk

2 tablespoons flour
1 teaspoon melted butter
¼ teaspoon salt
fat for frying

Wash, peel and grate chocho or cucumber. Add flour, salt, milk and melted butter. Fold beaten egg into mixture. Drop tablespoon by tablespoon into hot fat. Fry until golden brown on both sides. Drain on paper towel. Serve hot.

Spinach cakes

150 g (6 oz) spinach *or* bhagi
1 egg
½ teaspoon pepper
2 tablespoons butter
¼ cup milk
oil for frying

1 tablespoon chopped onion
½ teaspoon salt
½ cup breadcrumbs
½ cup flour
¼ teaspoon baking powder

Wash spinach leaves well and shred finely with a knife. Add beaten egg, onion and melted butter, then stir in dry ingredients sifted together. Add milk to make a very thick batter. Fry in hot oil till golden brown. Drain before serving.

Green corn fritters

2 cups boiled corn off the cob *or*
   canned whole corn
½ cup milk
2 cups flour
1½ teaspoons salt

½ teaspoon white pepper
2 teaspoons baking powder
1 tablespoon melted butter
2 eggs

Sift dry ingredients together. Beat eggs, add milk and gradually stir in flour, etc. Mix to a thick consistency and fry by spoonfuls in smoking hot oil. Drain on absorbent paper and serve at once.

Tannia or coco fritters

2 cups grated cocoes
2 tablespoons flour
1 teaspoon salt
few blades escallion

1 teaspoon baking powder
2 eggs
½ teaspoon white pepper

Wash, peel and grate vegetables finely. Chop seasonings and mix all ingredients. Beat well. Drop spoonfuls in smoking hot oil and fry until golden brown. Drain and serve at once.

Pancakes

Pancakes are traditionally made every year on Shrove Tuesday. This has been the custom for more than 500 years. Originally, pancakes were made from fats and eggs, etc., which had to be used up before Lent, but for many years they have rather been an aid to the menu during the Lenten period or at any chosen time throughout the year.

Pancake batter

2 cups flour
2 tablespoons melted margarine
2 tablespoons sugar
½ teaspoon salt

2 cups milk
2 eggs
fat for greasing pan

Sift flour and salt in bowl. Add sugar and blend. Beat eggs and essence in another bowl and stir in milk. Slowly add dry ingredients to the liquid mixture beating well. Pour the batter into a jug and allow it to stand for an hour or so before cooking. When ready melt a small bit of fat in a small omelette pan over the heat, and drain it off when it becomes very hot. Start to fry pancakes by pouring in some batter and allowing it to spread over the pan. Cook for about two minutes, loosening edges with a spatula. When bubbles appear on the surface turn or toss the pancake, cooking until pale brown. Sprinkle with lime juice and sugar or cinnamon and sugar. Roll and keep hot. Continue, until all the batter is used up but *without* adding any more fat to the pan. This quantity makes about 18 pancakes.

For *Orange Pancakes*, peel oranges thickly and remove fruit sections; cut them into thin slices, dredge with sugar and roll between the pancakes. Serve warm.

For *Savoury Pancakes*, put a little fish or cheese mixture on each pancake, roll and serve.

Tossing the pancake to turn it over in the pan is an art which has been unsuccessfully tried by many cooks. It adds interest to the making of pancakes and can be done with a little practice. When the under side of the pancake is finished, tip the pan downwards slightly and gently shake the pancake a little over the edge of the pan; then with a quick upward jerk of the pan, flip it over on the uncooked side and finish cooking.

19 Jams, jellies, preserves and candies

Most of the local fruits and vegetables are very suitable for making jam, jellies or preserves. The citrus fruits make good marmalade.

Many housewives grow some fruit in their own gardens, and it is economical as well as satisfying to use up any surplus by preserving it.

Bear in mind that the more acid fruit make better jams and jellies. They should be picked firm and *slightly* under-ripe for best flavour and the maximum of pectin, which is a substance which allows the jam or jelly to set after cooking. If the fruit is not very acid, use a tablespoon of lemon or lime juice per pound of fruit.

Use 500 g (1 lb) of granulated sugar to 500 g (1 lb) of fruit when making *jellies*, and about 375 g (¾ lb) sugar to 500 g (1 lb) for *jam*. Use a little more if the fruit is very acid. Cut fruit in small pieces for making *jam*. Cook until tender, then add sugar. Simmer until sugar is dissolved, then boil briskly.

Cut fruit in small pieces for making *jelly*. Just cover with water, cook slowly until fruit is very tender, 1 hour or more. Pour into a jelly bag and allow liquid to drip through for several hours or over-night, so that jelly will be clear.

Allow the fruit or liquid to boil quickly during cooking time, but do not allow it to boil before sugar is dissolved. Stir it often but do not stir unnecessarily while boiling, or the mixture will be cloudy. Use a wooden spoon for stirring.

Use aluminium, enamel or stainless steel heavy pans for cooking fruit and do not fill them more than half-full.

To test when jam is set, remove the pan from the heat. Put a little jam on a saucer and let it cool. The surface will wrinkle when pushed with the fingers. Test jelly by putting a little in a saucer with cold water. If it remains in a soft ball without disintegrating, the jelly is finished. If a thermometer is used, the temperature should register 104°C (220° F) in either case.

To sterilize jars for bottling, wash and clean them thoroughly, put in cold water and bring to the boil; boil for 15 minutes, *or* put them in a cold over and heat them gradually. Sterilize them just before ready for use. Fill them 6 mm (¼ in) from the top and wipe off with a clean damp cloth. Cover them with a round of waxed paper and put on a tightly fitting metal cover. Store in well-ventilated cupboards.

Pineapple jam

2 cups grated pineapple
1 cup water
1½ cups granulated sugar
2 teaspoons lime juice

Cook pineapple with water slowly until soft. Add sugar and lime juice; stir well. Cook until thick and set. Cool and bottle.

Mixed fruit jam

1 cup each finely cut banana, mango and pineapple
2⅓ cups sugar
¾ cup water
Piece of cinnamon

Cook fruit in water with cinnamon and sugar. Stir well. Boil until very thick. Bottle and cover.

Garden cherry jam

3 cups garden cherries (stoned)
4 cups sugar

Cook cherries with juice until tender. Add sugar and stir over low heat until sugar is dissolved. Cook until jam is thick and set. Pour into warmed jars and cover.

Gooseberries and other berries may also be used.

Watermelon jam

3 cups cubed fruit
¾ cup water
2¼ cups sugar
1 teaspoon grated green ginger

Use green part of water melon. Red part may be used in fruit salad. Peel off the green skin. Cut fruit in cubes and simmer with water and ginger until tender. Add sugar and stir until dissolved. Cook for 15–20 minutes. Cool and bottle.

Granadilla jam

1 granadilla
lime juice
granulated sugar

Wash the fruit; cut and remove seeds, drain. Scoop out the pulp.
Use ¾ cup sugar to each cup of pulp and juice. Boil together, adding
1 teaspoon lime juice to 1 cup fruit, until set. Pour into warmed jars.
Ripe pawpaw jam may be made similarly.

Golden apple jam

golden apples
salt
granulated sugar

Use under ripe apples. Peel and grate, remove strings. Use 1 cup of
sugar to 1 cup pulp plus ½ teaspoon salt. No water is necessary. Boil
until mixture sets and bottle.

Sorrel jam

900 g (2 lb) sorrel (cut without seeds)
1.35 kg (3 lb) sugar
water
piece of cinnamon

Wash sorrel sepals well and boil with about 1 cup water until they
are very tender and soft enough to crush to a pulp. Add sugar, stir
well and boil until mixture sets. Put into jars and cover.

Guava jelly

guavas (under ripe)
lime juice
granulated sugar
water

Wash, peel guavas, cut in halves and put in a saucepan. Cover with
water. Boil until guavas are soft. Strain through a colander and then
through fine muslin. Measure the juice and use 1 cup sugar to 1 cup
juice. Heat juice, add sugar and dissolve before it boils. Add ½ teaspoon lime juice per cup liquid. Boil briskly removing gum with
wooden spoon, until mixture jells. Test on saucer, bottle and cover.

Citrus fruit marmalade

675 g (1½ lb) fruit
1 grapefruit
2 lemons

1 large orange
6 cups water
1.35 kg (3 lb) sugar

Wash and peel the fruit, and shred the peel coarsely or finely according to taste. Cut up the fruit, tying the pips and any pith or coarse tissue in a muslin bag. Soak the fruit, peel and muslin bag in the water in a bowl for 24 hours. Next day, transfer to the preserving-pan and simmer gently for 1½ hours or until the peel is tender and the contents of the pan are reduced by about ⅓. Remove the muslin bag, after squeezing gently. Add sugar, stir over a low heat till dissolved. Bring to the boil and boil rapidly till setting point is reached.

Orange or tangerine marmalade

6 oranges or tangerines
sugar
½ cup lime *or* lemon juice
water

Wash fruit. Cut in quarters and remove seeds. Measure fruit pulp. Add 3 cups water to 1 cup of pulp. Bring to the boil and cook about ½ hour. Let it stand overnight. Measure 1 cup liquid to 1 cup sugar and 2 tablespoons lime or lemon juice. Bring fruit mixture to the boil. Add sugar and stir until dissolved. Boil rapidly, stirring occasionally until mixture jells in cold water or, if using a candy thermometer, it should register 104°C (220°F). Allow it to cool and pour into clean jars. Seal at once.

Guava cheese

very ripe guavas
sugar

Peel and grate guavas. Rub through coarse net or a sieve. Use 1 cup sugar to every cup of guava pulp. Boil until very thick and the mixture leaves the side of the pan. Stir occasionally while cooking. Test in cold water. Pour into a wet shallow tin about 1 cm (½ in) thick. Cut into squares. When cool, dredge with caster sugar.

Mango cheese

ripe firm mangoes
sugar
lime juice

Peel mangoes, cut off flesh and rub through a sieve. Use ¾ cup sugar to 1 cup pulp. Add ½ teaspoon lime juice to a cup. Boil until thick, stirring well, and until mixture leaves sides of the pan. Pour on to a wet tin sheet. Put aside to cool.

Marrow and ginger preserve

1.8 kg (4 lb) vegetable marrow (weighed after preparation)
1.35 kg (3 lb) granulated sugar

50 g (2 oz) green ginger (root)
3 tablespoons lemon *or* lime juice

Peel marrow and cut into 1½-inch cubes, after removing the seeds. Put the fruit in a heavy saucepan with very little water. Cover and steam over low heat until marrow is tender. Put the mixture into a bowl, cover with the sugar and let it remain overnight. To finish the cooking, crush the ginger, tie it in a muslin bag and put it into the saucepan with the marrow and lime juice. Cook it over low heat for about an hour until fruit is transparent and the syrup very thick. Remove the ginger, cool and pour into dry warm jars and cover.

Breadfruit blossom preserve

12 breadfruit blossoms or 'swords' (ripe but not dry)
450 g (1 lb) sugar

Soak breadfruit blossoms or 'swords' for 10 to 15 minutes. Scrape off rough skin. Cover with water and boil. When tender, put in sugar and cook gently until blossoms have absorbed the syrup. Drain and dry for 2–3 days in the sun or in a warm oven. Sprinkle with sugar before storing.

Pawpaws in syrup

green pawpaws
few pieces of orange peel
sugar

Scrape pawpaw skins deeply with a serrated knife, wash and parboil in water slightly salted. Discard the water. Cut the pawpaws in half and remove the seeds. Cut in halves again. Weigh pawpaws and put them in a pan with an equal quantity of sugar plus 1 cup water to each pound of sugar used. Simmer the fruit until it has absorbed nearly all the syrup. Cook a few pieces of orange peel with pawpaws to flavour them. If desired, pour some cane syrup (molasses) over the pawpaws to cover and allow them to steep in it for several days before using. Serve with syrup.

Shaddock rind

1 large ripe shaddock
granulated sugar

Wash the fruit and with a grater lightly grate off some of the rind. Cut in 5 cm (2-in) wedges. Soak in salted water overnight. Squeeze dry and put in fresh water next day and soak again for several hours. Discard and squeeze dry. Put rinds in cold water to cover and boil until tender.

Drain and squeeze well between 2 plates. Make a syrup with 675 g (1½ lb) sugar to 1½ cups water, without stirring it. Simmer the peel in it until the syrup has been used up. Then make a syrup with 1.1 kg (2½ lb) sugar to 2 cups water. Boil the rinds in it until most of it is absorbed. Lay them on a flat dish and pour over any remaining syrup. Put them in the sun or cool oven to crystallize.

Grapefruit and *Orange* rinds may be prepared in the same way.

Candies

Coconut sugar cake or coconut ice

2 cups light crystal *or* granulated sugar
¼ teaspoon vanilla essence
¼ cup water
1 cup grated coconut

Boil sugar and water together until syrupy. Test a few drops in a saucer with cold water; when it forms a soft ball, remove from heat. Cool a little, then beat mixture until very thick and it begins to crystallize. Stir in essence and coconut; blend well and pour into a greased shallow pan 20 × 20 × 2.5 cm (8 × 8 × 1 in). Mixture may be divided and half coloured pink, using a few drops of red dye, or a pink layer may be placed on a white layer to make a two-colour cake. Cut in 5-cm (2-in) squares. Work quickly and do not overbeat mixture.

Molasses sugar cakes

100 g (4 oz) sugar
1 cup syrup or molasses
2 cups grated coconut

½ teaspoon grated ginger *or*
½ teaspoon powdered spice

Boil sugar, molasses and spice until syrup spins a thread from a spoon dipped in it. Remove from heat. Cool a little, stir in coconut and beat until very thick. Drop spoonfuls on a wet shallow tin, and leave to set.

Peanut sugar cake

450 g (1 lb) white sugar
½ cup water
1 cup roasted peanut halves

Boil the sugar and water until syrup, when tested, forms a firm ball in cold water. Remove from heat. Cool a little, add peanuts and beat well until very thick. Drop spoonfuls on a wet shallow tin, and leave to set.

Chocolate fudge

2 cups sugar
1 teaspoon vanilla
1 cup milk

2 tablespoons cocoa
2 tablespoons butter

Combine sugar, cocoa and milk, and place over medium heat. Stir steadily until mixture begins to boil, lower heat and continue to cook gently, stirring occasionally. Test by dropping a little into cold water; if it makes a firm ball between the fingers, the fudge is ready. Remove from heat. Add vanilla and butter, beat with wooden spoon until very creamy and beginning to set. Pour into a buttered tin and cut into squares when cool. ½ cup raisins or chopped peanuts may be added before pouring out.

Marshmallows

1½ tablespoons gelatine
½ cup boiling water
¼ teaspoon of salt
icing sugar

2 tablespoons cold water
2 cups granulated sugar
½ teaspoon vanilla

Soak the gelatine in 2 tablespoons cold water until all the liquid has been absorbed. Boil sugar and water to the firm ball stage (110°C or 240°F). Add vanilla and salt to gelatine. Pour syrup slowly over the gelatine, beating constantly until cool and thick. Butter a shallow pan slightly and dust with icing sugar. Turn the marshmallow mixture into it, and smooth the top evenly. Dust with icing sugar and let it stand overnight. Cut into small squares and roll in icing sugar.

Toffee (Plain)

½ cup water
4 cups granulated sugar
½ teaspoon cream of tartar
1 teaspoon lemon essence

Boil water and sugar together, stirring until dissolved. Bring to boiling-point and add the cream of tartar. Boil to the 'small crack' stage (143°C, 290°F), add flavouring and pour into a greased tin. Cool, mark off in squares and when cold, break into pieces. ¾ cup of cracked peanuts may be added just before pouring out. At the 'small crack' stage, syrup should make a hard ball when tested in water.

Coconut toffee

2 cups granulated sugar
1 cup brown sugar
100 g (¼ lb) glucose

1 cup grated coconut
½ teaspoon almond essence
¾ cup water

Boil water and sugar together, stirring until dissolved. Add glucose and boil to the 'small crack' stage (143°C or 290°F). Remove the pan from the heat, stir in the coconut, and boil to the 'large crack' stage (156°C or 312°F). Add flavouring essence and pour on to buttered pans. When cool, mark off in squares, and break in pieces when cold. At the 'large crack' stage, syrup should make a very hard ball when tested in water.

Peanut brittle

2 cups sugar
½ cup water
1 cup chopped peanuts
2 tablespoons butter

¼ teaspoon cream of tartar
¼ teaspoon salt
¼ teaspoon bicarbonate of soda

Mix sugar, nuts, cream of tartar and water and boil to the 'large crack' stage (156°C or 312°F). Remove from heat and add salt, soda and butter. Pour on to a greased pan and when cold, break into pieces.

Barley sugar

4 cups granulated sugar
2 cups water
½ teaspoon lime juice

¼ teaspoon cream of tartar
few drops of yellow colouring
½ teaspoon lemon essence

Dissolve the sugar in water and boil to the 'small ball' stage (113°C or 238°F). Add the lime juice. Continue boiling to the 'large crack' stage (155°C or 312°F), then add cream of tartar, yellow colouring and essence. Pour on to a greased tin. When cool, cut into 1-cm (½-in) strips, twist into a spiral, and when cold, store in airtight bottles.

Tamarind balls

tamarinds (ripe)
white pepper
granulated sugar

Shell tamarinds, scrape off the pulp from the seeds. To 400 g
(1 lb) of sugar, add 100 g (¼ lb) pulp and ¼ teaspoon white pepper.
Mix together thoroughly to make a paste. Roll into balls, putting a
seed inside each. Sprinkle with sugar and store in a jar.

Pawpaw or lime balls

2 cups grated green pawpaw (peeled)   1 tablespoon lime juice
2½ cups granulated sugar   ½ tablespoon grated lime rind
red and green food colouring   ¼ cup water

Cook grated pawpaw for 3 minutes in boiling water. Strain and
discard water. Repeat. Press out all the water from pawpaw and
stand aside. Add ¼ cup water to the sugar. Heat it slowly and boil
until it spins a thread. Add the pawpaw to the mixture and cook it
until it leaves the sides of the saucepan. Remove from heat, add lime
juice and rind. Cool. Divide into 2 portions and colour in red and
green. Make into balls and roll in sugar.

Ginger squares

2 cups granulated sugar   15 g (½ oz) grated green ginger
¼ cup water   1 teaspoon lime juice
1 teaspoon butter

Boil sugar, water and ginger until syrup makes a firm ball in water.
When tested, remove from heat, add lime juice and butter. Beat well
and when very thick pour into a wet shallow tin. Cut into squares
when firm.

Kisses or soupises (Meringues glacés)

3 egg whites
1 cup granulated sugar
1 teaspoon vanilla essence
¼ teaspoon cream of tartar

Beat eggs with essence and cream of tartar until frothy. Gradually
add sugar and beat till mixture makes very stiff peaks. Drop table-
spoonfuls on ungreased paper on shallow pan. Bake in slow oven
(140°C, 275°F or Gas 1) for about 1 hour. Turn off heat and leave in
oven for another hour to become dry and crisp. To colour 'kisses',
add a few drops of food colouring near the end of whipping time.

In the islands and regions of the vast Caribbean area, the climate and food crops may range between tropical and Mediterranean, but from the early sixteenth century when West Africans were brought over as slaves by traders from some of the European countries, food crops of all kinds have been interchanged between the territories and grown and produced as required, and according to the suitability of the soil, rainfall, etc. Although food produce and dishes are similar throughout the area, methods of cooking vary according to the original influences. Different cookery methods are used in town and country. Cheap food produce regularly available, e.g. in rural areas, has influenced the traditional dishes there. On the other hand, the urban folk indulge in more exotic and highly seasoned foods prepared by modern methods.

Here is a variety of traditional dishes:

British Honduras

Sopa de Hess

900 g (2 lb) conch meat
450 g (1 lb) coco (tannia)
2 tablespoons tomato paste

salt and pepper to taste
1 large onion
1 lime

Clean the conchs with lime and salt and pound them well. Put to boil in salted water for about $\frac{1}{2}$ hour. When tender, discard water. Season with pepper, salt and tomato paste. Add onion cut in rings. Peel coco and dice. Add water to cover and allow to boil until coco is soft. Serve hot.

Codfish holiday

1 cup rice
$\frac{1}{2}$ cup codfish
$\frac{1}{2}$ cup English potatoes

225 g ($\frac{1}{2}$ lb) cabbage
1 small onion
2 small tomatoes

1 small red pepper
piece of thyme
pinch of black pepper

2 cups coconut milk
1 avocado pear (sliced)

Soak codfish in cold water for ½ hour. Clean and wash vegetables; cut potatoes into 2.5-cm (1-in) squares. Cut cabbage coarsely, and slice tomato, pepper and onion. Drain codfish and pour hot water over it. Clean, remove bones and flake into small pieces, then put with potatoes in saucepan to steam for 10 minutes, adding just enough water. Then steam cabbage on top for 10 minutes. Cook rice in another saucepan with coconut milk and seasonings. Combine mixtures and serve hot garnished with slices of avocado.

Pumpkin pudding

1 medium sized pumpkin
  (900 g or 2 lb)
2 cups flour
2 cups brown sugar
2 eggs

1 lime
1 teaspoon vanilla
4 tablespoons margarine
2 tablespoons rum
1½ cups coconut milk

Wash pumpkin, cut into 4 pieces and boil in salted water. When pumpkin is cooked, scrape from skin and put into a bowl. Add sifted flour and sugar and beat until smooth. Break eggs and add separately to mixture, again mixing smoothly. Add milk to mixture, juice of lime, butter and flavouring. Pour into large buttered baking dish and bake in a moderate oven for about 1 hour.

Johnny or journey cakes

1½ cups sifted flour
40 g (1½ oz) lard
50 g (2 oz) margarine
2–3 tablespoons grated coconut

½ cup coconut milk
2 teaspoons baking powder
¼ teaspoon salt

Sift flour, baking powder and salt. Add melted lard and margarine slowly, mixing well. Then add the coconut and stir in the milk gradually. Roll into small balls and flatten, decorate with a fork. Bake for 20 minutes in a hot oven (280°C, 450°F or Gas 8). Slice and butter cakes when hot. Serve immediately.

Jamaica

Ackee and salt fish

2 dozen ackees
450 g (1 lb) salt fish
piece of hot pepper
2 tablespoons butter

2 medium onions
few blades of escallion
½ green pepper

Boil fish after soaking in cold water to remove salt. Flake. Remove ackees from pods, seeds and red centre. Wash and put into cold water; boil for 15 minutes. (They may be tied in a muslin bag and boiled.) When cooked, place them over flaked fish and serve hot with the following dressing:

Chop onions and escallion finely. Toss lightly in 2 tablespoons butter with hot pepper. Garnish with pieces of green pepper.

Green corn dumplings

2 cups freshly grated corn
2 cups flour
milk *or* water

75–100 g (3–4 oz) beef suet
1 tablespoon salt

Remove husks and clean ripe corn. Grate on sharp grater; add flour and salt sifted. Mix in shredded suet. Pour in milk or water and mix to mellow dough. Shape into dumplings and cook in boiling water for 20 minutes.

Note: If corn is dry, soak in boiling water overnight. Dumplings may be served with soup.

Rice and beans

1 cup red beans
1 medium sized coconut
2 blades chives, thyme
2 bacon rashers
salt

2 cups rice
1 sweet pepper (small)
piece of hot pepper
1 clove garlic
2 cups hot water

Grate coconut and add hot water. Squeeze and strain off liquid. Add beans and enough water to cover. Cover and cook until beans are tender. Add all other ingredients except rice and cook for 10 minutes. Increase stock to 4 cups. Add rice, stir and cover. Cook over low heat until grains are soft. Garnish with slices of sweet pepper.

Pepper pot soup

1 bunch Indian kale
1 bunch callaloo
450 g (1 lb) fresh beef
225 g (½ lb) salt beef
8 cups water

few shrimps or a crab
2 cocoes
1 dozen okras (ladies' fingers)
seasoning (bunch of mixed herbs)

Boil the vegetables and meat till tender, then rub greens through a colander, pressing out all the pulp. Return to the pot and add seasonings. Boil till ready to serve. Cut okras in rings and fry lightly in butter. Add to soup 10 minutes before serving.

Jerk pork

This is a speciality of Portland, Port Antonio. A young pig about 13.5 kg (30 lb) in weight, cleaned and prepared for cooking, is used for 'jerking'. A mixture of blood, pepper, pimento seeds, escallion, minced onions and salt, is rubbed inside the belly cavity. A stand made of green pimento or other sticks, or 'pata' is fixed up over a coal fire and the pig is placed on the stand. The fat is allowed to fall in the fire. Men who prepare and sell this meat are known as 'jerk men'. They sell this delicacy in the market square and heat the meat in an oven at one of the local bakeries.

This jerk pork often lasts for several weeks.

Akkra

2 cups black eye peas
3–4 green peppers
salt to taste
fat for frying

Wash and soak the peas overnight in hot water. Remove outer skin. Soak again until fully swollen. Pound in a mortar until very smooth. Put aside in a bowl. Cut up peppers and pound them; add to pea mixture. Beat well until thick and creamy with a wooden spoon. Drop spoonfuls into hot fat and fry till golden brown. Drain and serve.

Banana pudding

6 grated green bananas
2 tablespoons flour
1 cup coconut milk
2 tablespoons shredded coconut
2 eggs
25 g (1 oz) margarine

1 cup brown sugar
½ teaspoon nutmeg
¼ teaspoon salt
½ teaspoon vanilla
2 tablespoons raisins

Add ½ cup milk to banana. Crush and beat until smooth. Add all other ingredients and blend well together. Pour into greased dish. Bake for 40 minutes. Decorate when cooled with grated coconut.

Totoes

3 cups flour
¾ cup molasses (cane syrup)
½ cup milk
1 cup dark brown sugar
1½ cups grated coconut
1 teaspoon mixed spice

2 beaten eggs
½ cup butter or margarine (melted)
3 teaspoons baking powder
1 teaspoon bicarbonate of soda
½ teaspoon salt

Sift together dry ingredients. Add sugar. Mix molasses, melted fat and a little milk. Blend with flour mixture. Add beaten eggs. Dissolve soda in rest of milk and add to mixture beating well. Stir in grated coconut quickly with a fork. Pour into well greased square tin and bake in a moderate oven for about 1 hour. When cool, cut in squares and remove from tin.

Leeward Islands

Creole sweet omelette

½ cup water
¾ cup flour
½ teaspoon baking powder
¼ teaspoon salt

50 g (2 oz) margarine
2–3 eggs
¼ cup raisins
fat for frying

Put water, salt and fat in saucepan; boil. Remove from heat; gradually stir in flour and baking powder. Return to heat and stir for 2 minutes. Remove and stir in well-beaten eggs and raisins. Drop by spoonfuls in hot fat and fry until golden brown. Sprinkle with sugar before serving.

Fungi

5 cups boiling water
salt to taste
okras (optional)

2 tablespoons shortening
2 cups cornmeal

To rapidly boiling water, add salt and sprinkle cornmeal slowly. Allow water to boil over meal a few minutes, stirring briskly to prevent lumping. When well combined, add shortening. Cover and steam for 5–10 minutes, stirring often. Serve hot. When okras are added, cut in small pieces and allow to boil for a few minutes before adding meal.

For *Sweet Fungi*, instead of okras, add ½ cup raisins and ½ cup sugar.

Boija

25 g (1 oz) dry yeast
4 cups flour
4 cups cornmeal
3 mashed ripe bananas
  (about 1½ cups)

1 cup grated coconut
2 teaspoons salt
½ cup sugar
1 cup melted shortening
warm water

Dissolve yeast in ¼ cup warm water. Add to 1 cup flour and mix to a batter. Allow it to rise. Add other ingredients and enough water to make a very stiff batter. Pour into greased pans and allow to rise to double in bulk before baking. Brush with milk and bake in a moderate oven for ¾–1 hour.

Duckanoo or Duckna

1½ cups grated sweet potato
1 small grated coconut
¾ cup sugar or to taste
1 teaspoon vanilla essence
½ teaspoon salt

½ teaspoon grated nutmeg
4 tablespoons margarine or oil
½ cup flour
milk to mix
banana leaves or plantain leaves

Mix together all ingredients adding milk last to make batter of dropping consistency. Put about 2 tablespoons of mixture on a piece of steamed banana leaf. Fold and tie securely. Steam for 30 minutes. Cornmeal may be used instead of potato.

Crab Gumbo (p52)

Crab Pelau (p52)

Curried Lobster (see p53 – Curried Shrimps)

Garnished salt fish

225 g (½ lb) salt fish
1 medium onion
1 large tomato

1 small avocado pear (ripe)
2 teaspoons cooking oil
pepper and salt to taste

Roast salt fish; remove skin and bones. Wash, drain and shred fish. Chop onion and cut tomato in small pieces. Mix all ingredients adding oil. Garnish with sliced avocado.

Seasoned rice

2 cups rice
100 g (¼ lb) salt beef
100 g (¼ lb) pig's tail
1 medium carrot
1 small egg-plant (225 g or ½ lb)
1 tablespoon fat
sprig of thyme

1 onion
50 g (2 oz) cabbage
1 large tomato
piece of hot pepper
salt to taste
few blades of escallion
4 cups water

Soak salt meat in water for ½ hour. Cut in pieces and cook in 4 cups water for 45 minutes or until tender. Wash and dice carrot and egg-plant. Cut onion, tomato and cabbage finely. Wash escallion, add to carrots and meat and cook for 10 minutes. Then add greens and egg-plant and cook for 5 minutes. Add rice, seasoning, margarine. Cook for about 25 minutes until rice is tender. Serve hot.

Windward Islands

Jack and Bluggoe broth

12 medium sized jackfish
12 bluggoe figs
25 g (1 oz) butter or margarine
1 large onion
8 cups of water

1 tablespoon oil
1 lime
pepper, chives, garlic
few small tomatoes

Clean, wash and season jacks with salt, lime and garlic. Marinate for 15 minutes. Heat oil and fry onions lightly. Boil bluggoes in water for ten minutes and add other ingredients. Cover and simmer for 25 minutes or more.

Lambie souse

4 lambies or conchs (900 g or 2 lb)
1 medium onion
1 cucumber
2 limes

1 green pepper
watercress or parsley
sweet pepper for garnishing
salt and pepper to taste

Clean away slime from lambies using salt and lime. Pound lambies well and boil till tender. Prepare souse pickle with cucumber and seasonings. Cool lambie and cut in small pieces. Put in pickle. Decorate with parsley and sweet pepper. Serve with breadfruit.

Stuffed jackfish

6 jackfish
2 limes
salt, pepper and herbs to taste

1 chopped onion
6 slices stale bread
fat for frying
2 tablespoons butter *or* margarine

Bone jackfish after cleaning. Marinate in a mixture of lime juice, salt and water for about 15 minutes. Drain and dry the jackfish thoroughly and butter the insides before stuffing.

Stuffing
Soak 6 slices of bread in salted water until soft. Squeeze dry and shred; then mix in 2 tablespoons butter or margarine, the chopped onion, a piece of hot pepper and herbs to taste. Fry the stuffing in some hot fat before the fish is filled with it. Fasten the sides of the fish together by sewing loosely or with small skewers. Baste the fish with butter and bake them in a shallow pan in a moderate oven (190°C, 375°F or Gas 5) until the fish are brown on both sides, basting when necessary. Serve with lime slices.

Breadfruit with coconut milk or oiled down

2 small ripe breadfruits
450 g (1 lb) corned pork
salt to taste

3 cups milk from
2 grated coconuts

Peel and wash breadfruits and cut into halves, removing centres. Arrange in large iron pot, pour on coconut milk, and place pork cut in pieces on breadfruit halves. Cover with tight fitting lid. Cook over low heat until coconut milk becomes oily and pork is cooked. Stir occasionally to prevent burning.

Smoked pork with yams

450 g (1 lb) smoked pork
900 g (2 lb) white yam
1 pepper (hot)
1 onion
2 blades chives

1 clove garlic
1 tablespoon lime juice
few cloves
4 small carrots (diced)
2 cups cold water
red pepper rings for garnishing

Soak pork for 1 hour to remove salt. Throw away water and wash. Put pork in cold water and put over a medium flame to simmer till tender. Cut in pieces, add sliced yam and carrot and boil for 30 minutes. Add remaining ingredients. Boil for 5 minutes more and serve hot. Garnish with red pepper rings.

Crayfish salad

6–8 crayfish	100 g (¼ lb) potatoes
salad oil	100 g (¼ lb) carrots
mayonnaise	100 g (¼ lb) beets
white pepper and salt to taste	2 large tomatoes

Boil crayfish with salt and when cooked, remove shell. Cut flesh in small pieces. Add oil, mayonnaise, white pepper and salt to taste. Dice cooked potatoes, beets and carrots. Slice tomatoes. Combine prepared crayfish with potatoes and carrots to make a salad. Arrange tomato slices and diced beets around dish. Garnish with parsley.

Fried frogs' legs

This dish is served as a delicacy in Dominica and Montserrat. The frogs are larger than the garden frogs and are caught in the mountains. They are also known as 'mountain chickens'. The legs are skinned, marinated in vinegar and salt, then seasoned with white pepper and fried in a batter or coated with egg and crumbs and fried. They are like chicken in taste.

Farine dumplings

2 cups farine (cassava meal)	¼ cup sugar
1 cup water	2 tablespoons margarine
1 beaten egg	fat for frying

Bring water to boiling-point. Add farine gradually to water and stir occasionally so that the mixture does not lump. When it resembles gluten, remove from heat and blend in egg and melted margarine. Add sugar and mix well. Fry in fat until golden brown, using a spoon for dropping batter as for fritters.

Arrowroot sponges

2 cups arrowroot starch	1 cup margarine
1 cup flour	2 egg yolks
1¼ cups sugar	1 teaspoon baking powder
1 teaspoon vanilla	½ cup milk

Cream margarine and sugar. Add each egg yolk separately with milk and essence, and mix to a smooth paste. Sift in arrowroot, flour and baking powder. Mix well. Put in greased shallow pans in moderate oven. Cut in squares and decorate as desired.

Barbados

Flying Fish (see p49–50)
Sea Egg (see p54)

Cou-Cou

2 cups corn meal
12 okras
6 cups water or more

1 tablespoon salt or to taste
2 tablespoons butter

Wash okras, cut off stems, slice into rings and boil with half the water and salt for about 10 minutes. Add the rest of the water and salt to the sifted corn meal and mix well. Remove saucepan from heat and stir in the corn meal mixture until well blended. Return saucepan to stove and cook mixture stirring ingredients with a wooden spatula over medium heat. When mixture becomes stiff and smooth, and breaks away from saucepan cleanly at bottom, it is finished. Put into a dish immediately and spread liberally with butter. Serve with Steamed Flying Fish.

Pudding and souse

Pudding

Thoroughly clean some of the intestines of a pig (turning skins inside out) with soap and water and then salt water and lime juice. Then soak in a salt water and lime solution for about 1 hour. Grate 900 g–1.35 kg (2–3 lb) of sweet potatoes in a bowl. For *Black Pudding*, strain some of the pig's blood mixed with water in it and add minced eschalots, thyme, red pepper, sweet marjoram, 4 tablespoons margarine, salt to taste, 1 tablespoon sugar and ½ teaspoon powdered cloves. Add water to make a mixture of loose consistency. Fill the skins (do not pack tightly) with mixture, tie at each end and steam or cook slowly in boiling water until potato is cooked and skins firm. Prick the skins in places when half cooked to expel air and prevent bursting.

For White Pudding, blood is not added to ingredients.

Souse

Divide a pig's head in half. Wash, scrape and clean well with a sharp knife. Remove the brain, and boil in salted water until the flesh begins to leave the bones. Plunge immediately into cold salted water to make the flesh crisp, and to cool. Then cut off the meat in slices and put into a large bowl of pickle made from salt water, lime juice, chopped onion, cucumber and a few sliced red peppers. Leave for several hours to steep before using. Garnish with parsley. This is a popular Saturday night supper. Pigs' trotters are also cooked and soused.

Jug-Jug

Jug-Jug is a corruption of the Scottish dish haggis, which was introduced by the Scots who were exiled in Barbados after the Monmouth Rebellion of 1685.

The original haggis is a savoury mixture of oatmeal, blended with minced liver, suet, etc., well-seasoned and steamed like a pudding.

In cooking Jug-Jug, whole grain ground guinea corn flour (millet) is substituted for oatmeal. Salt or fresh meat, local green peas, fat, herbs and other seasonings are minced and blended with the flour, stirred gradually with stock to make a very thick purée, as in making Cou-cou. Okras are sometimes chopped and cooked in this dish. This is a very rich dish and is served in a casserole topped with butter.

8 cups green peas
1 cup guinea corn flour
225 g (½ lb) salt beef *or* any other salted meat
100 g (¼ lb) fresh pork *or* chicken
2 tablespoons butter

2 medium sized onions
3–4 blades eschalot
1 bunch mixed herbs
salt and pepper to taste
about 4 cups water

Boil the pork or chicken in water; add the salt meat cut in pieces and soaked previously to remove the salt; also add the peas and herbs. Cook the mixture until peas are soft. Now strain it off reserving the stock. Mince the meat, peas and seasonings. Cook the guinea corn flour in the stock for about 10 minutes, stirring constantly. Add minced ingredients, stir and cook for about ½ hour stirring the mixture until it becomes a fairly stiff consistency. Cover and allow to steam for 5 minutes. Before removing from the heat, stir in some of the butter, then turn mixture out on a dish, spreading it smoothly with the rest of the butter. Serve hot with sliced ham and chicken. This is a traditional Christmas dish.

Doved peas

Boil some green peas in salted water until soft. Cut up a few bacon rashers or slices of ham with some minced onion, red pepper and sweet marjoram. Mix the seasonings together with the peas and fry them in hot fat. When dry but not crisp, stir in a little butter and serve hot with fried fish.

Fowl down-in-rice

1 chicken about 1.3–1.8 kg (3–4 lb)	2 tablespoons butter
4 cups rice	½ teaspoon mustard
100 g (¼ lb) onions	100 g (¼ lb) tomatoes
1 tablespoon salt	1 lime
8 cups water	bunch of herbs

Clean and wash chicken with salt and lime. Allow to stand for about 1 hour. Cook chicken in water for ½ hour. Clean, wash rice and add to chicken, with herbs and pepper and salt to taste. Cook until rice grains are soft. Make a sauce with sliced onions, tomatoes, butter, mustard and lime juice, mixed in ½ cup of water. Salt to taste. Cook for 5 minutes. Cooked giblets may be added. Remove chicken from rice and dissect. Pile rice on dish and arrange chicken pieces around it. Garnish with sauce.

Sea Moss Jelly (p93)

Conkies

It is traditional in Barbados for housewives to make conkies on Guy Fawkes Day, 5 November – although the origin of the custom is unknown. Conkie is probably a corruption of the West African word 'kenky' used up to the present day, for a similarly prepared corn meal dish.

2 cups fresh corn flour	100 g (4 oz) raisins (optional)
⅓ cup flour	325 g (¾ lb) brown sugar
325 g (¾ lb) pumpkin	1 cup milk
150 g (6 oz) shortening	1 teaspoon powdered spice
225 g (½ lb) sweet potato	1 teaspoon grated nutmeg
3 cups grated coconut (1 large)	1 teaspoon almond essence
1 teaspoon salt	

Grate coconut, pumpkin and sweet potato. Mix in sugar, liquids and spices. Add raisins and flour last and combine well. Melt shortening before adding with milk, etc. Fold a few tablespoons of the mixture in steamed plaintain leaves cut in squares about 20 cm (8 in) wide. Steam conkies on a rack over boiling water in a large pot or in a steamer until they are firm and cooked.

Falernum

¾ cup lime juice
2½ cups white rum
900 g (2 lb) granulated sugar

12 cups water
almond essence to taste

Boil sugar with half the water to a thick syrup. Allow to cool, mix in lime juice, essence, rum and rest of water. Strain, bottle and allow to stand for 3 weeks. Strain and bottle again before serving.

Trinidad

Callaloo

16–20 dasheen or eddoe leaves
100 g (¼ lb) pig's tail *or* salted meat
1 large crab
4 tablespoons cooking oil
1 lime
2 blades chives

1 tablespoon butter
8–10 okras
1 large coconut
1 green pepper
1 onion
sprig of thyme

Wash leaves and break into fine pieces. Grate coconut, add 2 cups of hot water and extract milk. Wash crab with lime. Extract crab meat and shred it. Cut up salt meat and okras. Place ingredients in saucepan, cover and leave to boil until leaves are tender. Swizzle and leave to simmer until smooth and okra seeds are pink. Serve with pounded plaintain.

Breadnut curry (Chataigne)

1 breadnut (just ripe)
2 tablespoons curry powder
1 tablespoon butter
salt to taste
oil for frying

2 cups coconut milk
1 large onion
2 blades chives
1 clove garlic
1 tomato

Peel breadnut and divide into pieces. Shred pulp, peel seeds, cut up seasonings and fry in oil with garlic. When brown remove garlic, add curry and stir until well flavoured. Put the shredded pulp and curried seeds with the coconut milk into a saucepan; leave to simmer slowly. When thick, add butter and cook a few minutes more. Serve with a border of rice.

Brule Jol

225 g (8 oz) salt fish
1 small chopped onion
2 medium sized tomatoes
1 avocado pear

1 tablespoon salad oil
1 lime
piece of red pepper
½ teaspoon white pepper

Soak fish overnight to remove salt. Clean and shred fish. Mix chopped tomato, onion, pepper and shredded fish in a bowl. Marinate with olive oil and lemon juice. Serve on lettuce leaves with slices of avocado.

Cascadura stew

6 cascadura fish
2 blades chives
few garden tomatoes
½ teaspoon clove
lime juice
1½ cups water

1 large onion
salt and pepper to taste
2 tablespoons cooking oil
2 tablespoons butter
1 tablespoon sugar

Wash fish well to remove mud. Clean as usual and marinate in lime and salt. Brown sugar in hot oil and put in fish. Brown on both sides. Put in seasonings and water and simmer for 15 minutes.

Sancoche

This is a very old plantation dish cooked with salt meat and seasonal vegetables.

450 g (1 lb) mixed pickled meat
1 tablespoon butter
4 cups water
675 g (1½ lb) mixed provisions
  (vegetables)

bunch of herbs
salt and pepper to taste
dumplings (p33)

Soak meat to extract salt and cook until almost tender. Cut vegetables in thick slices, lightly fry the seasonings in butter, mix together ingredients with meat and simmer until soft.

Accra and floats

Accra

2 cups flour
½ teaspoon salt
100 g (4 oz) salt fish
½ package dried yeast
1½ cups warm water
oil for frying

1 tablespoon chopped onion
1 clove garlic
2 blades eschallot
piece of thyme
piece of red pepper

Soak fish in hot water and drain; then scald and remove skin and bones. Crush fish and add the minced seasonings. Sift flour and salt. Dissolve yeast in a little warm water and stir into the flour with rest of the water to make a batter. Add fish mixture and beat a few minutes. Allow to rise for about 1½ hours. Drop into hot oil by spoonfuls and fry. Drain and serve with hot floats.

Floats

4 cups flour	½ package yeast (7 g or ¼ oz)
1½ teaspoons salt	warm water to mix
½ cup shortening	fat for frying

Sift together flour and salt. Add shortening and mix with a fork to resemble fine breadcrumbs. Use a little warm water to mix yeast and add to the flour mixture. Knead until smooth. Allow it to rise until double in bulk. Cut in pieces and roll into small balls. Allow to rise for 15–20 minutes. Flatten to 6-mm (¼-in) thickness and fry in hot fat. Drain and serve hot.

Bakes

1½ cups flour	2 teaspoons sugar
1 teaspoon baking powder (rounded)	1 tablespoon shortening
	¼ cup water
½ teaspoon salt	oil for frying

Sift flour, baking powder and salt. Rub in fat. Add dry ingredients and mix to make a soft dough. Knead lightly, with extra flour if needed. Break off pieces and roll into balls. Then flatten to 2 cm (½ in) thick. Fry in hot oil or bake on a hot greased tawa.

Pastelles

3 cups grated green corn or same quantity in corn balls	few capers or sweet pickles
	¼ cup raisins
450 g (1 lb) minced beef (cooked)	2 medium onions
450 g (1 lb) minced pork (cooked)	¼ cup cooking oil
2 large tomatoes	piece of sweet pepper
1 tablespoon vinegar	2 blades chives
½ teaspoon black pepper	plantain or banana leaves

Chop all green seasonings finely and mix with meat. Brown in hot oil; add chopped tomatoes, raisins and sweet pepper. Blend well together. Cut plantain leaves in 20-cm (8-in) squares, clean them with a damp cloth and steam them over hot water to make them pliable. Crush corn and dampen with a little salted water, butter the leaf squares and spread with the corn mixture. Place 2 tablespoons of the meat mixture on each square leaving a 2.5-cm (1-in) border. Fold over and tie securely into a parcel, using thread. Steam for about 1 hour.

Paimie

2 cups corn meal	¼ cup raisins
¼ cup shortening	salt and black pepper to taste
2 cups grated coconut	225 g (½ lb) fresh or salt meat
1 cup grated pumpkin	1 cup water
½ cup flour	plantain leaves

Mix together all ingredients and blend well. Prepare banana leaves and cut into 15–20-cm (6–8-in) squares. Put 2 tablespoons of mixture in the centre of each square. Fold over leaves and tie securely. Steam for about ¾ hour.

1 cup of sugar may be substituted for the pepper and meat to make Sweet Paimies.

Guyana

Pepper pot

This dish is an Amerindian speciality and has become one of the national dishes of Guyana. Its chief seasoning ingredient is cassareep, the thick syrupy residue from boiled cassava juice. The juice is extracted by grating the raw cassava, adding water and straining. Cassareep is seasoned with salt, pepper and sugar and is a preservative for meat.

Pepper pot lasts for some time provided it is boiled up every day. Freshly cooked pieces of meat may be added and simmered in it. No onions, vegetables or starchy foods must be used in it.

1.8 kg (4 lb) cow heel, stew beef,	½ cup cassareep
pork or pig trotters	1 or 2 hot peppers
225 g (½ lb) salt beef or pig's tail	1 stick cinnamon
2 tablespoons brown sugar	few cloves
1 lime	1 tablespoon vinegar
salt to taste	

Cut meat into pieces; wash well with lime juice and salt and put to boil well covered with water. Add cassareep and allow to simmer. When half-done, add other ingredients. Put in peppers with stems and remove before they burst or they may be put in a muslin bag strung over the side of the saucepan. Keep on boiling until meat is tender and liquid just covers it. Serve hot with boiled rice.

Metagee

450 g (1 lb) green plantains
1 small coconut
100 g (¼ lb) yam ⎱ or
100 g (¼ lb) cassava ⎰ dumplings
4 ochroes
100 g (¼ lb) pumpkin
sprig of thyme
1 tablespoon margarine

100 g (¼ lb) mixed meat (salt meat and pig's tail)
200 g (½ lb) salt fish or fresh fish
1 large onion
few garden tomatoes
piece of hot pepper
salt to taste

Clean and cut up mixed meat. Fry lightly in margarine, and then simmer in water to cover for about 15 minutes. Clean and soak salt fish for 15 minutes. Peel and wash vegetables. Grate coconut, add 1 cup of hot water and strain off milk after squeezing well. Remove pot from heat. Arrange vegetables, salt fish and seasonings in layers putting the plantains and cassavas at bottom and the salt fish on top. Add coconut milk and simmer for 30 minutes. Place pumpkin and ochroes on top of salt fish and allow to steam for 10 minutes. Serve hot.

Note: Dumplings, if used, are added last.

Garlic pork

1.8 kg (4 lb) pork
salt to taste, thyme
100 g (¼ lb) garlic

2 cups vinegar
fat for frying
1 lime

Chop the garlic and thyme and mix. Add salt to taste. Wash pork well in lime and salt and cut into small pieces. Parboil pork in water to cover for about 20 minutes. Remove pork from water, dress with seasonings and place in an earthenware bowl or jar. Pour on vinegar to cover pork, and allow to stand for 1–2 days. Remove from jar and fry in deep fat. Serve hot.

Shrimp Curry (see p53)

Foo Foo (see p73)

Cook-up rice

1 cup cooked meat
½ cup prepared shrimp *or*
2 cups rice
few garden tomatoes
2 tablespoons butter *or* fat
½ cup dried peas (soaked beforehand) *or* 1 cup green peas
4 cups water and coconut milk
1 chopped onion

100 g (¼ lb) salt meat (soaked
  beforehand)
2 blades chives
1 dessertspoon salt
piece of green pepper
1 small hot pepper
1 teaspoon lime juice
sprig of thyme and marjoram

Cut up seasonings and meat. Brown in the butter or fat. Add water
and milk, salt and peas; cook for 20 minutes. Add rice, lime juice,
tomatoes and hot pepper. Cover and cook until both rice and peas
are soft but grainy. Garnish with green pepper and serve hot.

Cassava pone

3 cups dry cassava flour
100 g (¼ lb) shortening
1½ cups sugar
3 cups milk and water
½ teaspoon powdered orange peel
  or rind of ½ orange

1 teaspoon salt
2 cups grated coconut
1 or 2 eggs
1 teaspoon vanilla essence
1½ teaspoons mixed spice

Mix dry ingredients together. Add melted shortening, milk, beaten
eggs and essence. Blend well. Pour mixture into greased shallow tin
and bake in a moderate oven for about 1½ hours. Glaze with sugar
and water before baking.

Note: When freshly grated cassava is used, decrease the amount of
liquid.

Conquintay porridge

¼ cup conquintay (plantain) flour
1½ cups water and milk
1 teaspoon butter

¼ teaspoon salt
1 tablespoon sugar
¼ teaspoon nutmeg

Heat liquid over low heat, gradually add the flour, salt and sugar and
stir until it dissolves. Continue stirring until mixture becomes thick.
Remove heat; stir in butter and nutmeg. Makes 2 servings.

Fly

1.1 kg (2½ lb) sweet potatoes (white variety)
1½ cups lime juice
2 teaspoons ground mace
6 litres (1¼ gallons) boiled water

2.7 kg (6 lb) granulated sugar
2 teaspoons whole cloves
3–4 pieces stick cinnamon
2 egg whites and 2 egg shells

Grate the sweet potatoes and squeeze out the starch, using the residue. Beat the egg whites with the shells of two eggs. Put these, the spices and the other ingredients in a jar. Stir well and cover loosely, i.e. with a piece of muslin. On the third day, strain off the liquid and pour it into strong bottles. Tie down the corks with wire and allow a few days for ripening. Chill this drink before serving. Makes 25–30 servings.

21 Exotic dishes from our Oriental Heritage

Chinese

After the abolition of slavery in the early nineteenth century, the Africans were refusing to work on the plantations in the larger islands. Chinese emigrants were then encouraged to do this work, but they were unable to withstand the hardships in the fields. They, however, remained and opened laundries, restaurants and provision shops. There are large communities of Chinese up to the present day in Jamaica, Trinidad and Guyana. Chinese food and cooking methods are very popular throughout the area. Fried rice, Chow Mien, Wan Tun Soup and a great variety of dishes flavoured with Soy Sauce are served daily. Chinese food requires long preparation, but the actual cooking is quicker. The vegetables are hardly cooked but blended in such a way as to ensure the maximum flavour and preservation of food nutrients.

Fried crispy noodles

225 g (½ lb) shredded cabbage
2 onions (sliced)
1 cup bean sprouts
225 g (½ lb) pork (cooked)
450 g (1 lb) noodles
lard or oil for frying
1 tablespoon soy sauce
salt to taste

Shred the vegetables and cut up the meat. Put the noodles into boiling salted water and boil for 5 minutes, then drain, and hold them under cold running water. Drain well. Fry in deep fat or oil for 5 minutes, until golden brown and crisp. Meanwhile fry the vegetables and meat together in 1 tablespoon oil for 5–10 minutes, adding the soy sauce halfway through. Serve this mixture on top of the crispy noodles.

Wan Tuns

Noodle Dough
2 cups flour
¼ cup water
2 eggs
1 tablespoon cooking oil

Sift flour and make a well in the centre. Break the eggs in it and put in the water and oil. Mix, stirring in the flour from the centre until a smooth dough is made. Knead dough until smooth. Let it stand a little. Roll out very thinly. Cut in 7.5-cm (3-in) squares. Put ½ teaspoon filling in a corner of each square, and fold over twice. Fold over the opposite side and turn under. Stick together with beaten egg white.

Filling

1 cup cooked pork or shrimps	½ teaspoon Ve-Tsin powder*
½ teaspoon salt	2 or 3 water chestnuts
½ teaspoon sugar	1 tablespoon chopped chives
½ teaspoon white pepper	½ teaspoon soy sauce

Chop ingredients together finely and mix.

Wan tun soup

4 cups stock from chicken carcass	1 cup thinly shredded cabbage
¼ cup sliced mushrooms and water chestnuts	few blades chives
	wan tuns as required

To boiling stock, put in wan tuns and cook for 8–10 minutes. Then add vegetables and cook for 3 minutes more. Garnish soup with chopped chives.

Crisp wan tuns

Wan tun may be fried in deep fat, drained and used as appetizer or party snacks.

POW (Pork dumplings)

Filling

1 cup finely diced roast pork	1 teaspoon Ve-Tsin powder
1 teaspoon soy sauce	1 tablespoon cornflour
½ teaspoon salt	½ cup water
1 teaspoon sugar	2 tablespoons cooking oil

Fry the pork in the oil, adding soy sauce and seasonings. Blend cornflour with water and cook about 2 minutes. Allow mixture to stand.

Dough

2 cups flour	½ teaspoon salt
1 tablespoon sugar	¼ cup water (hot)
1 teaspoon baking powder	2 tablespoons peanut *or* corn oil

* *Ve-Tsin* or m.s.g. (monosodium glutamate) is a Chinese gourmet powder made in Hong Kong. It enhances the flavour of foods. The powder is also obtainable as Accent (American), Aji No Moto (Japanese) and Stress (English).
Only a small quantity is needed for flavouring. It resembles bicarbonate of soda and is a vegetable product.

Sift flour with baking powder and salt in bowl. Make a well in the centre. Dissolve sugar in hot water. When cold, mix in the oil, and pour the mixture into the well. Mix to a soft dough. Knead a little and make into balls. Flatten into 7.5-cm (3-in) rounds. Put a teaspoon of the filling in each round. Draw the edges of dough together, closing in the filling by twisting and pinching the dough to form dumplings. Steam for 20 minutes.

Fried rice

4 cups cooked rice
100 g (4 oz) roast lean pork (cut in small pieces)
50 g (2 oz) cooked ham (shredded)
1 tablespoon soy sauce
1 egg

½ teaspoon salt
50 g (2 oz) fresh shrimps (cut up finely)
½ teaspoon Ve-Tsin powder
¼ teaspoon white pepper

Heat greased pan well, put in cooked ham, lean pork and fresh shrimps and sauté for 3 minutes. Add cooked rice, mix together and fry for 3 minutes again. Add soy sauce, Ve-Tsin powder, salt and pepper. Break egg and stir well into hot mixture. Fry for 2 minutes more and serve.

Chow Mien

225 g (½ lb) package egg noodles
½ cup diced chicken *or* cooked pork
½ cup diced celery
½ cup sliced onions
1 scrambled egg, shredded
1 cup chicken broth or water

½ cup bean sprouts
½ cup cabbage
50 g (2 oz) mushrooms
1 tablespoon corn starch
2 tablespoons soy sauce
fat for frying

Fry chicken or pork in fat; add celery, onion and chicken broth. Cover and cook till vegetables are tender. Add bean sprouts, cabbage and mushrooms, and bring to boil. Add noodles boiled for 5 minutes, drained and fried. Mix corn starch with soy sauce and add to hot mixture, stirring. Simmer for 2–3 minutes. Arrange in deep bowl and garnish with scrambled egg.

Pancake rolls

Pancake batter
1 cup flour
¼ teaspoon salt
1 egg
1 cup water

Sift flour and salt. Make a well in centre. Put in egg, add water gradually and stir well to make a creamy batter. Allow it to stand for an hour or so.

Filling

½ cup meat mixture (chicken, ham, pork, etc.)
2 tablespoons shrimps
½ cup bean sprouts, mushrooms and bamboo shoots
1 tablespoon cooking oil
2 medium onions, chopped
1 teaspoon soy sauce
¼ teaspoon grated ginger
salt and sugar to taste
½ teaspoon Ve-Tsin powder
1 tablespoon sherry
parsley

Cut meat into thin pieces. Cut mushroom and bamboo shoots in thin slices. Sauté onion in oil. Add meat, vegetables and shrimps; cook for 2 minutes, stirring. Season to taste, add soy sauce and sherry. Stir well off heat and cool.

To fry *Pancakes*, lightly grease pan and heat. Pour in 2 tablespoons batter and allow it to spread over the pan. Cook pancakes on one side only, and stand on rack on cooked side. To fill, put some filling on one-half of the cooked side, fold the other side over, sealing and pressing the ends together with some of the batter to make a roll. Deep fat fry the pancakes till pale brown. Drain on kitchen paper. Garnish with parsley.

Stewed spare ribs

900 g (2 lb) meaty spare ribs
1 tablespoon shortening
2 tablespoons brown sugar
2 tablespoons corn starch
½ teaspoon salt
⅓ cup vinegar
1 cup diced pineapple
¼ cup pineapple juice
¼ cup cold water *or* stock
1 tablespoon soy sauce
1 tablespoon meat sauce
½ cup cut green pepper
½ cup finely cut onion

Cut meat into small pieces. Cook in salted water for 1 hour approximately. Drain and brown in hot fat. Mix brown sugar, corn starch, salt together and add vinegar, water and pineapple juice, and condiment sauces. Add to meat and cook until mixture thickens, slightly stirring. Add remaining ingredients and cook until vegetables are tender and crisp.

Sweet and sour pork

325 g (12 oz) lean pork (in 2.5-cm or 1-in cubes)
salt and pepper to taste
½ cup flour
½ teaspoon Ve-Tsin powder

½ teaspoon ground ginger
1 tablespoon cooking sherry
groundnut oil for frying
salt to taste

Sauce and Garnish

1 tablespoon cornflour
2 tablespoons brown sugar
2 tablespoons vinegar
½ cup water
2 teaspoons soy sauce

½ cup pickled cucumber
¼ cup carrots
½ cup shredded pineapple
2 tablespoons oil

Make batter as for Pancake Rolls (p183)

Rub seasonings and sherry in pork and fry in shallow fat until brown. Drain and dredge with flour. Shake off and coat pork pieces with batter. Fry in deep fat until brown.

To make the sauce, shred the pickles, carrots and pineapple slices and cook in 2 tablespoons oil for 5 minutes. Add soy sauce, water, sugar and vinegar. Simmer for 15 minutes. Blend cornflour with 2 tablespoons water and stir in. Salt to taste and simmer for 5 minutes longer. Pour the sauce over the pork. Garnish top with the vegetables.

Chicken with pineapple

225 g (½ lb) chicken meat (sliced)
2 cups canned pineapple pieces
¼ cup bamboo shoots
½ cup water chestnuts
½ teaspoon Ve-Tsin
2 tablespoons peanut oil
1 tablespoon cornflour

½ cup celery (diced)
1 teaspoon salt
1 teaspoon sugar
1 teaspoon soy sauce
1 cup water
½ teaspoon paprika

Boil chicken meat in water for 3 minutes; sauté water chestnuts, bamboo shoots and celery in hot oil for 3 minutes. Mix well and add chicken meat, stock, salt, pepper, sugar, soy sauce and Ve-Tsin. Cover and cook for 5 minutes. Add pineapple and then slowly mix in cornflour made into paste with a little water. Cook for 3 minutes and serve hot.

Indian

East Indians were engaged as indentured labourers in the larger Caribbean territories soon after the Chinese arrived. They proved to be very keen and skilled agricultural workers, and up to the present time a great majority work on the farms and are very successful gardeners. Indian dishes include flour, rice, pulses and vegetables, and some meats. Meat curries, roti and dahl puri are specialities and are favoured by all nationalities.

Dahl puri

1 cup dry split peas *or* dahl peas
4 cups flour
1 teaspoon baking powder
salt and pepper to taste
1 teaspoon jira

1 clove garlic
2 tablespoons onion
1 tablespoon curry powder
water
2 tablespoons oil

Wash and soak peas overnight. Cover with water and boil with curry powder until soft. Crisp jira in the oven and grind. Add to minced onion, garlic, pepper and peas. Sift flour, salt and baking powder. Add oil and water to make a stiff dough. Form into balls, roll out 6 mm ($\frac{1}{4}$ in) thick and put about 2 tablespoons dahl mixture in each. Fold in edges to encase mixture and roll out again. Bake on tawa greased with ghee or oil. Turn occasionally. Bake till brown and risen.

Roti

2 cups flour
$\frac{1}{4}$ teaspoon bicarbonate of soda
$\frac{1}{4}$ teaspoon salt

milk to mix
ghee *or* oil to brush

Sift flour, soda and salt together. Add milk to mix stiff dough. Knead well. Form in 4 or 5 balls. Flour board and roll out balls very thinly and apply ghee or oil to surface, then roll up into ball. Allow tawa or hot-plate to heat in the meantime (3 minutes). Roll out dough again and place on baking hot-plate. Rub with oil again and turn frequently. Remove and clap with both hands until very pliable. Wrap in towel and keep warm. Serve with shrimp or meat curry.

Mutton Curry (p64)

Dahl with boiled rice

1 cup dry split peas *or* dahl peas
2 tablespoons onion
1 clove garlic
1 tablespoon curry powder

1 tablespoon ghee *or* cooking oil
1½ cups water
¼ teaspoon salt

Wash and soak peas overnight or for several hours. Boil with curry powder until soft. Add salt and chopped onion. Beat until smooth with wooden spoon and remove from heat. Burn the crushed garlic in the oil to extract the flavour. Then add oil to the dahl mixture and blend well. Serve hot with boiled rice.

Alu curry (Potato)

900 g (2 lb) English potatoes
2 teaspoons salt
2 tablespoons curry powder
 or massala

¼ cup coconut oil
2 cloves garlic
1 cup water
few slices green mango

Burn crushed garlic in hot oil, remove garlic and fry curry powder for 5 minutes. Add sliced potatoes, mangoes, water and salt. Cover and simmer till vegetable and mango are soft.

Fried channa

450 g (1 lb) channa peas
½ cup oil
salt and pepper to taste

Cover channa with water and allow to soak overnight. Pepper may be added. Remove skin and wipe peas dry. Put oil, pepper and salt in heavy pan. When hot, add channa and fry brown. Drain on absorbent paper. Keep in an airtight tin.

Phulouri

600 ml (1 pint) split peas
1 onion
oil for frying

2 cloves garlic
salt and pepper to taste

Soak peas overnight; drain off liquid and grind peas very finely with seasoning. Add salt, beat well and make into small balls. Fry in deep fat.

Metai

450 g (1 lb) flour
½ teaspoon baking soda
½ teaspoon salt

2 cups sugar
1 cup water
oil for frying

Sift flour and soda. Add enough water to mix a stiff dough. Knead dough well and let it stand for a few minutes. Roll out dough and cut into thin strips. Fry in deep fat.

Syrup
Put sugar and water in saucepan and boil until syrup forms a soft ball in saucer of water. Put in metai and stir until all strips are coated.

Jilebi

4 cups flour
15 g (½ oz) dry yeast
1 cup warm water
½ teaspoon salt
oil for frying

2 teaspoons sugar
¼ teaspoon powdered cinnamon
2 cups sugar
1 cup water

Dissolve yeast with sugar in a little warm water. Add salt, spice, flour and rest of warm water to make a thick batter. Allow it to rise two hours. Prepare a pan of hot oil. Beat batter lightly and add enough water to make it of pouring consistency. Pour batter through a funnel into hot oil, forming rings by circling the pot 3 or 4 times. Fry until golden brown. Drain on absorbent paper and soak in hot syrup for 5 minutes. When cool, jilebi will have a sugary coating.

Bhagi

225 g (½ lb) spinach leaves
2 tablespoons cooking oil
1 medium onion

salt to taste
piece of red pepper
1 clove garlic

Chop onion, garlic and pepper. Brown in hot oil. Add spinach leaves, torn coarsely and with the thick part of the stem discarded. Cover and allow to steam over low heat. Do not add water. When soft, serve hot with boiled rice.

Bara (Salt cake)

1 cup split peas
½ cup flour
3 tablespoons curry powder *or*
    massala

oil for frying
½ teaspoon baking soda
1 teaspoon salt
water

Soak peas overnight. Drain and grind very finely. Add other ingredients and mix to a stiff dough with water. Shape into balls. Roll out into round shapes, about 12–15 cm (5–6 in) in diameter and 6 mm (¼ in) thick. Fry in hot oil till brown. Drain on absorbent paper.

Curried chicken

1 chicken (1.35 kg or 3 lb)
2 tablespoons curry powder *or* massala
salt and pepper to taste
1 medium onion
1 clove garlic

2 tablespoons flour
ghee or oil for frying
2 cups water
few blades chives
few garden tomatoes

Clean and cut chicken in joints and marinate. Crush garlic, burn in oil. Remove garlic and brown massala and chicken pieces previously rolled in flour. Add rest of seasonings and water. Cover and simmer until tender. Stir occasionally.

22 From Britain to the Caribbean

Since the sixteenth century, Great Britain has had a powerful influence in the Caribbean. The British fought with other European colonists, and finally gained several island territories as well as British Honduras and Guyana on the mainland. They settled in the area and continued their methods of cookery, and eating habits have been handed down and adopted by the Caribbean community of mixed peoples.

Potatoes are widely used in stews, and boiled and baked. Bacon and eggs are served at breakfast. Roast beef with Yorkshire Pudding often appears on menus. English scones, pancakes, tea cakes, sponge cakes and biscuits are as popular as the local sweet breads and cakes. Rice pudding and bread and butter pudding are served especially for children's desserts. Tea is a well favoured hot beverage in the Caribbean. Plum pudding, rich fruit cake and mince pies are Yuletide specialities.

Here are other dishes sometimes used.

Steak and kidney pie

675 g (1½ lb) steak
225 g (½ lb) kidneys
few garden tomatoes
seasoned flour
rich shortcrust pastry (p132)

1 medium onion
bunch of herbs
1 tablespoon tomato ketchup
fat for browning

Cut meat into pieces and dip in seasoned flour. Allow to stand a little. Brown in hot fat. Add about 2 cups water, chopped onion, seasoning, etc., and simmer until almost tender. Pour into greased pie dish and cover with pastry. Leave a hole in the centre of the pie crust and a little gravy to pour into the centre of the pie before serving. Decorate pie with pastry leaves, brush with egg and bake in a hot oven (220°C, 425°F or Gas 7).

Irish stew

450 g (1 lb) mutton	225 g (½ lb) onions
8–10 potatoes (900 g or 2 lb)	225 g (½ lb) carrots
4 tablespoons oil	1 bay leaf
sprig of thyme	parsley
salt and pepper to taste	3–4 cups water

Dice the meat and slice the onions, potatoes and carrots. Brown the onions and meat in the heated fat, then put in the potatoes and carrots. Add water and flavour with bay leaf, thyme, pepper and salt. Simmer for 1–1½ hours until all the ingredients are tender. Serve sprinkled with parsley.

Shepherd's Pie (p211)

Yorkshire pudding

Use Coating Batter (p148) with egg. Melt some fat in a shallow pan or use dripping from roast beef. When it is smoking hot, pour in the batter and bake in a hot oven until batter is well-risen and crisp. Cut into squares and serve with thin slices of roast beef.

Stewed smoked herrings

4 herrings	1 tablespoon butter
1 onion	1 tablespoon flour
few small tomatoes	1 cup water
parsley	1 tablespoon vinegar
piece of red pepper	2 sliced hard boiled eggs
sprig of thyme	

Soak herrings in hot water to extract salt. When cool, remove some of the bones and flake. Brown sliced onions in the butter, blend in flour, stir, then add water, sliced tomatoes, pepper and vinegar. Add flaked herrings, stir gently and cook for 10 minutes. Remove from heat. Garnish with hard boiled eggs, parsley and slices of lime. Serve with boiled eddoes or green bananas.

Welsh rarebit

1 cup grated cheese	3 tablespoons milk
2 tablespoons butter	salt and pepper
mustard if desired	slices of toast
½ cup beer	

Place cheese, milk and beer in saucepan and melt slowly. Add pepper, salt and butter. When piping hot, pour it over the toast and brown under the grill.

Cornish pasties

225 g (½ lb) beef
225 g (½ lb) potatoes
1 teaspoon finely-chopped onion
mixed herbs to taste

salt and pepper
4 tablespoons gravy *or* water
225 g (½ lb) short crust pastry

Mince the meat finely. Dice the potatoes. Add the onion, herbs, salt, pepper and gravy to the meat and potatoes, and mix well together. Divide the pastry into 8 equal portions and roll them out 6 mm (¼ in) thick, keeping the portions as round as possible. Pile the mixture in the centre of each piece of pastry, wet the edges and join them together on the top to form a frill. Prick them with a fork and bake in a hot oven for 10 minutes, then in a moderate oven until brown.

Steamed jam pudding

2 tablespoons jam
½ cup margarine
½ cup sugar
1½ cups flour

1½ teaspoons baking powder
2 eggs
½ teaspoon vanilla essence
¼ teaspoon salt

Cream fat and sugar until soft and white. Whisk eggs to a thick froth and gradually beat them into the creamed mixture. Add vanilla. Lightly stir in flour and salt. Put jam into greased pudding bowl, add mixture, cover tightly with foil and place bowl into saucepan of boiling water. Cover and steam for 1½ hours.

Hot Cross Buns (p146)

23 Adoptions from European cuisine

The Europeans (mainly French and Spanish and to a lesser extent the Portuguese and Dutch) also settled in the territories they captured during the seventeenth and eighteenth centuries; and have passed on some of their delicious rich pastries, meat dishes, salad dressings and spicy methods of seasoning.

The following dishes are great favourites.

Ragôut of beef

1 cup sliced onion	1½ cups diced potatoes
3 tablespoons butter or margarine	1½ cups sliced carrots
2 cups left over gravy and water	1 cup raisins
1½ cups diced cooked beef	salt and pepper to taste
1 tablespoon lime juice or vinegar	1 tablespoon flour

Sauté onion in butter until just tender. Add remaining ingredients except flour. Bring to boil, cover and simmer for 20 minutes. Blend ¼ cup water with the flour. Stir into beef mixture. Bring to boiling-point, stirring constantly. Simmer uncovered for 5 minutes.

Chicken fricassée

chicken (1.35 kg or 3 lb)	sprig of thyme and sweet
2 tablespoons tomato ketchup	marjoram
2 medium onions	salt and pepper to taste
1 chopped sweet pepper	2 tablespoons vinegar *or*
1 clove garlic	cooking sherry
1 tablespoon soy sauce	fat for frying

Cut chicken into pieces and marinate in salt and vinegar. Drain and brown in hot fat. Sauté onions, sweet pepper, garlic; pour in 2 cups hot water, and add other ingredients. Simmer slowly until chicken is cooked. Serve with boiled rice.

Pilau

4 cups rice	2 tablespoons butter
1 1.35–1.8 kg (3–4 lb) chicken *or*	1 tablespoon sugar
900 g (2 lb) braising steak and pork	2 tablespoons vinegar

1 tablespoon soy sauce
salt and pepper to taste
8 cups water
1 tablespoon curry powder
2 onions
1 bunch herbs

1 clove garlic
few garden tomatoes
2 tablespoons raisins
piece of red pepper
fat for frying

Crush garlic and brown it in fat with sugar. When garlic is almost burnt, remove it. Put in marinated chicken or meat pieces and brown. Add half the water and all seasonings. Cover and simmer until meat is tender. Add the rest of water, bring to the boil, sprinkle in washed rice, stir well, salt to taste and finish cooking when rice grains are soft. Finally stir in butter, and serve hot.

Duchesse potatoes

4 cups hot mashed potatoes
1 tablespoon butter
2 beaten egg yolks
2 tablespoons butter, melted

To potatoes, add 1 tablespoon butter, egg yolks, and salt and white pepper to taste; mix well. Using pastry bag with star tube, pipe hot potato mixture around dishes to garnish.

Sprinkle potatoes with melted butter. Grill until lightly browned.

Mardi Gras salad

French dressing (½ cup)
6 tablespoons mayonnaise
900 g (2 lb) cooked potatoes (diced)
4 hard boiled eggs (chopped)
½ cup cooked carrots (diced)
½ cup string beans
1 red pepper

½ green pepper
225 g (½ lb) cheese (grated)
1 chopped onion
3 tablespoons chopped parsley
2 teaspoons salt
lettuce
radishes

Blend dressing and mayonnaise. Add potatoes and eggs, and allow to stand for 10 to 15 minutes. Add green pepper, cheese, onion, parsley and salt. Mix well. Put in salad bowl to chill. Toss well. Garnish with strips of red pepper and lettuce. Fill centre with radish roses or string beans and diced carrots.

French loaves

2 packages dry yeast
½ cup water
1 tablespoon salt
2 cups lukewarm water

7–7½ cups sifted flour
1 egg white
1 tablespoon water

Soften yeast in ½ cup lukewarm water. Combine salt and 2 cups lukewarm water; beat in 2 cups of the flour. Blend in yeast mixture, stir in 4–4½ cups of flour, or enough to make a soft dough. Turn out on lightly floured surface. Cover and allow to rest for 10 minutes. Knead till smooth and elastic for 5–8 minutes, working in remaining 1 cup flour.

Put aside to rise as usual. When well risen, divide in 2 portions. Roll each portion to a rectangle. Roll up tightly, beginning at long side, sealing well. Taper ends.

Place each loaf, seam side down, on greased baking sheet. With sharp knife, gash tops diagonally every few inches. Brush with egg white and water, cover and let rise again till double in size. Bake in a moderate oven (190°C, 375°F or Gas 5) until light brown. Brush with egg white mixture again. Finish baking until brown.

Garlic butter

Blend ½ cup soft butter or margarine with 2 cloves minced garlic. Spread on crispy or French bread.

French toast

8 slices stale bread	¼ cup sugar
4 eggs	1 cup milk
½ teaspoon salt	butter for frying

Beat eggs slightly; add salt, milk and sugar. Cut crust from bread and soak in mixture until soft. Fry in butter until brown on both sides. Use for breakfast, served with marmalade or jam.

Vichyssoise

4 leeks (white section) thinly sliced	4 cups chicken stock
1 medium onion, sliced	1 cup whipped cream
¼ cup butter or margarine	2 cups evaporated milk
4 cups sliced English potatoes	pepper and salt to taste

Cook leeks and onion in butter until soft; add potatoes, stock and salt. Cook 35 minutes.

Rub through a sieve and return to heat; add evaporated milk and season to taste. Bring just under boiling-point. Cool; strain. When cold, add whipped cream. Chill before serving. Garnish with finely chopped chives.

Spanish omelette

4 eggs
1 onion
1 tomato (large)
oil for frying
1 tablespoon salad oil

1 tablespoon raisins (cut up finely)
1 teaspoon olives (cut up finely)
¼ teaspoon nutmeg
1 tablespoon tomato sauce

Cook the onion, finely chopped, in the salad oil; add the chopped tomato, raisins, olives, nutmeg and tomato sauce. Remove from heat. Beat egg lightly with 1 teaspoon water and ¼ teaspoon salt. Make an omelette in another pan frying it in some hot oil. When almost set, lay on the mixture and fold the omelette in 3. Serve hot.

Spanish rice

6 slices bacon
1 cup finely chopped onion
¼ cup chopped green pepper
450 g (1 lb) sliced tomatoes
4 cups water

2 cups rice
½ cup chili sauce
salt and pepper to taste
1 teaspoon brown sugar
1 tablespoon vinegar

Fry bacon until crisp; remove from heat. Sauté onion and green pepper in bacon fat. Add rest of ingredients. Simmer until rice grains are soft. Garnish with pieces of bacon and parsley.

Tamale pie

Dough

2 cups corn meal
½ cup flour
1 teaspoon salt

1 teaspoon baking powder
¼ cup shortening
water to mix

Filling

1½ cups minced cooked beef
2 tablespoons minced onion
piece of red pepper (chopped)

½ teaspoon salt
1 teaspoon chopped herbs
2 tablespoons oil for frying

Brown meat in oil; add seasonings and cook for 3 minutes. Stand aside.

Mix together corn meal, etc., and make a dough. Form into balls, egg-size. Roll out 6 mm (¼ in) thick, cut in 7.5-cm (3-in) rounds. Put 2 tablespoons of mixture on one round, cover with another dampening edges. Press together and fry in hot oil. Drain on paper and serve hot.

Spanish rarebit

225 g (½ lb) stewing beef
225 g (½ lb) English potatoes
½ cup green peas
1 cup macaroni, in pieces
2 tablespoons butter
pepper and salt to taste

1 onion, sliced
2 large tomatoes
1 turnip
2½ cups water
escallion and thyme

Wash and dice potatoes. Wash peas. Wash beef and cut into small pieces. Melt butter in saucepan. Sauté onion and beef. Add water, peas, seasonings and tomatoes, and cook covered until beef is nearly tender (30 to 35 minutes). Add vegetables and macaroni, and cook until macaroni is tender.

Pastelitos

225 g (½ lb) cooked pork (cut in pieces)
1 small onion
salt and pepper to taste
2 tablespoons flour
1 tablespoon butter

7.5 cm (3 in) rounds of pastry
1 clove garlic
few small tomatoes
1 tablespoon olives (chopped)
1 tablespoon raisins
fat for frying

Mince together pork, onion, garlic, olives and raisins. Add crushed tomatoes and season. Cook in melted butter, sprinkling in flour and stirring for 2 minutes. Cool mixture and put 1 teaspoon on one side of each round. Fold over and press edges together, dampening them. Fry in deep fat.

Spanish cream

2 cups milk
2 tablespoons sugar
2 eggs
nuts, cherries *or* fruit pieces

2 tablespoons gelatine
½ teaspoon salt
1 teaspoon vanilla

Soften gelatine in 2 tablespoons of cold water. Add sugar and salt. Place in the top of a double boiler over gently boiling water. Separate the eggs, beat the yolks and add to the milk. Stir in the gelatine mixture until the custard coats the spoon. Remove from heat and cool. Add the vanilla. Whip the egg whites stiffly and fold into the custard. Pour into individual glasses and chill. Decorate with nuts or cherries or fruit pieces.

Portuguese eggs

3 very large tomatoes
6 small eggs
chopped parsley

salt and pepper to taste
butter

Cut the tomatoes in half and scoop out the pulp. Sprinkle a little salt, pepper and chopped parsley in the halves. Place on a buttered baking dish. Break an egg in each, dot with butter and bake in a hot oven till eggs are set.

Serve on fried bread or buttered toast.

Garlic pork (p178)

This dish is of Portuguese origin.

Paella

1 chicken (about 1.1 kg or 2½ lb)
1 medium-sized onion
2 cloves garlic (chopped)
2 tablespoons salad or
  vegetable oil
150 g (6 oz) shrimps or other
  shell fish
1 cup peas or beans (cooked)

a little yellow food colouring
225 g (½ lb) rice
water or stock
piece of green pepper
2 large tomatoes
2 tablespoons vinegar
salt and pepper to taste
1 tablespoon wine

Cut chicken in pieces. Marinate in vinegar and one teaspoon salt. Drain well. Brown lightly in hot oil in a heavy pan over medium heat. Add sliced onion and garlic and stir well. Add rice and when it has absorbed the oil add a little water or stock, stir and allow rice to cook and absorb the liquid until rice is about half-cooked. Then add shell fish, strips of green pepper, sliced tomatoes, wine, peas or beans, salt and pepper to taste and a little food colouring to make the mixture a pale yellow colour. Stir well, cover and steam over low heat until rice grains are soft but not sticky.

24 Recipes from North America

Since the beginning of the century, the Caribbean has been closely associated with Canada and the United States of America, mainly through trade with the former and through emigration to the latter. Tourism has also brought the people in these countries into closer union. It was natural for Caribbean visitors to introduce some of the food habits of the Americans in their home towns as they travelled back and forth over the years.

Serving meals buffet style, barbecues, hamburgers and a variety of rich cakes, salads and desserts are some of our culinary adoptions from the North Americans.

Here are some of the dishes most often used.

Baking powder biscuits

2 cups sifted flour
3 teaspoons baking powder
½ teaspoon salt

¼ cup shortening
⅔–¾ cup milk

Cut shortening into sifted dry ingredients until like coarse crumbs. Make a well; add milk all at once. Stir quickly with fork until dough begins to hold. Turn dough on to a lightly floured surface. Knead gently and form into a ball. Roll out 1.2 cm (½ in) thick. Cut with floured biscuit cutter, brush with milk and bake on baking sheet in hot oven for about 15 minutes.

Pancakes

1¼ cups sifted flour
3 teaspoons baking powder
1 tablespoon sugar
½ teaspoon salt

1 beaten egg
1 cup milk
2 tablespoons melted shortening

Sift together flour, baking powder, sugar and salt. Combine egg, milk and melted shortening; add to dry ingredients, stirring just till flour is moistened. Bake on a greased tawa or heavy pan. Makes about 12 pancakes.

Waffles

2 cups sifted flour
3 teaspoons baking powder
½ teaspoon salt
2 beaten egg yolks

1¼ cups milk
½ cup melted shortening
2 stiffly beaten egg whites

Sift together dry ingredients. Combine egg yolks and milk; stir into dry ingredients. Stir in shortening. Lightly fold in egg whites. Bake in pre-heated electric waffle maker. Makes about 8 waffles.

Club sandwiches

Use 3 slices of buttered toast for each sandwich. Put lettuce and cold sliced chicken or pork on the first. Spread on a little mayonnaise or salad dressing. Top with the second slice and add tomato and bacon slices. Top with the third slice, having added a little more dressing. Press together, cut in quarters diagonally and serve, points upwards.

Pineapple upside-down cake

To top cake

Melt 2 tablespoons butter in greased pan. Add ½ cup brown sugar. Halve 4 canned pineapple slices; place in mixture. Halve red cherries; place 1 piece in centre of each pineapple slice.

Cake

⅓ cup shortening
1¼ cups sifted flour
½ cup sugar
½ teaspoon grated lime peel

2 teaspoons baking powder
½ teaspoon salt
½ cup pineapple syrup
1 egg

Combine dry ingredients and add pineapple syrup, grated lemon or lime peel and 1 slightly beaten egg. Mix to make a thick batter and pour over pineapple. Bake in a moderate oven for 30 to 35 minutes or till done. Let stand for 10 minutes, then invert on plate.

Boiled frosting for cakes

2 cups granulated sugar
¾ cup water
¼ teaspoon cream of tartar

¼ teaspoon salt
2 stiffly beaten egg whites
1 teaspoon vanilla

Cook sugar, water, cream of tartar and salt over low heat, stirring till sugar dissolves. Cover pan 2 to 3 minutes to dissolve sugar crystals on sides of pan. Uncover; cook until mixture forms a soft ball in water. Gradually add hot syrup to egg whites, beating constantly. Add vanilla; beat till frosting is of spreading consistency.

Cookies (p127)

Lemon meringue pie

1½ cups sugar
3 tablespoons corn starch
3 tablespoons flour
¼ teaspoon salt
1½ cups hot water
3 slightly beaten egg yolks
¼ teaspoon grated lemon or lime peel

2 tablespoons butter
⅓ cup lemon *or* lime juice
1 22-cm (9-in) baked pastry shell
3 egg whites
1 teaspoon lime juice
6 tablespoons sugar

In saucepan mix the sugar, corn starch, flour and salt. Gradually blend in water. Bring to boiling-point over medium heat; stirring constantly. Reduce heat to low; cook and stir for 8 minutes more. Remove from heat.

Stir small amount of hot mixture into egg yolks; return to hot mixture. Bring to boil over high heat, stirring constantly. Reduce heat to low; cook and stir for 4 minutes longer. Remove from heat. Add lemon peel and butter. Gradually stir in ⅓ cup lemon juice. Cover entire surface with aluminium foil. Cool for 10 minutes. Now pour into cooled pastry shell. Cool to room temperature. Top with Meringue.

For *Meringue*, beat egg whites with 1 teaspoon lemon juice till soft peaks form. Gradually add 6 tablespoons sugar, beating until stiff peaks form and sugar is dissolved.

Bake in a moderate oven for 12 to 15 minutes, or till meringue is golden. Cool thoroughly before serving.

Iced Tea (p119)

Iced Coffee (p113)

Hamburgers

675 g (1½ lb) minced beef
2 tablespoons chopped onion
1 teaspoon salt
½ teaspoon white pepper

Mix together and shape into thick round cakes 6–7.5 cm (2½–3 in) in diameter. Cook over hot coals on greased grill for about 10 minutes turning over once. Makes 6–8 hamburgers.

Sauce to brush hamburgers
½ cup tomato sauce
1 teaspoon Worcestershire sauce
¼ teaspoon celery salt

Blend together ingredients and heat in pan. Split buttered buns and lightly toast. Put a hamburger cake in each. Brush with sauce. Serve immediately.

Cheeseburgers

450 g (1 lb) minced beef   ½ teaspoon white pepper
1 teaspoon salt   1 tablespoon Worcestershire sauce
cheese slices

Mix together ingredients. Make into 4–6 cakes. Place on greased grill. Cook over hot coals. Just before they are finished, lay a cheese slice over each cake to melt. Serve in grilled buttered buns.

Coleslaw

Shred 3 cups cabbage very finely, using a chef's knife or grater. Cover and chill to make crisp. Add ¼ cup chopped green pepper or minced onion *or* 1 cup grated carrot and ½ cup raisins. Toss in salad dressing before serving.

25 Traces from our African Origin

Since the arrival of West African emigrants to the Caribbean in the sixteenth century, the main ingredients of the original African dishes form a basic part of those of the Caribbean to the present day. These foods are cassava, corn meal, sweet potatoes, yams, plantains and bananas.

It is interesting to note that although these foods are commonly used in the Caribbean, similar dishes vary in names and methods of preparation according to various regions.

Originally West Africans in their native country ate cassava, yam or plantains as 'foo-foo' when the vegetable was cooked, crushed and moulded like a pudding. Cou-cou, a savoury corn meal dish with okras, is a corruption of 'foo-foo'. Fungi, another corn meal mixture may be sweet or savoury like Cou-cou.

Conkies and Paimies are similar sweet dishes containing corn meal and cooked in plantain or banana leaves.

Duckanoo is similar to Conkies and is made with sweet potato or corn meal.

Bambula cake or bammie is cassava bread.

The popular ackee of Jamaica and the mango, well known in the area, were originally imported from West Africa.

Jerk pork, for years a speciality of Portland, Jamaica, was long ago introduced by the Cormantee slaves from West Africa. In their homeland, these workers had been hunters. During their long journeys over the mountains, they cooked jerk pork which consisted of a whole pig with intestines and organs removed, cleaned, stuffed with blood and other seasonings, etc., and roasted over hot coals. This meat lasted for several weeks, and was therefore very useful as food during journeys.

26 Popular Christmas food and drink

Some of the food and drink used at Christmas time are the same as those traditionally used in Great Britain and North America, e.g. roast turkey, baked ham, roast chicken; duck and pork are also very popular. Plum pudding, mince pies and rich fruit cake have also been adopted among Caribbean peoples. Local cassava and corn puddings are also on the menu. Roasted suckling pig, garlic pork and pudding and souse are specialities in some areas and jug-jug and rice and peas or red beans all help to enrich the festive board. Local vegetables and salads are prepared as desired in the various islands.

A great number of beverages are consumed from house to house, and many are locally made, often by housewives.

Roast turkey or chicken (p68)

Note: Garnish with sautéd carrots, baked English potatoes and bunches of parsley. Serve with guava jelly, if liked.

Baked ham (p62)

Note: Serve with grilled pineapple slices.

Roast suckling pig

1 suckling pig, 4–6 weeks old	vinegar
(cleaned and prepared for cooking)	1 cup chopped mixed seasonings *or*
salt to taste	1 cup seasoning mixture (p16)

Rub the pig inside and outside with a mixture of salt and vinegar. Rub inside well with the mixed seasonings or seasoning mixture. Fill the cavity with stuffing, and skewer or sew together. Draw the legs together and skewer or tie them. Arrange the hands under the head, tie tightly together. Keep mouth open with a skewer. Brush the entire skin surface with oil. Cover with aluminium foil and bake in a moderate oven for about 40 minutes per 450 g (1 lb) of meat. Baste 2 or 3 times during baking period. About half an hour before it is finished, baste and sprinkle it lightly with sugar, raise the oven heat and allow the skin to become crisp. Set on a platter. Remove the skewer and place a baked potato or apple in the mouth. Garnish with parsley, slices of sweet pepper, grilled pineapple chunks, tomatoes, or as desired. Serve with a baked sweet potato dish.

Stuffing

6 cups breadcrumbs *or* ½ breadcrumbs and ½ mashed potato
2 large onions
2–3 cloves garlic
1 teaspoon hot pepper
1 tablespoon sour pickles *or* capers
salt to taste

2 teaspoons chopped herbs
¼ cup butter *or* fat
1 large tomato
½ cup raisins
1 tablespoon sugar
1 cup water

Mix coarse breadcrumbs with water to dampen. Chop the ingredients and mix together with salt, sugar and fat to taste. Stuff the pig loosely to allow for expansion of the stuffing.

Garlic Pork (p178)

Baked Pork (p60)

Pudding and souse (p171)

Note: Souse is sometimes made with salted pig's trotters. These are soaked in hot water for several hours or overnight to remove the salt, then boiled and pickled in the same way as the fresh meat.

Rice and Peas 1 (p75)

Rice and Peas 2 (p164)

Jug-Jug (p172)

Drinks

Sorrel 1 (p108)

Sorrel 2 (p108)

Ginger Beer (p107)

Egg Nog (p113)

Punch a Créme

3 eggs
½ tin (175 g or 7 oz size) evaporated
  milk
1 tin (325 g or 12 oz size) condensed
  milk

1 wineglass rum
piece of orange or lime rind
1 teaspoon bitters

Beat eggs well with the rind. Remove rind. Add milk. Stir well. Add
rum and bitters and mix thoroughly. Bottle. Chill and shake well
before serving. Makes 12–16 servings in liqueur glasses.

Falernum (p174)

Special rum punch

4 cups boiling water
1½ cups rum
1 small 40 cl (12 fl oz) bottle claret
  wine
3–4 bay leaves
1 bottle soda water
1 egg white

2 oranges
2 oz granulated sugar
1 large lime or lemon
1 tablespoon grenadine syrup
a little grated nutmeg
½ teaspoon bitters

Allow the water to cool. Then add the rum and bay leaves, soda
water, claret wine and stir in one egg white, beaten until frothy. Add
slowly 50 g (2 oz) granulated sugar dissolved in the lemon or lime
and orange juice. Add the rind of one orange, grenadine syrup and a
dash of bitters. Mix the ingredients together well. Serve in punch
glasses with chopped ice and a little grated nutmeg. Making 12
servings.

Tea Punch

1 tablespoon tea
2½ cups boiling water
1 cup granulated sugar

1 cup orange juice
1 bottle ginger ale (6 oz)
some shredded pineapple

Put 1 tablespoon of tea in a jug. Pour over it 2½ cups of boiling
water. Allow the tea to infuse for 5 minutes and strain the liquid over
a cup of sugar in a bowl. Allow it to cool and add the ginger ale and
orange juice before serving with chopped ice. Garnish with pieces of
shredded pineapple. Other fruit juices may be used for orange juice
and a wineglass of apple. Other fruit juices may be used for orange
juice and a wineglass of liqueur may be added if a stronger drink is
required. Makes 8 servings.

Orange liqueur

12 oranges (include 2 Seville or sour oranges)
1.35 kg (3 lb) granulated sugar
2½ cups rum

Wash, dry and peel the oranges thinly. Squeeze and strain their juice. Put the peel and sugar in alternate layers in an earthenware or glass jar. Pour over the rum, then the orange juice. Cover the jar closely. Leave it in a warm place (e.g. inside a closed cupboard) for about 3 weeks, shaking the mixture occasionally. Then strain off the liquid, bottle and cork it well. This liqueur improves with age. Makes 18–20 servings.

Fly (p179)

Rice wine

900 g (2 lb) raisins
900 g (2 lb) currants
2½ cups white rice
1 package yeast
1.35 kg (3 lb) granulated sugar
1 orange
1 lime
4.5 litre (1 gallon) water (boiled and used warm)

Put washed fruit, rice, yeast and sugar in a jar. Add the water while warm and stir well to dissolve the sugar. Peel the orange and lime, cut in halves and add with the rind. After 3–4 days remove the rind, and after 7 days remove the cut fruit and allow the mixture to stand in the jar for 21 days, stirring each day, with a wooden spoon and tasting it for sweetness. Sugar may be added if needed. Pour off the liquid and strain it. Allow it to settle and pour off again. Bottle and cork well before storing.

Plum pudding

225 g (8 oz) raisins
225 g (8 oz) currants
50 g (2 oz) mixed peel
100 g (4 oz) chopped suet
1 cup flour
½ teaspoon salt
2 cups breadcrumbs
2 teaspoons baking powder
225 g (8 oz) brown sugar
½ teaspoon nutmeg
½ teaspoon cinnamon
3 eggs
½ teaspoon almond essence
1 cup milk, ale *or* stout

Put fruit and suet in bowl; add breadcrumbs and spices and mix well. Blend in beaten egg, essence, liquid and stir. Add sifted flour, baking powder and salt; stir again. Pour mixture in greased pudding bowls. Cover with two thicknesses of greaseproof paper and tie down well or cover with aluminium foil. Steam for 3–4 hours in a large saucepan with boiling water or cook in a pressure cooker for 1 hour.

Rich fruit cake

900 g (2 lb) raisins
450 g (1 lb) currants
225 g (½ lb) prunes
100 g (¼ lb) glacé cherries
1 teaspoon spice (powdered)
1 teaspoon nutmeg
¼ teaspoon powdered cloves
675 g (1½ lb) brown sugar
10 eggs
450 g (1 lb) flour
1 teaspoon baking powder

225 g (½ lb) mixed peel
100 g (¼ lb) brown sugar
1 cup rum
100 g (¼ lb) chopped nuts (optional)
450 g (1 lb) butter
1 teaspoon salt
1 tablespoon vanilla essence
1 tablespoon almond essence
1 cup port wine or falernum
1 cup water
brown colouring

Mince the fruit and soak in 1 cup rum with the spices, essences, nuts and 100 g (¼ lb) sugar. Mix these ingredients well, put them in a glass or earthenware jar, cover and allow mixture to steep for three weeks or longer. When ready to bake the cake, cream the butter and sugar well, and add the eggs beating in one by one. Now add the fruit mixture which has been cooked over low heat with a cup of water for about 15 minutes, constantly stirring. This preliminary cooking of the fruit shortens the baking time of the cake and reduces the possibility of the cake burning in the oven. Stir in about ½ cup burnt sugar colouring to make the mixture light brown in colour. Add the flour sifted with baking powder and salt, last. Put the mixture into baking tins greased and lined with two thicknesses of waxed paper. Fill the pans, 2.5 cm (1 in) from the top. Bake them in a slow oven (140°C, 275°F or Gas 1) for 2 to 3 hours according to the size. Test with a skewer before removing them from the oven. As soon as the cakes are removed from the oven, prick them well with a skewer and pour slowly over them a mixture of rum and port wine or falernum which the cakes will absorb. Allow them to remain in the pans for 3 to 4 days, after which they may be covered with a layer of almond icing or marzipan, then iced with Royal Icing.

Marzipan

225 g (½ lb) ground almonds
225 g (½ lb) icing sugar
1 or 2 egg whites
½ teaspoon almond essence

Beat the egg whites stiffly with the essence. Add them to the almonds and sugar. Mix to a stiff paste and knead well, using more sugar if necessary. Roll out to a circular shape with a rolling-pin. Cover the top of the cake, having first brushed it over with beaten egg white.

Knead the rest of the paste and roll thinly to cover the sides. Allow to dry for 1 day before icing.

Royal icing

450 g (1 lb) icing sugar
2 egg whites
1 dessertspoon lime juice or
½ teaspoon cream of tartar

Beat the egg whites until frothy. Gradually add half the sugar sifted with cream of tartar, beating well. Add the lime juice and rest of sugar and continue beating until the mixture stiffens and forms into peaks. Smooth the icing on the cake with a spatula dipped in hot water and shaken occasionally during icing. A second layer of icing may be applied when the first is thoroughly dried. The cake may now be decorated as desired.

Mince pies

Mincemeat filling

100 g (4 oz) raisins	1 teaspoon nutmeg
100 g (4 oz) currants	1 teaspoon spice
100 g (4 oz) prunes	¼ cup rum
50 g (2 oz) mixed peel	½ cup wine
100 g (4 oz) brown sugar	2 tablespoons lime juice
100 g (4 oz) suet	1 tablespoon lime rind

Chop fruit and suet finely or mince. Add sugar, spices, rum, wine, lime juice and grated rind. Mix well together. Put in glass jars, cover closely and allow to stand for about 3 weeks before using.

Rich Short Crust Pastry
200 g (8 oz) rich short crust (p132)
beaten egg
granulated sugar
mincemeat filling

Roll out pastry and cut in 6 cm (2½-in) rounds and fit into patty pans. Put in a rounded teaspoon of filling. Moisten edges with water and fit rounds on top, pressing them on; brush with beaten egg, sprinkle with sugar and bake at 230°C, 450°F or Gas 8 for about 25 minutes.

27 Rechauffée dishes

Rechauffée dishes are reheated dishes, and these may consist *either* of whole dishes prepared the day before *or* dishes made up from bits and pieces of left-over food.

It is desirable to plan for the immediate requirements of meals, but this is not always practicable, so left-over food and pre-prepared dishes are common experiences in most homes. To avoid wastage and extra expense, left-overs may be used to good advantage. Be sure always to keep these foods covered, cool and away from insects; use them as quickly as possible to prevent deterioration in the warm humid atmosphere of the area. Remember that harmful bacteria, which cause food poisoning, thrive under warm conditions.

When, therefore, it is expedient for dishes to be prepared in advance (e.g. meat pies, milk and fish dishes, gravies, etc.), they should be thoroughly and quickly cooled before storing in a refrigerator and thoroughly heated in an oven before they are served. These precautions will hinder the development of bacteria.

In the preparation of made-up dishes:

1 Make sure that all the food used is in good condition.
2 Add milk, butter, cheese, egg and seasonings to moisten and replace any loss of flavour. Make them tasty and attractive.
3 Mince or cut up the ingredients and blend them well together. Make rissoles, curries, fritters, add to soups, etc., but *do not* add fresh meat which requires long cooking.
4 Heat the made-up dishes *as quickly as possible*, and serve hot. *Never reheat* a second time.

Suggestions for left-over foods
Cooked meats and fish

Mince meat and use to stuff vegetables for baking, e.g. Stuffed Sweet Pepper (p83). Use fish or meat as fillings for pies, pancakes, omelettes, fritters. Dice pieces of meat to enrich and flavour soups. Meat bones, poultry carcases and fish bones may also be used for making stock for soup or gravy.

Shepherd's pie

2 cups cooked meat
1 medium onion, chopped
900 g (2 lb) cooked mashed potatoes
1½ tablespoons butter

1 beaten egg
salt and pepper to taste
1 cup meat gravy

Cut the meat into small pieces. Add gravy, onion, pepper and salt to taste. Put in a buttered oven dish. Mix potatoes with nearly all the butter and egg. Add a little salt to taste, and mix well. Spread the mixture over the meat. Lightly butter the top, stroking with a fork to decorate. Brush on the rest of the egg and bake in a moderate oven.

Meat croquettes

2 cups cold beef *or* mutton
2 tablespoons butter *or* fat
¼ cup flour
1 cup gravy *or* water
salt and pepper to taste

1 teaspoon chopped mixed herbs
1 tablespoon tomato sauce
1 beaten egg
breadcrumbs
parsley

Mince the meat. Melt fat in saucepan; add flour and cook; add gravy or water. Stir and boil for 3 minutes. Put in the meat, seasonings and herbs. Stir for 2 minutes. Pour mixture on to a shallow dish. Cool and form into croquettes. Coat with beaten egg. Dredge well with breadcrumbs, pressing well in. Allow to stand for ½ hour. Fry in deep hot fat until brown. Drain on paper. Garnish tops with pieces of parsley.

Ham and egg pie

100 g (4 oz) fresh button
    mushrooms
¼ cup milk
salt and pepper to taste
150 g (6 oz) cooked ham
½ cup cooked green peas (congo)

1 medium sliced onion
2 hard boiled eggs
1 teaspoon prepared mustard
225 g (8 oz) rich short pastry (p132)
beaten egg

Trim and prepare fresh mushrooms and simmer them for 10 minutes in the milk with salt and pepper *or* drain canned mushrooms and add them to the milk. Dice ham and mix with peas, sliced hard boiled eggs, mushrooms, mustard and seasoning. Divide pastry into 2 unequal portions. Roll out the larger piece and cover a pie dish, trimming the edges. Prick well. Put in the filling. Roll out the rest of the pastry. Cover the pie. Trim and scallop edges. Make slits on top to decorate. Brush with beaten egg and bake for 45 minutes in a hot oven, reducing heat to moderate during the last 10 minutes.

Babootee

1 cup left-over cold meat (any mixture)
1 medium chopped onion
1 egg
2 teaspoons butter
1 dessertspoon curry powder
½ teaspoon minced red pepper
1 slice stale bread
salt to taste
milk to moisten
breadcrumbs

Mince the cold meat, add the seasonings, chopped onion, 1 teaspoon butter and the curry powder. Beat the egg and mix with the meat mixture. Soak the slice of bread in cold water, squeeze dry, shred finely and add it with a little salt to taste, and some milk to moisten the mixture. Grease a small casserole with a bit of butter, put the mixture in, sprinkle the top lightly with breadcrumbs and dot with the rest of butter. Bake this uncovered at 180°C, 350°F or Gas 4 until lightly browned. Serve as a supper dish.

Fish scallops

1 cup cold fish
¾ cup crushed yam
1 tablespoon butter
1 small onion
1 beaten egg (optional)
1 teaspoon lime juice *or* vinegar
1 teaspoon chopped parsley
¼ cup milk
salt and fresh pepper to taste

Crush the fish with a fork and stir in the yam, lime juice, milk, seasonings and half the butter. Mix well together, put into greased individual scallop shells and dot with the rest of the butter. Brown them under the grill or in a moderate oven. To serve, sprinkle with chopped parsley.

Cooked vegetables

Green cooked vegetables and pulses make useful additions to salads and soups. These should be used up the same day whenever possible. Pieces of sweet potato, yam and other roots help to bind the mixtures for fish or meat balls, rissoles, pies, etc.

Cooked rice

Use left-over rice in soup, pudding, kedgeree, rice fritters, etc.

Cooked-up rice

1 cup cooked meat
½ cup prepared shrimps (cut in pieces)
2 cups rice
few garden tomatoes
sprig of thyme and marjoram
½ cup dried peas (soaked) *or*
1 cup green peas

4 cups water (part coconut milk, optional)
1 chopped onion
2 blades chives (chopped)
1 dessertspoon salt
piece of green pepper
2 tablespoons butter *or* fat
piece of hot pepper

Cut meat into pieces and sauté in fat. Cook peas in water until nearly soft; add meat and extra boiling water and coconut milk (if used) to make 4 cups. Add all seasonings, bring to the boil and sprinkle in rice. When about half-cooked, add shrimps and cook until rice grains are soft.

Chocolate-rice dessert

1 cup milk
¼ teaspoon salt
4 tablespoons cocoa
2 egg yolks
2 egg whites

5 tablespoons sugar
1 cup cooked rice
½ teaspoon vanilla
½ cup whipping cream

Combine the milk, salt and cocoa. Heat in the top of a double boiler until the cocoa is melted. Add the slightly beaten egg-yolks and the sugar. Cook until the mixture coats a spoon, while stirring constantly. Add the rice and vanilla. Remove from the heat. Cool. Put to chill in refrigerator. Before serving, fold in the stiffly-beaten egg-whites and whipped cream. Pile in serving glasses. Decorate with a little whipped cream and a cherry.

Hard cheese

Cheese which has hardened may be grated, stored in an airtight bottle in a cool place and used for salads, toppings, for puddings and cheese dishes.

Bread and cakes

Stale bread is useful for making puddings and may also be toasted and ground to make breadcrumbs for dredging fried foods and au gratin dishes. Stale cake may be used in fruit trifles or puddings.

28 Suggestions for vegetarian menus

For religious and other personal reasons many people become vegetarians. There are two types of vegetarians – those who are very strict, eating no animal products at all, e.g. meat, fish, eggs, cheese or milk; the less strict use dairy products but no meat or fish in any form.

The strict diet gives very little scope for planning meals, as the diet may only include the use of vegetable proteins, e.g. cereals, peas, beans, lentils and nuts cooked with vegetable oils. Rice, macaroni and spaghetti may be combined with the pulses for the main dishes. Fruit and vegetables of all kinds may be used. Many tinned varieties of vegetarian foods are available and very useful in the preparation of quick meals.

The less strict vegetarian may enjoy a more varied diet as many tasty dishes are made from cheese, milk and eggs. These foods may be seasoned with herbs and onions, etc., for added flavour.

Select vegetarian menus from vegetables, fruits, cereal and sweet dishes, also those including milk, eggs and cheese as required. All salads, including green and yellow vegetables and fruit, with dressings may be used liberally. Peanuts should be used regularly.

Suggested recipes

Peanut Soup (p36)
Lentil Soup (p36)
Pigeon Pea Soup (p33)
Split Pea Soup (p34)
Mock Chicken (with peanuts) (p79)

Peanut salad

1 small cabbage (225 g or $\frac{1}{2}$ lb)
1 teaspoon flour
1 teaspoon mustard
1 teaspoon sugar
2 cups peanuts

4 tablespoons vinegar
1 teaspoon butter
$\frac{1}{2}$ teaspoon white pepper
2 egg yolks
pepper and salt to taste

Chop cabbage and peanuts finely; add salt and pepper. Cream the butter, mustard, sugar and flour together and stir in the vinegar. Cook in double boiler until very thick, add beaten egg yolks; blend in thoroughly. When warm pour over nuts and cabbage, and serve.

Baked cheese and peanuts

1 cup grated cheese	1 cup finely ground peanuts
1 cup breadcrumbs	1 tablespoon butter
1 teaspoon chopped onion	1 tablespoon lime juice
salt and pepper to taste	

Cook the onion in the butter and a little water until tender. Stir in other ingredients, and moisten with water, using the onion stock at 190°C, 375°F or Gas 5. Pour into a greased shallow dish and brown in the oven.

Peanut rissoles

2 cups breadcrumbs (soft)	1 teaspoon salt
4 tablespoons peanut butter	1 well beaten egg
1 cup grated coconut	1 cup finely ground peanuts

Thoroughly mix all ingredients, make into rissoles and fry in deep fat or bake in a moderate oven until golden brown.

Corn Pudding (p78)
Red Pea Loaf (p77)
Baked Rice Pudding (p112)
Carrot Pudding (p101)
Banana Coconut Custard (p100)
Stuffed Avocado Salad (p83)
Potato Salad (p85)
Moulded Vegetable Salad (p85)

29 Barbecue cookery

Cooking whole meals out of doors is gradually becoming more popular. It is an occasion for informality; hosts and guests alike share the chores and the fun.

A simple removable grill fitted over a large iron coal-pot may be used for a small party, or more elaborate grills or barbecues may be acquired.

The dishes are always freshly prepared and well-seasoned.

As the food is cooked over direct heat, cooking time is short, hence all meat cuts and joints served must be tender, e.g. steaks, chops, spare ribs, broiler chickens or small whole fish. These are some of the popular choices. Minced beef is used in making hamburgers and cheeseburgers. Frankfurters serve as hot dog fillings.

Grilled bacon and frankfurters

4 slices bacon	sliced cucumber pickles
8 frankfurters	hot sauce
8 rolls	prepared mustard

Cut slices of bacon in half, and place on a griddle or under a grill, using low heat until they are crisp; drain on kitchen paper. Slit each frankfurter and put in a piece of bacon and a slice of cucumber Add hot sauce to taste and spread about ½ teaspoon mustard on the top.

Hamburgers (p201)

Cheeseburgers (p202)

Steaks

Choose steaks about 2.5 cm (1 in) thick. If frozen, allow them to thaw out to room temperature. Score the fat edge. Heat grill and grease it. Put on the steaks. Grill one side, then the other. Sprinkle salt and pepper to taste after grilling. Allow 10–15 minutes for each steak, rare to well done.

Chicken

Choose broiler chickens weighing about 675–900 g (1½–2 lb). Clean and prepare birds for cooking. Use halved chickens; break the joints to keep them flat. Season with celery salt and white pepper. Brush with butter. Place on grill, skin side up. Grill over slow heat. When browned on under side, about 25 minutes, turn and brown the skin side, 25 minutes more basting with butter. Remove from grill when flesh feels soft.

Sauce for chicken

⅛ cup Worcestershire sauce   ¼ cup salad oil
2 tablespoons lemon juice   1 small clove garlic (minced)
¼ teaspoon salt

Shake all well together and brush chicken before serving hot.

Vegetables

These may be roasted whole in their skins, each kind on a separate spit, if a rotisserie is available. Alternately, choose small sweet potatoes, English potatoes or yams. Scrub the skins, brush them with cooking oil, wrap each securely in aluminium foil and bake on the grill for 45–60 minutes *or* on top of the coals. Turn them occasionally. When cooked, split open at the top, add salt and butter. Onions and tomatoes may be grilled similarly.

Grilled tomatoes

Use halved tomatoes. Brush with Italian Salad Dressing (p17). Sprinkle with salt and pepper. Place cut side up on greased grill over hot coals for about 10 minutes.

Grilled onions

Use small onions. Melt some butter or margarine in a pan on grill. Season with salt and white pepper. Cook slowly until of golden colour, turning often.

Salads

Fresh green salads or moulded salads, potato salad, sweet pickles, radishes and olives are ideal accompaniments for barbecued meats.

Bread and rolls

Crispy French-type bread is sliced and buttered for eating outdoors. Long sweet toasted rolls are split to hold sausages or frankfurters for hot dogs. Garnish these with prepared mustard, sliced onions and tomato ketchup. Round toasted split rolls are excellent for hamburgers. Toasted garlic bread is also delicious. Toast crispy bread slices and spread with Garlic Butter (see p195).

Typical Caribbean kitchen Equipment

Old cookery methods are still commonly used in the area as certain types of equipment have been handed down from generation to generation.

The *smokeless fireplace* consists of hearth stone in concrete with a fire-box at one end, in which a wood fire is made, and a flue at the other end, to draw out the smoke. Cooking is done on top of the heated stone. This is used in many rural areas.

The *Caledonian stove* is an old-fashioned large cast iron range. Wood or coals are used in the fire-box. A flue at the back draws out the smoke and allows the fire to burn. The heat is controlled by a damper. It has a built-in oven and 4 to 6 burners.

Coalpots in cast iron and clay are still used in both urban and rural areas. Fuel costs are low when compared with oil, gas or electricity and often the latter facilities are not available.

From tradition and custom, iron coalpots are still used in modern and well-equipped homes, for cooking pepperpot, stews and dishes which require long hours of simmering. Fuel costs are thus reduced.

In many rural areas the *box oven* is the only type of oven used. This is made from a wooden crate lined with zinc or tin, fitted with wire shelves, and heated by a coalpot set on the floor of the box, With a little patience and skill, these ovens work very satisfactorily.

The *dutch pot* (buck, stewing pot) is a shallow (7.5–10 cm or 3–4 in deep) flat bottomed, cast iron pot generally used, on any type of stove, or over coals on a trivet on a coalpot, for stewing, frying or pot-roasting.

The *three-legged iron pot* (dutch pot) is very deep, standing on legs which rest on the coals or on a trivet over a coalpot.

The *cast iron saucepan*, with a tin cover and long handle at one side, is used on any type of stove, as well as over a coalpot.

The *yabba pot* made in glazed clay to withstand great heat is also very familiar in rural areas. Glazed mixing bowls in clay are still popular. Large jars for storing, water coolers, water jugs, canarees or casseroles, are other articles in clay.

The *tawa* is a flat iron girdle 25–30 cm (10–12 in) in diameter, used for baking cassava bread, roti, scones, bakes, etc.

The very large *mortar and pestle* is seen in many homes where pounded plantain (foo-foo) is regularly made.

Glossary

Avocado A pear-shaped fleshy fruit used as an *hors d'oeuvre* and in salads. Known also as pear, zaboca, and alligator pear.

Bammie Cassava bread.

Bananas The small variety are known as figs, and silk figs. The stout variety, which is used for cooking, is known as bluggoe fig and sometimes called bird fig.

Bhagi An Indian name for the leaves of a local weed used in Indian cookery in the same way as spinach.

Bluggoe figs A species of banana, also known as bird figs. They are stout reddish-purple and used in cooking as a vegetable.

Breadfruit A large green fruit with rough skin, which grows on a large tree. The round fruit is boiled or roasted. When sliced thinly and fried it may be substituted for bread.

Breadnut The fruit of a tree which grows in tropical America and the West Indies.

Callaloo A dish made of dasheen or eddoe leaves, okras, salt meat and other seasonings, all chopped and simmered together. Callaloo is also an alternative name for spinach.

Cashew A yellow or red juicy pear-shaped fruit which is really a swollen flower stalk with a heart-shaped seed projecting at the top. The flesh is slightly acid, tough and stringy but the fruit is stewed or used for making jam. The seeds, which are roasted and shelled, are the popular cashew nuts. Cashew is sometimes known in the Caribbean as Christmas apple.

Cassareep Thick black seasoned syrup used for colouring especially when cooking pepper pot. It is processed from cassava root.

Cassava Long tuberous roots of the cassava plant, sometimes called cassava 'sticks'. There are two varieties, sweet and bitter. The sweet variety, which has brown roots about 2.5 cm (1 in) to 4 cm (1½ in) in diameter, is used as a vegetable and boiled. The bitter variety, which is black and rough-skinned with much longer and stouter roots, is known to be poisonous when cooked in the same way as the sweet. It is, however, processed, and produces cassava flour and starch.

The grated roots of bitter cassava are covered with water and allowed to stand overnight. The mixture is then strained and the water squeezed out thoroughly by wringing it in a thick cloth over a container until only damp flour remains. This is spread out on a tin tray and dried in the sun or in an oven.

The sediment which settles in the water after the cassava has been wrung out is starch. The water is carefully drained off and the starch allowed to dry out before packaging.

Chocho A member of the melon family which is also known as crisophene. It is a green pear-shaped fruit used as a vegetable.

Coco Also known as Eddoe. A small round starchy root vegetable, brown-skinned and hairy, with white flesh.

Coconut cream Coconut milk.

Conch A shell fish of the mollusc family. It lives in a large spiral shell and may be a variety of sizes.

Conkies Paimies (see page 177).

Conquintay The creole name for plantain flour which is made from just under-ripe plantains. They are sliced, allowed to dry thoroughly in the sun or oven and then ground into flour. The flour, which is used for making porridge, is now factory processed in Guyana.

Dasheen A large root tuber with a dark brown rough skin. The flesh is dark, and when cooked, is not quite as tasty as other root vegetables.

Eddoe See *Coco*.

Egg Plant A dark-skinned fleshy vegetable also known as melongene, bolangere, garden egg, or aubergine.

Escallion Spring onions or chives.

Eschalot Another name for escallion.

Foo-foo Pounded plantain.

Granadilla The large fruit of a climbing plant. It is pale green, resembles a melon and grows from 20–25 cm (8–10 in) in length. The flesh has a delicious, slightly acid, flavour and is chiefly used for making drinks and ices. It is also called Barbadine.

Groundnut Peanut.

Ground provisions All starchy root vegetables.

Jira The small dry spicy seeds from a sweet herb, used in making *Roti* and in other Indian dishes.

Mango A tropical fruit with thick skin, yellow flesh which is firm and sweet, and a flat hairy seed. There are many varieties. It is available tinned in many countries.

Mauby A drink made from the bark of a tree which grows in some areas of the Caribbean. The bark is dried and sold in pieces and is very bitter.

It is boiled with spices and sugar and made into a syrup which is added, in small quantities, to water, sweetened to taste, iced, swizzled and served as Mauby Drink (see p107).

Molasses Cane syrup.

Okra Also called ochroes or 'ladies' fingers'. They are finger-length green-ribbed and hairy pods which grow profusely. They are best when picked young and freshly boiled. They are also used in the dish *Cou-cou* (see p171).

Otaheite apple Also known as pomerac, plum rose and molly apple, this is a pear-shaped red fruit with white flesh. It grows to about 7.5–10 cm (3–4 in) in length and is used chiefly for stewing and making jam.

Paw paw A large round or oblong melon-like fruit which grows from its tree trunk between umbrella-shaped leaves. The thick yellow juicy flesh has a delicious flavour and there are numerous black seeds in the centre of the fruit. The green paw paw is sometimes used as a vegetable, also as a preserve. See *Paw paws in syrup* (p157). It is also called papaya.

Peas

Black eye peas Tropical white peas with a black patch which grow in long pods. The dried peas are available in many countries.

Congo peas Green, pigeon or gunga peas.

Channa peas Also known as Chick peas, they resemble dried whole peas but are slightly larger. They are chiefly used in Indian cookery.

Gunga peas Tropical green peas, also dried and available in many countries. Sometimes called Congo peas.

Pepper Pot A very hot meat stew with cassareep (see p177).

Pepper Pot Soup Callaloo style dish, such as on page 165.

Plantains A member of the banana family. The large fruits are not eaten raw but cooked when ripe. They are also cooked when green or under-ripe, especially in the preparation of the dish *Foo-foo*.

Red Peas The Caribbean name for red beans.

Shaddock A member of the citrus family which resembles a grapefruit but is much larger, and the flesh is sometimes pink in colour. It is used as fruit and the skin and pith are made into a preserve. See *Shaddock rind* (p157). Also called pomelo.

Soursoup A large dark green heart-shaped fruit with spiny rough skin. The pithy flesh is slightly acid and juicy with black seeds. It is very popular when made into punch or ice-cream because of its refreshing flavour.

Tamarind The fruit of a very large tree, it is a brown pod about 7.5–10 cm (3–4 in) long which grows in bunches. When ripe the pods may be cracked easily to reveal black seeds covered with brown pulp which is used in making some condiments. The seeds may also be steeped in cane syrup for several months to preserve them. See *Tamarind balls*, a preserve, on page 161.

Tannia A tuberous root, similar to eddoes but large, used as a vegetable.

Some alternative names

All Spice pimento
Breadnut chataigne
Coco-Plum fat pork
Dunk Coolie plum, governor plum, dumb fruit
Garden Cherry cherry, West Indian cherry
Genip ackee, channet
Goat mutton goat
Golden Apple Jew plum, pomme cythere, golden plum
Gooseberry raspberry, jimbillin, sour cherry
Red and Green Sweet Pepper paprika (also in powdered form)
Rounceval carili, bodi, cowpea, bora
Sapodilla naseberry
Spice cinnamon
Star-Apple kaimet
Sugar-Apple sweetsop

Index

Gail Duff
Gail Duff's Vegetarian Cookbook £3.50

Vegetarian eating is economical as well as nutritious. Beans, pastas, rice, eggs, cheese, vegetable curries, salads and more allow plenty of scope for the most mouthwatering menus.

'Develops meatless eating into authentic cuisine' THE TIMES

'Really imaginative . . . recipes anyone would be tempted to eat, vegetarian or not!' STANDARD

Theodora Fitzgibbon
Crockery Pot Cooking £1.50

Creator of the famous *Taste of* . . . series, Theodora FitzGibbon explains how the crockery pot works, how to get the best out of it and adds a mouthwatering selection of recipes. The perfect kitchen handbook for every cook who has – or is thinking of having – an electric crockery pot cooker.

Elisabeth Orsini
The Book of Pies £1.95

To prepare this veritable encyclopaedia of piecraft, Elisabeth Orsini has traced the pie back through history, discovering the immense variety of traditional pies and tarts that have graced the tables of cottage and castle with distinction. She has adapted over 200 recipes to suit today's cook, suggesting a mouthwatering variety of fillings and offering guidance on preparing the all-important pastry.